A SAVAGE
EMPIRE

ALSO BY ALAN AXELROD

A SAVAGE EMPIRE

Trappers, Traders, Tribes, and
the Wars That Made America

Alan Axelrod

THOMAS DUNNE BOOKS

St. Martin's Press

New York

THOMAS DUNNE BOOKS.
An imprint of St. Martin's Press.

A SAVAGE EMPIRE. Copyright © 2011 by Alan Axelrod. All rights reserved. Printed in the United States of America. For information, address St. Martin's Press, 175 Fifth Avenue, New York, N.Y. 10010.

www.thomasdunnebooks.com
www.stmartins.com

Design by Phil Mazzone

Library of Congress Cataloging-in-Publication Data

Axelrod, Alan, 1952–
    A savage empire : trappers, traders, tribes, and the wars that made America / Alan Axelrod.—1st ed.
        p. cm.
    Includes bibliographical references and index.
    ISBN 978-0-312-57656-1 (alk. paper)
    1. Fur trade—North America—History—17th century. 2. Fur trade—North America—History—18th century. 3. Fur traders—North America—History—17th century. 4. Fur traders—North America—History—18th century. 5. United States—History—Colonial period, ca. 1600—1775. 6. United States—History—Revolution, 1775–1783. I. Title.
    HD9944.N62A94 2011
    381'.45685—dc23

                                                                                    2011026771

First Edition: December 2011

10 9 8 7 6 5 4 3 2 1

For Anita and for Ian

Contents

Contents

Acknowledgments

Both author and reader have had the good fortune to benefit from the work of two great editors, Rob Kirkpatrick at Thomas Dunne Books and copyeditor India Cooper. The first helped shape *Savage Empire* and the second redeemed it from any number of mysteries and outright errors. On behalf of readers, the author thanks them.

A SAVAGE
EMPIRE

Mr. Pepys's Hat

———◆———

SAMUEL PEPYS WAS JUST the kind of Englishman the English themselves cherish—extraordinary in his ordinariness. While he rose high above his humble birth, he avoided doing so with any spectacle or flamboyance. For this reason, among others, his celebrated *Diary,* which he began on January 1, 1660, and stopped in May 1669, after his eyesight went bad, is truly representative of London life during a decade both extraordinary and ordinary.

He wrote about both. He wrote about the Great Plague and the Great Fire, and he also wrote about his hat. Obviously, plague and fire are extraordinary, but Pepys's hat, as it turns out, was not so ordinary a subject as it may at first seem. If plague and fire brought mass death, Pepys's hat was the very stuff of mass death—and also boundless ambition, great enterprise, profoundly consequential discovery, and, in the end, epoch-making revolution.

Samuel Pepys was born in London on February 23, 1633, to a tailor father and to a mother who was the daughter of a Whitechapel butcher. Although his corner of the family got their living by trade, his father did have a socially prominent cousin, Richard Pepys, who became a member of Parliament, Baron of the Exchequer, and Lord Chief Justice of Ireland, and whose influence was doubtless crucial to enrolling young Pepys in Huntingdon Grammar School in 1644, and then in St. Paul's School two years later. Sooner or later when one Englishman meets another, the question will be asked: *What school did you attend?* With Huntingdon and St. Paul's behind him, the young man's rise commenced.

In 1649, Samuel Pepys witnessed a momentous occurrence, the beheading of a king, Charles I, but so did many other Londoners, which made this event less extraordinary than it might otherwise have been. Two years later, he enrolled in Magdalene College, Cambridge, and was awarded a bachelor of arts degree in 1654. Shortly after his graduation, Pepys went to live with another of his father's prominent cousins, Sir Edward Montagu (who would soon be created first Earl of Sandwich), and brought into the Montagu household fourteen-year-old Elisabeth Marchant de Saint-Michel, whom he married in 1655.

No doubt, marriage was for Pepys a major event, as it is for everyone who marries, but even more momentous in his life at this stage was the removal of a "bladder stone" on March 26, 1658, in a harrowing surgery without either anesthesia or antisepsis and therefore with very little prospect of a happy outcome. That he lived through the ordeal and recovered was a fact he understandably celebrated lifelong. Later in the year, Pepys began his professional career, moving from the Montagu home to Axe Yard (near modern Downing Street), where he became a teller in the exchequer. From this position, thanks to the patronage of Sir Edward, he rose to become Clerk of the Acts to the Navy Board in 1660—essentially secretary to the Navy Board, a key administrative post. His salary of £350 was munificent indeed, and it was in 1660 as well that he commenced his diary.

Much of great moment occurred during the decade in which he kept the diary. There was the Second Dutch War (1665–67), of nearly ruinous cost in men and money, both to England and Holland; the Great Plague of 1665, which carried off some hundred thousand people, a fifth of the capital's population; and, in 1666, the Great Fire of London, which razed seventy thousand of the eighty thousand buildings in Pepys's own haunt, the central City of London. As an intimate window onto these events, Pepys's *Diary* is of inestimable value, yet the legions of historians and enthusiasts who have pored over the nine volumes of the published book treasure it less as a picture of extraordinary cataclysm than as a chronicle of the strictly quotidian, as when, for example, on Tuesday, October 29, 1661, Pepys recorded how he prepared to attend "my Lord Mayor's feast" by putting "on my half cloth black stockings and my new coat of the fashion, which pleases me well, and . . . my beaver." It was only with the addition of the latter that Pepys deemed himself "ready to go."

By "beaver," Pepys meant his hat, but not just any hat. It was a hat suited to the wardrobe of a prosperous gentleman, to a personage worthy of an invitation to "my Lord Mayor's feast." Pepys's patron, Montagu, had earlier in the year suffered the misfortune of having had his "beaver" stolen, a mishap made the more vexing to him because the thief had had the temerity to leave an ordinary hat in its place! In his entry of June 27, 1661, Pepys recorded that Joseph Holden, a haberdasher of Bride Lane (a London street noted for its fine men's furnishers), "sent me a bever, which cost me 4*l*. 5*s*." This figure alone explains Montagu's vexation, for an ordinary hat of felted fabric, presumably the kind left by the thief, could be had for a mere thirty-five shillings.

The historical value of money is notoriously difficult to calculate realistically, but consider that Pepys earned £350 from his job on the naval board, deemed at the time a very handsome salary, and had shelled out more than 1 percent of that yearly income for a mere hat. What did other things cost in Pepys's day? Some detailed figures can be found in a "Statement taken before Charles Talber for Hugh May, Esq., Clerk of the Markets to His Majesty's Household," on August 21, 1625:

A kilderkin [18 gallons] of good ale or double beer with carriage [delivery charges].	3s 4d
A full quart of the best ale or beer by measure sealed.	1d

A full quart of single ale or beer by measure sealed.	½d
A full pound of butter sweet and new the best in the market.	3½d
A pound of best cheese in the shop or market.	2½d
A stone [8 pounds!] of the best beef at the butchers.	1s 2d

. . .

A hundred good oak boards with carriage.	8s
A hundred good elm boards with carriage.	6s
One thousand bricks.	14s

An accounting from 1630 listing the cost of emigration from England to New England put the expense of four pairs of new shoes (or one pair of men's boots) at nine shillings. So: four pounds, five shillings for a *hat*? Must have been some hat.

On Saturday, April 26, 1662, the diarist recorded a very pleasant outing to Southampton, where he toured Lord Southampton's parks and lands, then had dinner with the mayor. In all, Pepys could think of only two causes for complaint. First: While his meal of sturgeon had been well prepared, the caviar he was served was "neither . . . salt[ed] enough, nor [were] the seedes of the roe broke, but [were] all in berryes." Second: "After dinner to horse again, being in nothing troubled but the badness of my hat, which I borrowed to save my beaver."

Consider the second complaint closely. So highly did Pepys value his beaver hat that he borrowed an embarrassingly "bad" substitute for it so that he would not have to hazard his own elegant headgear on a day trip just outside of London.

In the April 26 entry, Pepys did not specify whether he feared for the well-being of the beaver he had purchased so dearly the year before or another, which he had acquired just seven days before the Southampton excursion. On Saturday, April 19, 1662, he went to a "draper's [dry goods] shop" in Aldgate, pausing in his errand to watch a triple execution. Three of the men who had signed the death warrant of King Charles I, John Barkestead (Barkstead), John Okey, and Miles Corbet, were "drawn towards the gallows at Tiburne; and there they were hanged and quartered. They all looked very cheerful; but I hear they all died defending what they did to the King to be just; which is very strange." As condemned traitors, Barkestead, Okey, and Corbet would have been dragged on wooden frames, called hurdles, to Tyburn, London's traditional place of execution, then hanged by the neck until not quite dead. After being cut down, the dazed prisoners would have been slowly gutted and castrated, their entrails and genitalia roasted before their eyes. Following this, the trio would have been beheaded, their bodies then quartered, cut into four separate parts. After witnessing this spectacle, Pepys noted nothing more than that it was on "to the office and then home to dinner. . . . Then abroad about business."

So much for a day that included the singularly grisly execution of three regicides. Yet what apparently made more of an impression on Pepys was what occurred that evening, when, he recorded, he "did get a bever, an old one, but a very good one."

The hat was given to him by Sir William Batten, the sailor son of Andrew Batten, a Royal Navy master. Pepys noted that he "must give him [Sir William] something" in return for the beaver, with which he confessed himself "very well pleased."

Prosperous as he was, Samuel Pepys was not too proud to accept a hand-me-down hat, provided that it was made of beaver fur. Short, stout, with a round face and a broad, somewhat bulbous nose, his full lips set in a pendulous frown, here was a man who hardly cut a dashing figure of the type that might have been drawn from the lines of a Restoration drama. Moreover, as if he were always conscious of having been raised up from the tradesman's class, Pepys was decidedly cautious with money, the pages of his diary liberally laced with meticulous daily accounts of pence and shillings spent and pence and shillings taken in. Happy to accept a used beaver hat, he was also willing to lay out a significant part of his income for a brand-new one. So much, after all, was expected of a gentleman in his position.

We know almost nothing of what either of Samuel Pepys's beaver hats looked like. Even making a guess as to their appearance is hazardous, because the fashion in English hats changed rapidly in the course of the seventeenth century, especially during the period of the Restoration. We do know for certain that hats were of paramount importance in European society of the era and that their wearing, as well the precise manner of their doffing and donning, was governed by a code of etiquette sufficiently convoluted that, in the early part of the century, James I of England created the court office of Master of Ceremonies, one of whose duties was personally to instruct foreign ambassadors in the requisite courtly protocol, including when, where, and how to remove and replace one's hat when in the presence of the king.

The English Civil War of 1641–49 pitted the Cavaliers (supporters of King Charles I) against the Roundheads (supporters of Oliver Cromwell). Whereas the Anglican Cavaliers sported a hat with a flamboyantly lofty crown, rich in ornamental trim, including a large plume, with a broad brim jauntily flipped up on one side—the kind of hat depicted in any number of paintings by the Dutch masters—the Puritan Roundheads wore more somber headgear, void of ornament, the crown substantially lower, and the brim narrower and never, ever turned upward on one side or any side. The contrasting styles reflected the sharply different cultural and religious orientation of the two factions. Cromwell's Puritan Commonwealth endured from 1649 to 1660, when the restoration of King Charles II brought back at least some of the exuberance of the Cavaliers. This was evident in the hats men of substance wore. Although Restoration crowns were generally lower and brims somewhat narrower than the Cavalier originals, throughout the 1660s the millinery fashion migrated farther from the Puritan pole and closer to the style of the Cavalier, with brims widening markedly by the middle of the decade and the crowns beginning their rise anew.

Both Cavalier and Restoration hats were architectural tours de force, requiring a material sufficiently supple to accept an exuberant shape, yet sufficiently stiff to hold that shape. For reasons we are about to see, beaver fur was the ideal medium for such hats, whereas the humbler Puritan-style headgear, with its steeped crown and simpler stiff brim, could, if necessary, be fashioned of less costly material.

The Puritan hat symbolized the ideal of frugal industry that characterized ultra-Protestant religion and ethics; nevertheless, the more prosperous among the Puritan brethren insisted on beaver even for their much-modulated headgear. It is true that the demand for beaver hats waned somewhat during England's Puritan interregnum of 1649–60, but it was still substantial. Among other things, the Restoration served first to restore and then to increase the demand for beaver, even though hats made of the material remained high-end merchandise. At the time that Pepys acquired his beaver hats, the fur for their manufacture was imported mostly from the far northern reaches of Russia and Scandinavia and was therefore very dear. An expanding market made hatters as well as importers of beaver pelts especially anxious for new, cheaper sources of supply. The French and English exploration and early colonization of North America promised to yield just that, and if Pepys had been able to put off his purchase for a decade or so, when beaver pelts from America were supplanting those from Europe's frozen north, he would have paid considerably less than the "4l. 5s." he invested in 1661.

The first flowering of the North American trade in beaver pelts during the seventeenth century was a direct response to the European demand for this high-end commodity, which grew during the English Restoration and which would continue to expand, through the period of the American Revolution and well into the nineteenth century. Although beaver fur was used in many articles of dress, including the trim on collars, cuffs, and boot cuffs, most of it was worked into hats, and as the European middle class prospered and increased, the clamor for this emblem of wealth and social position intensified as well. From the later seventeenth century through the early nineteenth, it was a good time to be a hatter and an even better time to be a fur trapper.

It was not, however, a good time to be a beaver. At least not in North America.

As furs go, beaver is hardly the most beautiful. It lacks, for instance, the regal richness of ermine and the sheer sensuality of marten and mink; but then, it was not the beauty of beaver fur that drove the demand for this commodity. The desirability of beaver was a structural rather than a superficial attraction.

Beaver fur consists of two types of fiber, an outer coat of coarse "guard hairs" and an inner coat of soft underfur, called beaver wool or duvet. All hair, animal or human, has a scaly outer layer of a fibrous structural protein called keratin, but if you examined beaver fur under a high-powered microscope, you would see that the surface of its keratin is uniquely barbed. Moreover, the microscopic barbs readily hook together, so that the beaver's underfur tends to mat quite naturally into the nonwoven cloth we call felt. Obviously, therefore, beaver fur is an ideal material for all felt products, including elaborately shaped hats.

Ask any seventeenth-century hatter, and he would tell you: Felting is the foundation of his art and trade. In one version of the story, Saint Clement, who became the fourth pope and bishop of Rome about the year 88, began his religious life as a monk. While he was leading a pilgrim army on a long and weary trek, the pain of the blisters on his feet at length became unendurable. Clement sought relief by putting some sheep's wool in his sandals, and by the time he reached his destination, he discovered that the motion of his bare feet had combined with their sweat to mat the wool into a solid fabric, one that was both durable and readily shaped. Without having meant to do so, Saint Clement had invented felt, and for this reason, beginning in the fifteenth century, the hatters of Europe adopted him as their patron saint.

While the barbed keratin in beaver underfur naturally lends itself to felting, a good deal of labor-intensive processing is still required to transform the beaver wool into finished felt. Not surprisingly, the best beaver fur for making felted hats came from animals trapped during the winter, when their undercoats were at their thickest. However, choosing premium pelts was not quite as simple as buying only those from the winter crop. North American beaver pelts fell into three categories, *castor gras* (or "coat"), *castor sec* ("parchment"), and *bandeau*. The pelts designated "coat" were not only from beaver trapped in the winter, but were pelts that had actually been worn by the trappers—typically Native

Americans—throughout the winter trapping season. Such usage wore the outer guard hairs off of these pelts, which meant that fewer had to be removed manually in the felting process later on. Moreover, although the beaver keratin naturally inclines the fibers to mat, the action of human perspiration on the keratin breaks down the protein structure in a way that promotes even more thorough matting, or felting. Thus, coat pelts were easier to process and generally made better felt than parchment pelts. It was a rare case of secondhand merchandise being more valuable than the brand-new item.

The only difference between coat (*castor gras*) and parchment (*castor sec*) pelts was that the latter, although they were skinned and scraped clean, had never been worn. In contrast to the coat pelts, made pliable by the friction of wear and contact with human sweat, the parchment pelts (true to their name) were stiff and therefore required significantly more labor to process into usable, let alone supple, felt. All of the guard hairs had to be removed, and the beaver wool had to be separated, but even then the keratin would not have been as beautifully broken down as in a coat pelt. It was not until Western European importers of beaver pelts discovered a special combing process that separated beaver wool from the guard hairs—long the closely held trade secret of the Russian furriers—that parchment pelts became desirable. Thanks to the special combing process, by the early to mid eighteenth century, this class of pelt actually overtook the coat pelts in value. (Always running a distant third in value were the cheapest and least desirable pelts, the *bandeau,* which were hastily and often incompletely scraped clean prior to shipment and therefore were prone to a good deal of rot before arriving in Europe.)

Once a pelt arrived at the hatter's establishment, it underwent three main stages of manufacture. First, the raw pelt was *prepared;* then the prepared fur had to be *felted.* Finally, the felted beaver fur was *shaped, dyed,* and *finished* into a hat. The complexity of this process and the high demand for hats elevated the hatter's trade well above the level of a cottage industry. We know, for example, that the city of Rouen, France, had in 1752 eighteen master hatters, who employed a total of one hundred journeymen, plus uncounted numbers of unskilled female laborers.

The first step in preparation was to pull out whatever guard hairs remained in the pelt, and then to tear or to shave the beaver wool from the pelt. This material would be collected in balls that were called beaver fluff. None of this first-step work required much skill, and so it was relegated to the lowest-paid workers, typically women, who might be employed on their own account or be used as unpaid labor by husbands or fathers who were journeymen or master hatters.

The beaver fluff was next subjected to a noxious and hazardous process called carroting. Mercury salts were dissolved in nitric acid and applied to the fluff to perform instantly what human sweat accomplished slowly: the breakdown of some of the keratin scales on the fiber, which thereby allowed the fibers to interlock—to felt—more readily. Carroting had to be carried out with great discretion and judgment because it inevitably compromised the quality of the fur by imparting to it the orange tint from which the process derived its name. For this reason, the highest-quality coat pelts, which required little or no carroting, were sometimes perceived as of greater value than the parchment pelts, even after the widespread dissemination of the Russian method of combing.

There was another price, hidden and hideous, to be paid for carroting. When hatters later applied steam to the felt in order to shape it, the mercury imbedded in the carroted fibers was released in the form of fumes, which, slowly and cumulatively, poisoned those who worked with the material. Exposure to mercury over long periods damages the endocrine system, the kidneys, and other organs, but most of all, it attacks the central nervous system. Those working in the hat trade so commonly suffered from uncontrollable trembling that the condition was labeled "hatters' shakes." Along with this, hat makers were often conspicuously clumsy and uncoordinated, their speech slurred like that of a drunkard. The teeth of a hatter might loosen and fall out. Memory loss and depression as well as fear and irritability to the point of paranoia—all of this was so frequently the hatter's lot that the phrase "mad as a hatter" entered into the English popular lexicon.

After carroting, the fluff was sorted by color and, at this point, might also be mixed with noncarroted coat fur, so that some of the beaver's natural oils (called castoreum) would be imparted to the fluff to make it shiny and water-repellent. The separated fluff was weighed and combed—"carded"—in order to agitate the fur in preparation for felting. The agitation was continued and intensified by "bowing." In a clean room free of drafts, the ephemeral fluff was laid out on a table that had slots cut into its top. A journeyman would pass a hatter's bow over the fluff piles. The tool resembled an oversized fiddle bow, and as he passed it over the fluff, he would repeatedly pluck the bow's single string, thereby agitating the fibers until they progressively matted together. As the agitation process matted the fibers, it also cleaned the fabric by knocking loose any dirt that adhered to the fluff, sending it through the slots in the table and onto the floor below.

After it had been matted, the fluff was called a batt. For each hat to be made, the journeyman bowed enough fluffs to make four batts, two large ones for the body of the hat, and two smaller ones to be used for finishing the hat's joints and details. Once the journeyman was satisfied with the quality of his batts, he covered them with a damp cloth or a piece of leather, placing them on top of one another over a small source of heat. This process, called basoning, used moist heat to promote further bonding of the fibers as the batt shrank into a more tightly felted fabric. Next, in a procedure called planking, the now shrunken batts were immersed in a metal basin filled with a nasty mixture of wine sediment and hot water. Using their hands as well as stirring planks, workers called *fouleurs* agitated the batts into "felts." The immersion caused them to shrink further and to felt ever more densely.

After planking, the felts, heavy and malodorous from their planking in wine waste, were stretched over wooden molds to be shaped—that is, blocked—and dried. The result was a crudely shaped hat, which had to be further manipulated into a finished product through a series of additional shaping processes. After initial blocking, the hat bodies were heated over a fire, then rubbed with a pumice stone to produce a smooth surface. Next, they were trimmed, then dyed. After the dye dried, a stiffening agent was applied using steam, which sealed the hat, rendering it somewhat waterproof and sufficiently stiff for final shaping. The last step was trimming, which involved lining the hat (typically with silk) and adding decorative details, including ribbons, bands, and, of course, feathers.

The manufacture of a beaver hat was a complex, dirty, unhealthy, labor-intensive operation, but, much like the classic recipe for rabbit stew that begins with the instruction "First, catch your rabbit," the process depended entirely on first trapping a beaver, and as demanding and even hazardous as making a hat was, obtaining the raw material for it was far more arduous and far more dangerous for hunter and hunted alike.

The largest rodent in North America, the beaver reaches an adult weight of sixty pounds—although some hundred-pounders have been recorded—and it can grow to more than a yard in length, from head to the rear end of the body. The distinctive, nearly hairless flat tail may add as much as another twelve inches. The animal uses it as a kind of fifth leg, to maintain balance, especially when it is gnawing on trees, and it may also slap the tail against the water to signal danger or to warn away predators. Its round, cuddly appearance belies a creature admirably adapted to a hard life in and near the water. The front legs are short, looking more like vestigial arms, with sharp, heavy claws nearly as well articulated as a pair of hands—though absent thumbs. The hind feet are generously webbed, capable of propelling the beaver swiftly through the water. The animal is at home on as well as under the water. Fleshy valves in its nose and ears close when it submerges, and underwater a transparent membrane covers its eyes. The beaver can even cut and chew submerged wood without getting water in its mouth; it simply draws its loose lips tightly behind its characteristically protruding front teeth. The prized fur of the beaver is rendered virtually waterproof by secretions of oily castoreum from its scent glands. In addition, a thick layer of fat under its skin provides insulation, which is crucial to survival in water that is often near freezing.

Behind its alert face, the beaver harbors sharp bucktoothed incisors with which it gnaws tree bark and cambium, the soft tissue beneath the bark. Willow, maple, birch, aspen, cottonwood, beech, poplar, and alder are the barks of choice, and the animal's stomach and gut have evolved to digest the cellulose component of tree bark. Beavers also consume other vegetation, including certain roots and buds, as well as various water plants.

Beaver life is centered on the family, called a colony, which consists of a breeding male and female plus their offspring. The colony is always located near water and food. As the colony exhausts the food supply immediately around it, members range farther from the colony in search of forage. This exposes them to predators—including trappers—but only when a wide area is totally depleted will the colony migrate in search of a new home.

Beginning at age three, beavers find a mate and mate for life (which may be as long as two dozen years in the wild), a circumstance that brings stability to the colony; however, they carry fidelity to a practical limit. When one mate dies, mourning is kept to a minimum. In short order, the survivor seeks a new spouse. The female gives birth to a litter of kits once a year, typically between April and June. She prepares for the birth—gestation is three months long—by making a soft bed in the lodge. The kits emerge with eyes wide open, and they start swimming within twenty-four hours of birth. After a very few days, they accompany their parents in exploring outside of the lodge. After only two weeks, the kits are fully weaned, but the young beavers remain with their parents for at least two full years.

The beaver's prodigious industry in building is legendary. The species's ambition is driven by an absolute need for two to three feet of water year-round to survive. At this depth, the water serves as a refuge from predators as well as an avenue to sources of food. Beavers also horde winter stores of food in caches they dig out underwater. To ensure that their habitat always has the requisite water level, beavers build dams, working either alone or with family members. The animals labor exclusively at night, using their short forepaws to carry mud and stones and their teeth to carry timber. Sometimes they float substantial logs considerable distances to get them to their dam. Natural engineers, they often build primary as well as small secondary dams to maintain the required water levels. Tightly constructed of such material as driftwood, green willows, birch, and poplar, the dams are sealed with mud and stones so that the structure is often nearly impossible to destroy—but even if it is breached, beavers will usually rebuild it in the course of a single night's work. The typical size of trees used for dam building ranges from four to twelve inches across the stump, but observers have recorded beavers using trees up to 150 feet tall and five feet across. Generally, they do not try to move very large trees, contenting themselves instead with stripping off and eating their bark. As for smaller trees, they use their formidable incisors to cut them into conveniently portable pieces, which they drag into the water for transportation to the construction site. If necessary, they may excavate canals—entirely new artificial waterways—in order to float very heavy logs and branches. All of this work is done mainly in the fall.

The trappers of old as well as modern biologists have long believed that the sound of moving water stimulates beavers to begin construction of a dam, although recent experiments suggest they also respond to other stimuli. In the early 1980s, experimenters inserted a pipe through an existing beaver dam, thereby allowing water to pass silently through the dam; the beavers used mud and sticks to plug the pipe and stop the flow of water. Under normal circumstances, beavers diligently maintain their dams, repairing any damage, and as long as the sound of water continues to be heard, they build the dam higher until they achieve silence. During periods of high water, however, the beavers allow some water to flow freely over the dam, lest the water level rise too high.

Beavers build dams in a variety of configurations, the shape apparently depending on the strength of water flow. In slow-moving water, they build nearly straight dams, whereas in stronger currents they curve their dams, bowing the structure so that its convex side points upstream. The size of dams ranges from modest to staggeringly grand in scale. Near Three Forks, Montana, for instance, a single dam 14 feet high, 23 feet thick at the base, and 2,140 feet wide—nearly a half mile—was recorded.

The beaver colony does not live in the dam but constructs a separate den, which serves as food cache, nursery, and home. In streams or rivers, beavers dig so-called bank dens, excavating these into the bank, then laying sticks, mud, and rocks over the top of the excavation. Bank dens usually have a number of exit and entrance tunnels, with at least one built above the high-water mark and another below the low-water mark. A den averages two feet wide by three feet in length and is about three feet high.

In the still or slower-moving water of ponds and lakes, beavers construct full-blown lodges at some distance from the shore. Like bank dens, lodges have one living chamber, and they also have tunnels above the waterline and below it—with one tunnel sufficiently deep to prevent its opening from freezing in the winter. Beavers use their deepwater tunnels to gather food and also to evade predators. Lodges are built to last and may be occupied by the same beaver colony for years. Not only do beavers continually repair their lodges, they tend to expand them yearly, so that a long-established lodge may be quite large. Comfort is also an important consideration. Typically, the floor of the main chamber of a beaver lodge is located somewhat above the level of the water and is liberally covered with wood chips, which absorb moisture. At the top of the dome-shaped lodge, the beavers leave a vent to draw in fresh air.

Beavers have long attracted the interest of naturalists, but one of the most enthusiastic admirers of the species was an engineer by profession. Brigadier General Hiram Martin Chittenden (1858–1917) graduated from West Point in 1884 and from the Army Engineering School three years later. He spent his military career not in combat but in flood control on the Missouri and Ohio rivers and in Yellowstone National Park. Intrigued by what he considered nature's most prodigious engineer, the beaver, and by man's interaction with this creature, he wrote *The American Fur Trade of the Far West,* a massive three-volume history that was published in 1902.

There was a time when the beaver ranged throughout North America, from East Coast to West, from the Gulf Coast to the Arctic Circle. Within a few years of the first extensive trade contacts between Euro-Americans and Native Americans, by the end of the seventeenth century, the beaver population had drastically thinned along the East Coast, and Native trappers pressed steadily westward. By the end of the American Revolution, the animals had been trapped to near extinction throughout the inland East as well as the coast, and the fur trade moved even farther west. Chittenden observed that by the first third of the nineteenth century "every stream of the West was as rich [in beaver] as if sands of gold covered its bottoms." He continued, "If gathered with judgment and not to the degree of extermination," the supply of fur-bearing beaver "would renew itself by natural increase."

Up to the French and Indian War of 1754–63, along the eastern seaboard, beaver trapping was characterized not by careful judgment but by naked rapacity—an unbounded economic, cultural, and political ferocity that drove a genocidal lust for land and that certainly did not scruple at bringing about in many places the extinction of all fur-bearing animals. In the two decades separating the outbreak of that war and the American Revolution, the quest for pelts moved men to endure spectacular hardships as they probed vast inland tracts of undiscovered country from which, often as not, they had little hope of ever returning. It also moved men to the same heartless, heedless rapine that had characterized the fur trade back east. With each passing year, trappers—Indian, white, or, more often, a genetic and cultural hybrid of the two races—had to journey farther west, farther from civilization, deeper into a country of forbidding topography, man-killing climate, and hostile "savages."

At the center of all a trapper's adventures, hardships, dangers, horrors, and audacities was the beaver. Whatever else a trapper had to know about surviving the wilderness, about living through biting cold, about finding food where none was to be found, about transforming hostile men into trading partners, and evading those who could not be transformed, he had first and foremost to become (as Chittenden wrote) "very expert in . . . knowledge of the habits of the little animal and the best methods of taking him." Trappers learned to tell, "from the appearance of a [beaver] lodge, the probable number of inmates and where they could most successfully entrap them." If the fur trade was lonely and dangerous, it was also grindingly arduous, just plain hard, dirty, miserable labor. Picture it. Through the winter silence of the Iroquois woodland, the muffled crunch of moccasin boots in the snow. A lone figure covered in fur—a "robe" of animal pelts loosely draped from his shoulders—crunches to the riverbank and eases down to the frozen river. He steps on the ice, stopping at what would be midstream in a warmer season, looks upstream toward a snow-covered beaver dam, then down at his feet.

From his shoulder, he lowers an iron ax—gotten from the Dutch in exchange for a good pelt—takes it in both hands, lifts it high over his head, then brings it down heavily into the thick river ice. He strikes blow after blow, chipping out a hole perhaps a foot and a half in diameter. The sound of the flowing river burbles up through it. The Iroquois lays the ax beside the hole, reaches into his robe, and withdraws a thick wooden club. He drops to his haunches, lays the club across his thighs, and looks into the hole. He waits. It is very cold, but he waits.

There are few sounds: the purling stream, the occasional crack of a branch or bough weighted heavily with snow and ice. Marked by the course of the pale winter sun, hours pass. The Iroquois, resting on his haunches the whole time, waits and watches.

At length he hears a faint splashing. He kneels, placing the club beside him. Suddenly, a bucktoothed, furry face appears above the rim. Plunging his hands into the icy water, the man seizes both of the chubby animal's short forepaws in his fists.

It is a beaver, eyes wide with fright.

Holding fast to the animal's paws, the Iroquois springs to his feet, swinging sixty pounds of living wet fur in front of him, over his head, then down hard, very hard, onto the ice. The stunned creature is motionless. The man takes up his club and brings it down sharply onto the beaver's skull, once, twice, splashing the snow-dusted river ice in scarlet.

This was the way of the Iroquois fur hunter early in the second third of the seventeenth century, as the Dutch traders reckoned time. For the Iroquois hunter, such historical reckoning meant nothing. To him, it was nothing more or less than morning in the late winter season. Now he would wait for another beaver to emerge through the hole he had cut, kill it as he had the first, then repeat the process with a third and perhaps a fourth before he hefted his heavy load and carried it back to his village, where he could at last warm himself by the longhouse fire.

He knew, as he hovered by the hole, that more beaver would come to him. He knew that they swam well under the ice, but, like every other flesh and blood creature, beavers have to breathe, and so they could not resist a patch of blue sky shining through the ice.

By the approach of the American Revolution, nearly a century and a half after this winter morning on the ice, trappers, whether Indian, white, or of mixed race, had adopted the steel trap as "universal mode of taking the beaver." Chittenden describes the typical trap of the late eighteenth century and early nineteenth: "a strong one of about five pounds' weight . . . valued [at the beginning of the nineteenth century] at twelve to sixteen dollars. The chain attached to the trap is about five feet long, with a swivel near the end to keep it from kinking."

As was the case 150 years earlier, winter was the prime trapping season, and this meant wading into icy streams to set the trap, so that no tracks would be apparent. The trapper "plants his trap in three or four inches of water a little way from the bank, and fastens the chain to a strong stick, which he drives into the bed of the stream at the full chain length from the trap. Immediately over the trap a little twig is set so that one end shall be about four inches above the surface of the water. On this is put a peculiar bait, supplied by the animal itself, castor, castorum [castoreum], or musk, the odor of which has a great attraction for the beaver."

The beaver reaches for the bait by raising his mouth toward it, "and in this act brings his feet directly under it. He thus treads upon the trap, springs it and is caught. In his fright he seeks concealment by his usual method of diving into deep water, but finds himself held by the chain which he cannot gnaw in two, and after an ineffectual struggle, he sinks to the bottom and is drowned." It is a cruel death, but one that is easy for neither the beaver nor the trapper. Often, the animal "wrests the chain from the stake, drags the trap to deeper water before he succumbs, or, taking it to the shore, becomes entangled in the undergrowth. In such cases he may cause the trapper much laborious and uncomfortable search, particularly if he has to wade deep streams in cold weather."

Usually, the trapper himself would skin the beaver near the place of its capture. This was to save space and weight. He wanted to carry back to camp only the commercial parts of the animal, nothing but the pelt, the tail, and the castoreum glands. In camp, the skins would be cleaned, dressed, cured, and marked. By the outbreak of the American Revolution, pelts gathered by white trappers were customarily assembled for sale into hundred-pound packs. On average, there were eighty skins to a pack. The packs had to be made up with meticulous care, the choicest furs always placed inside, the less valuable ones forming the outermost layers. Camp required vigilant guarding, since a single marauder could easily make off with a pack, which might represent an entire year of dangerous and difficult labor for a trapper.

In his 1836 epic of the fur trade, *Astoria; or, Anecdotes of an Enterprise Beyond the Rocky Mountains,* Washington Irving observed, "Two leading objects of commercial gain have given birth to wide and daring enterprise in the early history of the Americas; the precious metals of the South, and the rich peltries of the North." Those who pursued these two commodities, Irving declared, "have . . . been the pioneers and precursors of civilization. Without pausing on the borders, they have penetrated at once, in defiance of difficulties and dangers, to the heart of savage countries: laying open the hidden secrets of the wilderness; leading the way to remote regions of beauty and fertility that might have remained unexplored for ages, and beckoning after them the slow and pausing steps of agriculture and civilization."

Writing in the twilight of European literature's Romantic Age, Irving imbued the American fur trade with a romance he, as an American writer, desperately wanted to import into the literature of his native country. In this desire, he was by no means self-deluded or -deceived. For the story he had to tell was indeed filled with romance—with genuinely romantic and inspiring vision, with majesty, with courage, with feats of superhuman endurance and ambition, as well as craven greed, cruelty, and horror that would put to shame any gothic fiction of the era. Nor did Irving exaggerate the importance of the fur trade as a driver of enterprise, of settlement, and of competing empires. What America's first great writer did overlook, however, was the very start of the story: Samuel Pepys's beaver hat.

Monday, May 26, 1662, was a busy day for Pepys. He was up by four in the morning to tackle the tangled accounts of his patron, Edward Montagu, the Earl of Sandwich. Next, he attended to other business before going to Trinity House, seat of the Corporation of Trinity House, which had (and, to this very day, still has) responsibility for administering lighthouses and other navigational aids in English waters. At three in the afternoon, Pepys, a member of the corporation, sat to dinner with "the Brethren" there, taking care to plant himself near old William Prynne. The author of some two hundred books and pamphlets, Prynne was a prominent Puritan foe of the Catholic-leaning church policy of the former archbishop of Canterbury, William Laud, and thereby had attained high office in the government of Oliver Cromwell after the Civil War. Much to the chagrin of "General Ironsides," however, Prynne soon emerged as a critic of the Interregnum's military government, and in consequence Cromwell threw him into one of his prisons for a time. This bitter experience helped convert Prynne into a supporter of the Restoration, and so, under Charles II, the rehabilitated man was rewarded with appointment as Keeper of Records in the Tower of London. Pepys, who loved nothing more than the most delectable (and preferably scurrilous) records of history, suspected that old Prynne would have something most interesting to say at dinner.

He was not disappointed.

Prynne discoursed "upon what records he hath of the lust and wicked lives of the nuns heretofore in England, and showed me out of his pocket one wherein thirty nuns for their lust were ejected of their house, being not fit to live there, and by the Pope's command to be put, however, into other nunnerys." Much as he might have liked to hear more on this subject, Pepys had another engagement and "could not stay to end dinner with them." He "rose, and privately went out, and by water to my brother's, and thence to take my wife to the Redd Bull, where we saw 'Doctor Faustus.'"

Christopher Marlowe's play had been written more than half a century earlier, but in Pepys's day it was already a classic and frequently performed. Unfortunately, in Pepys's judgment, the performance he and his wife saw was "so wretchedly and poorly done, that we were sick of it." No matter, the disappointed theatergoers drove leisurely "homewards by coach, through Moorefields, where we stood awhile, and saw the wrestling. At home, got my lute upon the leads, and there played, and so to bed."

Even a bad performance of *Doctor Faustus* yields many memorable lines, the most memorable of which is spoken by Faustus himself as Mephistopheles delivers up to him a vision of Helen of Troy: "Was this the face that launched a thousand ships?" the world-weary scholar asks. So we might do precisely what Washington Irving did not—deliver up a vision of the beaver hat Samuel Pepys so treasured at four pounds, five shillings.

We do not know exactly what it looked like, but we may safely assume that it was considerably more elaborate than the modest headgear that had prevailed during the Puritan Interregnum but less ornate than what the Cavaliers had worn just before that. Was this, then, the hat that launched a thousand ships?

All told, the number of ships launched in quest of fur for hats like that of Samuel Pepys was certainly far greater than a thousand, especially if some 350 sixteenth-century Newfoundland coastal fishing vessels and untold numbers of small river craft over the centuries are added to the great galleons and doughty transports of the transatlantic voyagers. To be sure, New World exploration, settlement, and exploitation, as well as the creation of white and Indian alliances and enmities, were not driven exclusively by a quest for beaver fur, but when the initial dreams of gold and spices petered out—and they evaporated quickly—fur lingered as a powerful American lure. It beckoned the ships, and it recruited veritable armies of hunters and trappers, men solitary and very nearly superhuman, who were willing to journey westward, always westward, as the peltries of the East diminished. It moved Indians to tolerate and even to befriend some white trapper-traders while marking others as enemies to be killed. It created alliances and enmities that quite literally made history.

The fur trade, Irving observed, was the herald of civilization. Yet the second line of Marlowe's famed couplet is all too relevant as well:

Was this the face that launched a thousand ships,
And burned the topless towers of Illium?

If Mr. Pepys's hat launched a civilization, it summoned up as well—like the allure of Helen that brought down Troy—the dark side of that civilization in the multifarious guises of greed, cruelty, ecological devastation, and revolutionary warfare. Some of these revolutions, from the Beaver Wars to the French and Indian War, verged on genocide. The final revolution, what we celebrate as the *American* Revolution, was also enormously destructive, but it did produce a nation.

What follows is the story of the launching as well as the killing, the devastation and the creation, too. It is the story of a peculiar, fascinating, and deadly dangerous political, commercial, ecological, and military enterprise that helped to define the century and a half of American history culminating in the violent birth of the United States.

1

The Middle Ground

———✦———

FROM 1492 TO 1580, the year Philip II, king of Castile and Aragon, united for the time being the bulk of Spain with Portugal, thereby consolidating the vast New World holdings of all Iberia, Spain held a monopoly on American conquest and thereby came to control the largest empire in geographical extent the planet has ever known. Founded mainly on agriculture, the cultivation of cotton, sugar, and tobacco, and the raising of cattle, it was maintained by slaves, black as well as Indian. The empire was based on slave labor in one form or another, yet the lure that drew Spain westward was neither vegetative nor fleshly, but metallic overlaid with something resembling divinity. Driving the many Spanish voyages into the sunset lands was gold, gold plated with the thinnest layer of God.

Never mind that few of the Spanish expeditions actually returned with the coveted ore. A handful of discoveries was quite sufficient to inspire many more, the most seductive of which were those of Hernán Cortés. When in 1519 he landed a small force at what is today Veracruz, Mexico, he was greeted by ambassadors of the Aztec king Montezuma II, who bore dazzling gifts, mostly of gold. Doubtless, they were intended to appease the newcomer. Cortés, however, was anything but sated.

"Send me some more of it," he reportedly told Montezuma's minions, "because I and my companions suffer from a disease of the heart which can be cured only with gold."

From this point on, the story is a familiar one, perhaps too familiar any longer to generate much excitement. Driven by this sickness at the heart, a disorder all of us understand, Cortés and his companions marched on Tenochtitlán, the Aztec capital known today as Mexico City. The conquistador took care first to bore holes in the hulls of his ships ("Shipworm!" he told his men) so that none of them, least of all he himself, could turn back. He recruited allies among the ever-warring city-states of the far-flung Aztec realm, winning some by promising to make common cause against the Aztecs, others by sheer terror, as when he slaughtered three thousand Cholula tribespeople in the space of two hours, stopping only when volunteers answered his call to arms. Perhaps it was word of this and other bloodbaths that made Montezuma go weak in the knees. Or perhaps he believed the Spaniard to be the incarnation of the birdlike god Quetzalcoatl, who created man out of his own blood. In response to whatever prompting, the Aztec ruler threw open Tenochtitlán to Cortés and his conqueror band.

For Montezuma, it meant his death; for his people, their ruin. For Cortés, it meant mountains of gold. For those in Spain who spoke to Cortés—he returned twice to his homeland—or who heard of the reward of his audacity, it inspired envy and emulation. So powerful yet so familiar did the story of Cortés and the conquest of Mexico become that for a long time gold outshone all else as a motive for risking everything on a voyage to the New World. Its glow suffused sober history itself, and generation after generation has been satisfied with this formulaic justification for New World exploration and conquest: *It was all about gold*.

Gold and spices.

In every grade-school text, a dash of spice completed the recipe. European exploration and settlement of the Americas was all about gold *and spices*.

Naturally, the gold was always easier to understand. Universal shorthand for value and worth, when monetized, it is value and worth themselves: a commodity fully fungible, capable of instant conversion into real property, the service of slaves or kings, and the satisfaction of every desire.

Spices—well, that requires explanation. Food is life, but food is also dead, and, like all things dead, food rots. Spice fights rot, slows rot, and what it can neither fight nor slow, it disguises with strong taste and intoxicating aroma. Like gold, then, spices possessed power, and their power exercised allure. Ounce for ounce, pound for pound, spice, sovereign against the rot of death and therefore an elixir of life, was even more valuable than gold.

Yet as a motivator of contact and commerce between people uprooted from the Old World and those rooted in the new, neither gold nor spice was as enduring as fur.

Between 30,000 and 130,000 years ago, a member of the subspecies *Homo sapiens neanderthalensis*—Neanderthal man—compared himself to a furry mammal, found his own nakedness wanting, and began clothing himself in fur. The physical advantages are obvious enough. Animal hide provides protection against superficial injury, and fur, which traps air in the spaces between its fibers, is a superb insulator, enabling the wearer to conserve one of life's most precious commodities: the energy represented by body heat.

The symbolic, emotional, and cultural advantages of fur are far more speculative. Anthropologists and historians have pointed out that Native American (among other) hunters frequently made it a practice to consume the heart of a freshly killed animal in the belief that by doing so they would take on some of the beast's strength, ferocity, and courage. The early hominid hunters who appropriated animal fur certainly derived the physical advantages of their prey's coat, but perhaps they were driven as well by a belief—at some level of consciousness—that they were also taking on certain aspects of the animal's being, spirit, nature, or virtue.

Through history, fur has been associated with warriors, conquerors, and kings. Such modern trappings as the fur trim on the highly ornamented pelisse (jacket) of the hussar—the type of light cavalry soldier that emerged in Hungary in the fifteenth century and rose to prominence in the early nineteenth—and the busby (tall fur headdress) of the British Horse Guard are meant to convey a kind of animal ferocity. In a far more general context, clothing made of leather or fur connects the wearer to the natural world (though vegans and antifur activists are quick to point out the paradox that this connection comes at the price of nature's destruction). The value of gold is so universally perceived as inherent that it is readily monetized. Although today the value of spices is as a flavor enhancement, for most of history they were inherently valued as powerful food preservatives. The inherent value of fur is chiefly in the warmth it provides, rendering the coldest climates survivable. Yet, as with gold and spices, fur has always had a value beyond its inherent physical properties. Its emotional allure may well be rooted in the intimate connection fur creates between the wearer and the animal world, but, in the course of history, it also became a widely sought emblem of cultural and economic status. Like other badges, articles of fur both denote and confer authority, power, and status. For men of the time and place Samuel Pepys occupied, for example, a fine beaver hat was both token and mojo, symbolic of as well as productive of cultural and economic stature above the ordinary. So the material commanded a sufficiently high price to drive people to cross the ocean, to penetrate the frontier, and to dare death in the many forms the wilderness deals it.

In *The Ambiguous Iroquois Empire* (1984), a study of the "confederation" between Indian tribes and the English colonies, Francis Jennings dismisses "the fur trade" as a "misnomer" for "what is usually meant," namely "exchange between Indians and European, Euramericans, or Euro-Canadians." Jennings observes that there "were many kinds of such exchange, involving many different commodities," not just fur. True, of course. Yet Richard White, in his history of "Indians, Empires, and Republics in the Great Lakes Region, 1650–1815," *The Middle Ground* (1991), explains that the fur trade "bound people to each other" in unique ways. "Furs . . . acquired a special social meaning because, more than any other goods produced by the Algonquians [by which White means the largely

French-allied Indians of the Great Lakes region], they could be transformed into [the] European goods" the Indians so strongly desired.

By the seventeenth century, the fur trade was transforming American civilization in ways more profoundly consequential than the trade in gold, spices, or other commodities. For both suppliers and buyers, for Indians and Europeans/Euro-Americans alike, fur was so culturally charged a commodity that it drove the creation of what White calls the "middle ground," a society, culture, and civilization that blended Native, European, and Euro-American destinies, creating a network of cultural, economic, genetic, and military relationships—blends, alliances, and enmities—that would ultimately express themselves in the revolution by which the colonies broke free from Europe to create a new American nation.

However, it was not to America that Europe looked first to find the furs it craved.

During the early Middle Ages, before Europe knew of the New World, Russia and, to a lesser extent, Scandinavia were the major suppliers of pelts not only to Western Europe but to Asia. Before the seventeenth century, Russian furs were hunted primarily in the west and included wolf, fox, rabbit, squirrel, and marten in addition to beaver. By the mid-seventeenth century, Russian trappers and hunters were venturing into Siberia, and their exports accordingly expanded to include lynx, Arctic fox, sable, and ermine (stoat). Sea otter also came into demand, prompting the Russians to push beyond the Siberian coast and across the Bering Sea to Alaska, the only Russian exploitation of North American peltries.

Russian and Northern European fur so stimulated the Western European demand for the commodity that it soon exploded beyond the capacity of the Old World to supply the market. When this happened, Europeans at last looked west, to America, with which they were already familiar as the source of yet another living commodity: cod.

At least since approximately A.D. 800, Vikings had been fishing, eating, and trading in cod. Norwegian fishermen perfected the art of drying the fish, and by the eleventh century a vigorous market in dried cod had developed throughout Europe, well down to the south. It was a Norwegian, Bjarni Herjulfsson in 986, who is generally believed to be the first European to set eyes on North America, though, according to the medieval *Grœnlendinga Saga* (*Greenlanders Saga*), he did not go ashore, and no one back in Norway took much interest in this New Found Land—except for the Iceland-born Greenlander Leif Ericson, who about 1002 or 1003 landed at a place he named Vinland, believed to be the present L'Anse aux Meadows on the northern tip of Newfoundland. Ericson and his crew of thirty-five erected a clutch of huts in which they wintered before returning to Greenland in the spring. A few years later, Thorfinn Karlsevni, another Greenlander some believe was Ericson's brother, settled in Vinland, passing two years there, exploring the Newfoundland coast and battling a local people who called themselves the Beothuk, but whom Thorfinn and the other Norsemen dubbed Skrælings, an Old Norse word meaning "dwarfs" or, even less flatteringly, "wretches."

After Thorfinn was killed in an encounter with a Skræling, the Norsemen were discouraged from making further settlements, but they did take notice that cod was the staple food of the Beothuk, and that may have further spurred exploitation of the cod fisheries along the coast of north Norway, trade that was, by the fourteenth century, monopolized by the powerful Hanseatic League. As for the New World, for some five hundred years before Columbus's first voyage in 1492, the Old World largely ignored it. Some historians do believe that Basque fishermen began exploiting the Canadian cod fisheries by the early fifteenth century, *before* Columbus set sail, but the main phase of the European cod fishing in North America began here shortly after the Great Navigator's voyages. On June 7, 1494, Spain and Portugal concluded the Treaty of Tordesillas, which resolved a dispute between the two kingdoms over possession of claims in the New World. The treaty drew a line of demarcation that divided all "newly discovered" lands outside of Europe along a meridian halfway between the Cape Verde Islands (already claimed by Portugal) and Cuba and Hispaniola, islands claimed by the Spanish crown. Lands lying east of the meridian would henceforth be Portuguese; those to the west, Spanish. Four years after the treaty was concluded,

King Manuel I of Portugal granted a letter patent to João Fernandes, giving him leave to explore the Atlantic east of the Tordesillas line. In company with another Portuguese mariner, Pêro de Barcelos, Fernandes discovered and probed Labrador in 1498—a name derived from the Portuguese *lavrador,* "landholder," which was thereafter appended to Fernandes's name, so that he is known to history as João Fernandes Lavrador. He did not long enjoy his acquisition or his title. In 1501, this time bearing letters patent from England's Henry VII, João Fernandes Lavrador embarked on a new voyage in search of lands to claim in the name of England. He never returned.

The discoveries of the ill-fated Portuguese mariner inspired Manuel I to send Gaspar Corte-Real to follow in the earlier navigator's wake, specifically to search for a Northwest Passage to Asia. For the fifteenth- and sixteenth-century monarchs of Spain as well as Portugal—and for many powerful and influential men who followed them—the New World did not seem a discovery sufficiently valuable in itself. While it might offer many attractive commodities, not the least of which was cod, the land mass was also regarded as an obstacle between Europe and Asia, a proven source of spices and other very fine things. So, like many men after him, Corte-Real, with his brother Miguel, explored Labrador and Newfoundland for the purpose of finding the shortest possible water route to Asia. In the process, he captured sixty Natives to sell as slaves—for, as Columbus himself had pointed out to his patrons Queen Isabella and King Ferdinand—the "Indians" of America were among the most valuable commodities the New World offered. After packing his human cargo onto two of his three ships, Gaspar Corte-Real sent them back to Portugal under the command of Miguel while he continued to explore. Like João Fernandes Lavrador, Gaspar Corte-Real went missing. In 1502, Miguel returned to search for him. Neither brother was ever heard from again.

Nevertheless, though Newfoundland and Labrador seemingly consumed those who sought to possess them, Manuel I sent yet another voyager, João Alvares Fagundes, to Newfoundland and what is today Nova Scotia, enticing him to set off on the hazardous voyage in March 1521 with a grant of exclusive rights to and ownership of whatever he might find.

. . .

Unlike the other Portuguese who came before him, Fagundes did not disappear without a trace. In 1607, the French explorer, diplomat, and entrepreneur Samuel de Champlain stumbled upon "an old cross, all covered with moss, and almost wholly rotted away," which he believed Fagundes had erected eighty years earlier at a Nova Scotia village now called Advocate.

Champlain, however, was not following in the footsteps of the Portuguese explorer, but in those of a fellow Frenchman. Jacques Cartier was born on December 31, 1491, in Saint-Malo, on the coast of Brittany. Unlike many of his seafaring brethren, Cartier enjoyed a certain respectability and even prominence in his community; he was frequently called upon to bear witness at local baptisms and was more than once even enlisted as a godfather. Indeed, he was highly enough regarded to merit the hand of Mary Catherine des Granches, daughter of one of Saint-Malo's leading families, in 1520, and in 1534, when Brittany was united with France by the Edict of Union, Cartier was thought sufficiently important in the community to warrant an introduction to King Francis I. He was presented by the bishop of Saint-Malo, Jean le Veneur, who informed the king that Cartier possessed ample ability to "lead ships to the discovery of new lands in the New World."

Veneur well knew that Francis had, ten years earlier, invited Giovanni da Verrazano to explore North America in the name of France, and he also understood that Cartier had accompanied the intrepid Italian and had therefore seen a long stretch of the eastern seaboard, from South Carolina north to Nova Scotia. With Verrazano, he had also sailed to Newfoundland. The king was sold, and later in 1534 he commissioned Cartier to— what else?—seek out a Northwest Passage to Asia, admonishing him to take care as well to "discover certain islands and lands where it is said that a great quantity of gold and other precious things are to be found."

On this first voyage, which explored parts of Newfoundland and parts of what are now Canada's Atlantic provinces, Cartier and his men encountered a New World bounty of natural abundance—the profusion of birds at what today is called Rocher aux Oiseaux (Bird Rock) in the Magdalen Islands—and responded to the wonder by wantonly slaughtering perhaps a thousand birds of all kinds. On a note of greater humanity and hope, Cartier and his crew briefly made two contacts with some Micmac Indians on the north side of Chaleur Bay and, in what was the first exchange of its kind, traded knives for their furs.

These exchanges were peaceful and productive, but when, on July 24, Cartier planted on the shore of Gaspé Bay a large cross inscribed with the legend "Long Live the King of France," the Indians who looked on—members of an Iroquoian tribe—were clearly displeased. Noting signs of their growing hostility, Cartier summarily kidnapped the two sons of the Indian he referred to as "their captain," apparently intending to hold them hostage to ensure the good behavior of the locals. Surprisingly, the "captain" told Cartier that he could take his sons with him back to France on condition that he return not only with them but with goods to trade.

Cartier did return in the spring of 1535, with a crew of 110 (and the "captain's" sons) in three vessels, which carried a modest cargo of trade goods. This time, he called on an Iroquoian chief, named Donnacona, then ventured to Hochelaga—the site of Montreal—arriving there on October 2, 1535. He was met by more than a thousand Indians, with whom he did some trading. Here, he noted, at Hochelaga, the St. Lawrence River roiled into a wild rapids, which prevented further navigation, yet also, however incongruously, persuaded Cartier that he had discovered the Northwest Passage. The idea that, once a way was found to negotiate the rapids, the river would set a person en route to China proved enduring. Sometime in the mid-seventeenth century, the town that sprang up along the riverbank at this point, along with the rapids, was named Lachine—la Chine, French for China—and today is a Montreal neighborhood still known by that name.

Cartier spent a bitter winter in the area, during which scurvy broke out both among the local Indians and among his own crew, all but ten of whom fell seriously ill. Domagaya, one of the hostages Cartier had taken to France and returned, introduced Cartier to a native medicine made from the bark of the arborvitae tree, which he called annedda, and promised it would cure the scurvy. It did. Eighty-five of 110 Frenchmen survived the winter.

When he returned to France in May 1536, Cartier took Chief Donnacona with him. The Indian told King Francis I of the existence of the Kingdom of Saguenay, north of his own realm, where there was to be found an abundance of rubies, gold, and other wonders. This was quite sufficient to prompt the French monarch to send Cartier back to Canada in the spring of 1541. The objective this time was to locate not the Northwest Passage but the "Kingdom of Saguenay" and also to establish a permanent settlement on the St. Lawrence. Cartier built a fortress town at the site of present-day Cap-Rouge, Quebec, and set up a modest fur-trading operation there, concentrating on obtaining the kinds of fur that were used to trim cloth coats. That he largely ignored beaver, the stuff of hats, coats, and other major articles of clothing, suggests that he was more interested in dispatching his men into the countryside to look for jewels and gold rather than seek out Native hunters with beaver pelts to offer.

Cartier's men soon returned with quartz and fool's gold, which, taking them for diamonds and real gold, the eager Frenchman immediately sent back to France aboard one of his five ships. At this point, however, the local Iroquoians suddenly called a halt to the friendly trading that had so recently begun. There was apparently a battle, in which something like thirty-five Frenchmen were killed before everyone was able to retreat into the safety of the fortified town. Cartier returned to France, disheartened, but cheered by the prospect of the boatload of "gold" and "diamonds" that was waiting for him. There is no record of his disillusionment, but that this proved to be the final voyage of the still-vigorous fifty-year-old suggests he had written off Canada.

Although Cartier made tentative French inroads into general trade with the Indians of the Montreal area and also began dealing specifically in fur, the great European demand for beaver fur that developed during the mid-sixteenth century came not from Cartier and other river-borne and overland explorers but from those who worked the cod fisheries off the

Newfoundland coast. The Basque fishermen in particular developed advanced drying techniques that made these remote fisheries economically viable by preserving the fish well enough so that the cargo could withstand the long voyage from the Grand Banks of the North Atlantic to Europe. The Basque cod industry depended on volume, and that meant securing suitable harbors with ample supplies of lumber for the fires required to dry large quantities of cod. This need increased both the opportunities for and the necessity of contact between the fishermen and the local Indians. Trade naturally followed.

The fishermen were fishermen, not traders, but they learned to equip themselves with the mostly metal items—knives, axes, pots and pans, and other implements—the Indians wanted. These were traded for beaver robes, finished items of apparel fashioned from sewn-together tanned pelts. The fishermen used the robes to fortify themselves against the icy North Atlantic on their return voyages to Europe, then, upon arrival in port, unstitched the robes and sold the individual beaver pelts, which the French called *castor gras* ("coat beaver"), to furriers and, especially, hatmakers.

For the Basque fishermen, the beaver trade was always a sideline, but its profitability was highly instructive, first to the French and then to the English. By the sixteenth century, European demand for fur, especially beaver, had already outrun the capacity of Russian and Scandinavian producers, and the North American beaver sold off the backs of fishermen was hardly sufficient to meet the demand. The increased availability of pelts, therefore, served to stimulate rather than satisfy the clamor.

Cartier and the Basque fishermen traded with Iroquoians, who, by the sixteenth century or perhaps earlier, were members of five tribes, the Mohawk, Oneida, Onondaga, Cayuga, and Seneca, loosely confederated and living in what is today upstate New York and parts of Canada. When the French, increasingly cognizant of the growing demand for fur, decided to make another run at trading with the Indians for the pelts, they turned not to the Iroquois but to the Hurons and Petuns, who were rivals of the Iroquois and, by the end of the first third of the seventeenth century, on the verge of a ruinous war with them.

The leader of this second wave of French fur trading was Samuel de Champlain. Born into a family of mariners in Brouage, a port town in the French province of Saintonge, sometime between 1564 and 1580 (the year is much disputed), he accompanied his uncle-in-law on voyages to the West Indies and Mexico during 1598–1600. The enterprising young man covertly took extensive notes on operations in these Spanish colonies, which he turned over to King Henri IV on his return, receiving by way of reward a generous royal stipend. This money nicely supplemented a large inheritance from his uncle-in-law, who died in 1601, giving Champlain something few other explorers have ever had: independence.

Not that he forgot his duty to his king. From 1601 to 1603, he served as royal geographer, gleaning much information from fishermen who worked the waters off northern New England to Newfoundland. He became acquainted with the colonization efforts of Pierre de Chauvin de Tonnetuit, to whom Henri had granted a fur-trading monopoly for New France in 1599. In 1602, the monopoly passed to Aymar de Chaste, whom the king appointed his viceroy in Canada and lieutenant governor of New France. Aymar de Chaste quickly exploited his royal fur monopoly to create the Canada and Acadia Trading Company, the first formally constituted, investment-backed fur-based trading enterprise in the Americas. With the king's endorsement and blessing, Champlain secured from de Chaste a place aboard one of his North America–bound ships.

The leader of de Chaste's fur-trading expedition was François Gravé Du Pont, who had been Chauvin's partner. His long hair and longer beard gave him the air of a teacher more than of an explorer, and in America Du Pont took Champlain under his wing, tutoring him in everything from riverborne navigation to bargaining with Indians. Champlain proved a quick study. With Du Pont to guide him and following in the footsteps of Cartier, he drew the first detailed map of the St. Lawrence River, destined to become the great avenue of the North American fur trade, and he wrote a narrative to accompany it, which was published in 1603 as *Des Sauvages; ou, Voyage de Samuel Champlain, de Brouage, faite en la France nouvelle l'an 1603* (Concerning the Savages; or, Travels of Samuel Champlain of Brouage, Made in New France in the

Year 1603). Strikingly evident in this book are the friendly relations the French established with the Montagnais (also called Naskapi or Innu people) along the north shore of the Gulf of St. Lawrence. This was in stark contrast to the hostility of the Iroquoian Indians Cartier had encountered. In particular, Champlain managed to kindle a personal friendship with a Montagnais chief, Begourat.

Champlain joined a second expedition to New France in 1604, spending several years exploring the region south of the St. Lawrence River, the area that would later be known as Acadia. He was attached to the dashingly handsome Pierre Dugua, sieur de Mons, to whom Henri IV granted a fur-trading monopoly in Acadia. At Dugua's behest, Champlain scouted out and selected a site for winter settlement, St. Croix Island in the St. Croix River. After that first winter, the settlement was moved across the bay as Port-Royal, the place from which Champlain launched several exploratory expeditions.

In 1608, Dugua financed a flotilla of three ships bearing as passengers a small army of workers for the purpose of establishing a new colony on the St. Lawrence. He put Champlain in command of the flagship, *Don-de-Dieu* (Gift of God), with Du Pont—by now a close friend—in command of the *Lévrier* (Hunting Dog). After landing at the so-called point of Quebec on July 3, 1608, Champlain hastily built three two-story wooden buildings and surrounded them with a wooden stockade and moat. This was the beginning of Quebec City. From here, in 1610, Champlain sent Étienne Brûlé—he would have been about eighteen years old at the time—to live among the Hurons in exchange for a young Huron youth Champlain called Savignon, who lived among the French. Champlain had a radical plan. He meant for Brûlé to learn as much about the Indians as possible, including their language and their customs, and, for his part, he intended to teach Savignon the ways of the French. Champlain offered a military alliance with the Hurons against their Iroquois enemies, especially the Onondaga and the Seneca, but he wanted to establish an even deeper relationship with them through Brûlé—and, later, other young men as well—founded on intimate cultural knowledge. In this, Champlain set the pattern for French-Indian relations that would endure through at least the mid-eighteenth century. Unlike the Dutch and the English, who (with some exceptions) held themselves aloof from the Indians with whom they traded, Champlain sought to embrace them and deal with them on an equal footing.

Of Étienne Brûlé little is known. He was born about 1592 in Champigny, France, and he came to New France aboard a ship Champlain commanded, sailing from Honfleur on April 13, 1608. Some records suggest that he was Champlain's servant; in his own writings, Champlain refers to him only as "the young lad Brûlé." In 1609, Brûlé was with Champlain when he helped a group of Montagnais, allied with the Hurons, defeat a band of some one hundred Iroquois near his Quebec settlement. Aided by Champlain's military advice, the Montagnais prevailed, capturing fifteen Iroquois. The rest of the enemy were either killed in battle or drowned trying to escape. The unlucky prisoners were slowly tortured to death, save one, for whose life Champlain successfully argued. Of the other fourteen, at least one was not only tortured and quartered but also eaten. Far from horrifying Brûlé, the savage spectacle apparently awakened in him a desire to live among the Indians. He got his chance in 1611, when Champlain negotiated Brûlé's swap with Savignon. Champlain believed that this cultural exchange would put him in an advantageous position to establish profitable trade. Not only would Brûlé become familiar with the Indians' country, including the location of the great peltries, he would also earn their trust and learn their language, thereby staking out the "middle ground," the part Native, part European cultural space in which untrammeled trade could take place.

For most of the next twenty-two years, Étienne Brûlé accompanied the Huron and their chief, Iroquet, on journeys throughout much of Quebec, Ontario, and Michigan. He was almost certainly the first European to see all of the Great Lakes. He was gone for years at a time, though he reported faithfully and amply to Champlain whenever the two managed to meet. His success living among the Huron persuaded Champlain to establish as a regular policy the integration of young men among the

Indians, "to make the acquaintance of the people, to learn their mode of living and the character and extent of their territory."

On September 8, 1615, Brûlé set off with twelve Hurons to make contact with the Carantouannais, potential French and Huron allies who lived under constant threat from the surrounding Onondaga and Seneca in what is now Bradford County, Pennsylvania. Brûlé was not only willing but apparently eager to risk death among the Hurons' enemies. As the late nineteenth-century historian Willshire Butterfield observed, "Savage life had positive pleasures for [Brûlé], and its perils only intensified his liking for it." Whatever thrill it gave the young man, his hazardous mission produced a firm alliance between the Carantouannais and the Hurons, with Champlain and his French contingent participating in it.

Thanks to Brûlé, some five hundred Carantouannais warriors joined Champlain and the Hurons in combat against the Onondaga and Seneca. In October 1615, Brûlé returned with the Carantouannais to Carantouan, their village in present-day Bradford County, and, restless for new adventure, he set out alone on a birch bark canoe voyage southward on the Susquehanna River. He had become an expert navigator in this native vessel, stout ribbed but ultralight, its sweepingly upturned beaks fore and aft making for both speed and shallowness of draft, so that the canoe could negotiate the fiercest of rapids as well as the most still of shallows. Moreover, depending on its size, the birch bark canoe could be easily carried by one or two men, who could thus transport it overland from one river to another—making a *portage,* the French would say—which meant that travelers did not have to limit their long journeys strictly to the routes and junctions of rivers. Just as Champlain recognized the need for cultural as well as economic exchange, using agents like Brûlé, so he was quick to see the utility of the birch bark canoe. Thanks to him, this Native conveyance became the primary vehicle of French exploration and trade in the seventeenth and eighteenth centuries.

In his canoe, Brûlé traveled as far south as the Chesapeake Bay and saw both Maryland and Virginia, then returned to Carantouan. Early in April 1616, he set out from here to return to the Huron villages, with five or six Carantouannais serving as guides. En route, they were set upon by

Seneca in a violent exchange that seems to have tested the limits of the bond between Brûlé and the Carantouannais.

This much is certain. In the melee, Brûlé became separated from his guides. Far less certain is whether or not the separation was an accident. It seems highly likely that Brûlé made a purposeful decision to separate himself from the Carantouannais in the belief that doing so increased his chances of survival.

Perhaps Brûlé was right. Whether due to a stratagem of every man for himself or dumb luck, the Frenchman survived (as did the Carantouannais). Yet he survived only to realize quite suddenly that he was (in the words of Butterfield) "now alone in the interminable woods and greatly bewildered."

Whatever else the wilderness might do to a man, it could always "bewilder" him. Brûlé was unable to find any trail leading in any direction, neither forward to the Hurons nor back to the Carantouannais. After wandering aimlessly for days, without food and on the verge of despair, he happened upon an Indian footpath. He had no way of knowing whether it led to friends or enemies, but he concluded that any fate was better than dying lost and alone in the wilderness. He therefore followed the trail and, at length, encountered three Indians loaded down with fish. They were Seneca. They were the enemy.

No matter. Brûlé ran after them and "made the depths of the forest ring with a shout, according to the custom of savages, to attract their attention." If his objective in this was to show that he meant no harm, it worked. The three Seneca laid down their bows and arrows, and Brûlé likewise set down the Indian weapons he carried. He then unfolded his story to them. By way of response, he was offered food and a pipe, and he accompanied the men back to their village.

In forest depths, men were equals, it seemed, and could be friendly. Once Brûlé was in the Seneca village, however, he was swarmed by those curious to see an Adoresetoüy—a "Man of Iron," as the Seneca called the French, referring not to will or physical strength but to the metal implements the Frenchmen carried with them and offered in trade for beaver and other goods. Brûlé was bombarded with questions: "How did you happen to lose your way? Do you not belong to the Adoresetoüy, who make war on us?"

Brûlé replied that he belonged to a "better nation than the French, which nation was yearning to make their acquaintance and to make them their friends."

The villagers did not believe him. With good reason, of course. On the face of it, it *was* a lie. Yet on another level, it was a profound truth. Brûlé had by this time lived for years among the Indians. He had learned their language and their ways. He had fought beside them. He was certainly no Indian, but neither was he any longer simply a Frenchman. He was a citizen of another nation, and perhaps, given the time and place in which he lived, it was indeed a better nation than the French.

This, however, did not occur to the Seneca villagers, who threw themselves upon Brûlé, bound him, tore out his fingernails with their teeth, set glowing firebrands upon his flesh, and, hair by hair, plucked out his beard.

Such torture was ritual, and it was inevitably the prelude to—often the means of—death. Yet everything changed when a Seneca grabbed for the crucifix the Frenchman wore around his neck. Brûlé was by no means a religious man, and he would have gladly traded the ornament for his life, but, writhing as he was, Brûlé nevertheless retained the presence of mind to notice that before the Indian reached for his crucifix, he asked what it was.

"If you take it," Brûlé gasped out, "and kill me you will yourself immediately die—you and all your kin."

The threat bought but a moment's hesitation. That turned out to be just enough.

According to the account Brûlé later gave Champlain, the day had been fair, clear, and sunny when, suddenly, "darkness brooded o'er the scene." Thick clouds gathered and were instantly accompanied by lurid lightning and fierce thunder "so violent and long-continued that it was something strange and awful."

Without even taking time to unbind Brûlé, his torturers fled. He did not exult, however, but instead called after them in the gentlest tone he could summon. The Great Spirit was indeed angry for the torment they had caused him, he said, but he would intervene with the Spirit and save them all.

His tormentors now bound up his wounds, fed him, and nursed him. Before he left the Seneca village, Brûlé swore to them all that he would bring peace between them, the French, and the Hurons as well as their allies.

By the time he returned to the Hurons in 1618, Brûlé had been in the far wilderness almost continuously for eight years. Champlain soon approached him and asked him to return to "the savages." So, in company with another Frenchman, known only as Grenolle, Brûlé journeyed farther west than any white man had yet ventured. He was in search of two things Champlain badly wanted: copper mines a Montagnais had told him about and the "North Sea," the ocean that would take him to China. The copper mines turned out to be real, but the North Sea was a freshwater lake of staggering size—Lake Superior—though certainly no ocean.

While Brûlé was swallowed up in the world of the Native, Champlain was swept up in the tide of French history. Armand-Jean du Plessis de Richelieu, cardinal-duc de Richelieu, artfully intrigued against Charles, duc de La Vieuville, chief minister to the feeble King Louis XIII, exposed him as corrupt, and swiftly fell into his place as the king's principal minister. The king was weak, without will, and that was just the way Richelieu wanted it. He was the archetypal power behind the throne, bent on consolidating and centralizing power in France while simultaneously elevating the country to European dominance at the expense of the Hapsburgs, monarchs of Austria and Spain. Unlike Louis XIII and his father, Henri IV, before him, neither of whom had shown interest in New France except as a source of reward for pliant nobles, Richelieu regarded the New World as the very key to an imperial greatness that would eclipse that of ancient Rome. Accordingly, he supported Champlain in his efforts at building the French colonies, but he also ensured that no man—not even Champlain—would ever again control a monopoly of French trade and colonization. In 1627, he created the Compagnie de la Nouvelle France, consisting of one hundred wealthy investors and therefore universally known as the Compagnie des Cent-Associés: the Company of One Hundred Associates. Champlain was appointed the company's commander in New France, and he prepared to welcome its great fleet of colonization and supply.

Those ships sailed from France in April 1628, over the fretful objections of some of "the hundred," who pointed out that war with England, which had commenced in 1627, put the fleet at great risk. It was known that King Charles I of England had issued letters of marque, creating a flotilla of privateers—state-sanctioned pirates—dedicated not only to seizing French shipping but also to raiding French colonies.

While Richelieu had voiced support for Champlain, the winter of 1627–28 was nevertheless marked by critically low supplies at Quebec. Come the summer of 1628, English merchants descended on Cap Tourmente on the north shore of the St. Lawrence River in what is today the Charlevoix region of Quebec. They looted supplies intended for Champlain and his struggling colony. On July 10, the Kirke brothers, powerful English merchants armed to the teeth, demanded that Champlain surrender Quebec.

The Frenchman had almost nothing. Food was dwindling, and a mere fifty pounds of gunpowder stood between him and utter defenselessness. Should he not now throw himself and his colony on the mercies of the English merchants?

He did nothing of the kind. Instead, Champlain assumed a haughty air and deigned to make no response to the Kirkes' demand, refusing even to see them. This grand bluff persuaded the merchant brothers that Quebec's defenses were stout, and instead of storming the settlement, they withdrew.

It was, however, only the slightest of reprieves for New France. The Kirkes and their mercenaries took ship, intending to set up shop farther to the south, but once off the coast they ran into the Compagnie supply fleet, which they handily pirated. Supplies intended to sustain Quebec for a full year were now in English hands. Champlain and his people struggled through the summer and fall and weathered the winter of

1628–29, but spring brought what looked to be the final crisis. Supplies ran so low that Champlain sent some of his colonists to Gaspé to live among the Indians. Fortunately, thanks to "lads" like Brûlé, the Native community did not turn the refugees away.

In the meantime, Champlain sent word to France for help, but the Kirkes intercepted the ship carrying his dispatch, and on July 19, 1629, the brothers, now fully aware of the desperate straits of the French, renewed their demand for surrender. Champlain this time complied and was taken by the Kirkes, along with many of his colonists, back to England. Whereas the colonists were soon packed off from London to France, Champlain remained in the English capital working to regain his colony. He had learned that a peace treaty had been signed between the English and the French in April 1629, fully three months before his surrender. This meant that Quebec and everything else the Kirkes had taken that summer were supposed to be returned; the brothers, however, as well as every English crown official Champlain confronted, demurred, and it took nothing less than an entirely new treaty, that of Saint-Germain-en-Laye, signed on March 29, 1632, to compel England to live up to the original treaty of 1629. Quebec was returned to France, and Champlain returned to Quebec; lest the Kirke brothers be left out in the cold, King Charles I knighted David Kirke in 1633 and four years later presented him with a charter to colonize Newfoundland.

By the time Samuel de Champlain reclaimed his position as commander in chief of New France in March 1633, Étienne Brûlé, vanguard of the young men Champlain had cast into the wilderness to compound a new civilization out of French and Native culture and blood, was dead.

He had been killed—and not by the Iroquois, the Onondaga or the Seneca, but by his friends, the Hurons. No one knows why his friends turned on him, but Gabriel Sagard, who lived and worked during 1623–36 among the Hurons as a missionary of the Franciscan Recollect Order, wrote in his *L'historie du Canada* (1636), that, once slain, Brûlé was eaten, "eaten by the Hurons, whom he had so long served as interpreter. . . . I do not know what offense he committed against them." John Gilmary Shea, the nineteenth-century Irish American father of American Catholic history who (among many other projects) collected and collated the annals of North America's Catholic missionaries, upped Sagard's ante. He did not blandly observe that Brûlé had followed "the customs of the country" when he lived among the Hurons but boldly opined that the Frenchman had "given himself wholly to savage life." Moreover, this new identity had not only failed to save him, it may have led to his death when "at last he gave offense to his new countrymen, and they not only killed, but ate him." Shea's implication is clear. Brûlé had shed his racial and national identity to become himself a "savage"—to make them "his new countrymen"—and for this he reaped a savage reward.

The place of his death and the consumption of his flesh was Toanche, on the southeastern tip of Georgian Bay in what is now Simcoe County, Ontario, at the time well beyond the pale of European settlement, though not out of the reach of missionary-borne religion. Some have guessed that his downfall was related to his capture in 1616 by Seneca after he separated himself from his Huron-allied Carantouannais guides. Others believe that it was the consequence of a later, unchronicled, contact with or capture by Iroquois. In either case, some have speculated that the Hurons failed to believe the story of his escape from death. Who could blame them? Everyone knew that once captured by the Iroquois, no one escaped death. So the Hurons of Toanche believed Brûlé had betrayed them and intended to steal the French trade away from them and give it to the Iroquois.

Alternatively, it may be that Brûlé spent at least some of the years between 1616 and 1632 trying to make good on his pledge to his Seneca captors, that he would make peace among them, the French, the Hurons, and the allies of the Hurons. In that case, blessed though the peacemakers may be, they often suffer cruelly on account of their efforts.

As for Toanche and its people, in 1634, Father Jean de Brébeuf tried to reestablish a mission in this most remote of Indian communities, where he himself had lived from 1626 to 1629. When he arrived, however, he found nothing except "the vestige of his little bark chapel." All else was desolation, burned to the ground, the people having fled "to a spot some distance away, where they had built a new town—all because they feared some terrible judgment would overtake them if they longer remained where Brûlé was killed." This, at least, was what Brébeuf believed as he located what he thought was the very spot on which "poor Brûlé" had died.

Perhaps in looking at this spot and pondering the fate of "poor Brûlé," Brébeuf had some premonition of his own death, which would come at Iroquois hands in 1649 and cause his elevation to sainthood. Who can say? What *is* certain is that Father Brébeuf saw Brûlé as the victim of a people who needed to be changed—converted—from what they were into what they should be, transformed from heathen into Christian, from savage to civilized. What is also certain is that *this* was not what Samuel Champlain had intended when he sent "the lad" to live among the Hurons. His intention, his hope, had been to create a middle ground, a place in which *both* Native and Frenchman would be converted, changed into something entirely new, a new people compounded of two peoples, who would bring by means of beaver fur, copper, cod—by whatever else the New World had to offer—all the profit and more that the Frenchman Cartier and the Spaniards before him had in vain hoped to reap from gold, spice, and a shortcut to China. In this new, hybrid civilization, upon this middle ground, Champlain became the first of a select succession of traders, trappers, and entrepreneurs who labored to redeem America, staking their lives in this struggle, not for the pious sake of religion or the patriotic cause of empire but for wealth and power, sustained, perhaps even everlasting.

2

Employees, Martyrs, and
Four Hundred Rifles

——◆·◆——

ON AUGUST 9, 1934, at the invitation of a committee of citizens of Green Bay, President Franklin D. Roosevelt spoke to commemorate the man credited with having "opened up" Wisconsin to Europe. His name was Jean Nicolet. Few Americans had heard of him. Before 1852, when a handful of antiquarians poked around the history of the Green Bay area, no one even knew that he had wandered into what became Wisconsin. It is no wonder that President Roosevelt (or one of his New Deal speechwriters) had to dig with a broad shovel to connect Nicolet to much of anything that seemed truly significant in a Depression-burdened nation that couldn't see much further back than October 1929, when the stock market collapsed.

FDR proclaimed Nicolet the first of "the men and women who established civilization in Wisconsin and in the Northwest" at the very beginning of what would become the United States of America. This launched the president on the theme announced in the title of the speech—"A Wider Opportunity for the Average Man"—and, thus launched, FDR sailed his subject through narrative seas that had been thoroughly charted by popular historians and Hollywood. Nicolet, he said, was a "pioneer" who had to "fight against Nature" in order to "fight for his rights," which included living "a life . . . less fettered by the exploitation of selfish men." The pioneers "shared a deep purpose to rid themselves forever of the jealousies, the prejudices, the intrigues and the violence, whether internal or external, that disturbed their lives on the other side of the ocean."

In only his second year in office, having ushered through Congress in his first "Hundred Days" sheaves of social legislation and now flogging even more, FDR saw history through the lens of the New Deal, and it was important to him that others should see it this way, too. The New Deal was new, and Roosevelt understood that people were at once drawn to and frightened by whatever was new. He took every opportunity to connect the New Deal with American history, American traditions, the old, familiar "American way." So he appropriated Jean Nicolet, took him from the past, and used him for his own present purposes, transforming him into the New Dealer as Pioneer/Pioneer as New Dealer.

The president was hardly the first person to tailor history to suit a special interest. A few times before, Nicolet had been the subject of civic oratory. At the dedication in July 1915 of a tablet commemorating Nicolet's 1634 passage through the Straits of Mackinac, a senator spoke of his "deeds of valor and knightly heroism," a judge pronounced Nicolet an "intrepid explorer and Christian hero," and another speaker defined him as a "fearless and heroic pioneer of Christian civilization." The tablet itself described him as "the first white man to enter Michigan and the Old Northwest."

So Jean Nicolet, of whom few Americans had heard in 1934 or 1915 or today, was variously proclaimed a hero of the common man, a knight, an avatar of Christian civilization, and a pioneer of white hegemony in the Old Northwest. Another speaker at the 1915 dedication, present to flesh out the historical record, was Father Thomas J. Campbell, SJ. He dutifully noted that Nicolet's Jesuit contemporaries wrote admiringly of the man, but Campbell, no less admiringly, brought him down to earth. "Jean Nicolet was not a great explorer, like Champlain . . . [not a] picturesque Governor, like Frontenac, . . . daring fighter, like Iberville, . . . successful discoverer, like Marquette, . . . martyr, like his [Jesuit missionary] friends Brébeuf, Jogues, Daniel, Garnier, and Garreau." He was, Campbell declared, "simply an employee in a trading post; an Indian interpreter."

Campbell had hit upon a key truth of early American civilization. It was the product of trade. While Nicolet was an employee, however, he was not just any employee. He was a highly motivated employee. No small part of his value to the trading enterprise was his willingness to learn the language of the local Indians, to become "an Indian interpreter." Those Europeans willing to engage Native culture were, by and large, motivated by their desire to engage Native commerce, to sell and to buy, whether it was trade goods for beaver fur or Christian dogma for Indian souls.

Jean Nicolet de Belleborne was born about 1598 in the Norman port city of Cherbourg, where his father, Thomas, served as "messenger ordinary of the King between Paris and Cherbourg." In other words, Jean was a mailman's son. When, at nineteen, the young man signed with the Compagnie des Marchands, which sent him to Quebec, it was not as an explorer but as a clerk, who subsequently agreed to train as an interpreter. As his father served the king but was a humble mailman, so Jean Nicolet served a trading monopoly that was owned by French lords but was himself their humble minion. Almost immediately on his arrival in Quebec, they sent him to Allumette Island, a fur-trading outpost on the Ottawa River, to learn the language of the Algonquians. He remained there for two years, accompanying his Indian hosts on their travels. Clearly, he won acceptance among them; around 1622, they put him at the head of a delegation of four hundred of their number to negotiate a peace treaty with the Iroquois.

Apparently, the negotiation was a success; however, on July 19, 1629, when Quebec fell to the Kirke brothers, who seized it for England, Nicolet was either instructed to move or moved of his own volition northwest, to the Lake Nipissing area, between the Ottawa River and Georgian Bay in present-day Ontario, where he lived for more than eight years among the Huron (also called the Nipissing) tribe.

He lived in what contemporary records describe as a "cabin apart," engaging in fishing and trading. That he was, however, adopted by the tribe is evident in two facts. First, he took full part in all tribal councils. Second, he lived with a Huron woman he (or those who wrote about him) called Sauvagesse Nipissing. The couple had a daughter, Madeleine Euphrosine Nicolet. In this, there was also nothing unusual. Many, probably most, French traders took Indian wives. There was no moral stigma for either the Natives or the French colonists, and the children produced by such unions were generally accepted. Men like Nicolet were creating a hybrid civilization. The trading relationship was sufficiently valued by both sides that the Indians accepted the French into their community, and the French embraced such integration.

From a Huron or someone of a neighboring tribe, Nicolet learned of a people known as the Winnebago. Today, this tribe has shed "Winnebago," a name bestowed by Fox, Sauk, and Ojibwa neighbors, and calls itself by its original name, the Ho-Chunk. The French translated "Winnebago" as "people of the stinking water" or "people of the smelly water," which Nicolet (perhaps along with other Frenchmen of the period) chose to interpret as "people of the sea," reasoning that saltwater smelled bad.

After the 1632 Treaty of Saint-Germain-en-Laye returned New France to French control and restored Samuel de Champlain as its governor, Nicolet was summoned back to Quebec, where he served as an interpreter and mediator between the Indians and French secular and religious authorities. At this time, Champlain announced his intention to press his exploration of North America westward, both to claim more territory for France and to find the ever-elusive Northwest Passage, the through route to Asia. This was Nicolet's cue to tell Champlain what he had learned about a "people of the sea," and he persuaded the governor that these Indians either had knowledge of or actually controlled the Northwest Passage, which, he reasoned, must be hidden along the vast shore of the unexplored western Great Lakes. Champlain named him his right-hand man for an expedition of exploration.

Two fleets of canoes left Quebec on July 1, 1634, and ascended the St.

Lawrence River, to what is now Trois-Rivières, Quebec. Here Nicolet diverted onto the Ottawa River, paddling as far as a portage with the Nipissing River, which empties into northern Lake Huron. In company with seven Huron warriors, he coasted along the Lake Huron shore until he reached the straits leading into Lake Superior. From here, he ventured to Sault Ste. Marie (today a city at the eastern end of Michigan's Upper Peninsula opposite the Canadian city of the same name), rested, then crossed to the top of Lake Michigan at Michilimackinac, the Straits of Mackinac, then pushed southward along the western shore of Lake Michigan and into Green Bay, home of the Winnebago.

Reportedly—though the report is subject to historical dispute—Nicolet had prepared himself for the meeting with the people he believed commanded a direct route to China by arraying himself in fine Chinese silk robes and firing ornate pistols into the air (for he knew that the Chinese had long possessed gunpowder). The Winnebago were reasonably impressed, though doubtless not for the reason Nicolet had intended. They feted Nicolet for weeks, lavishing food upon him, including feasts of beaver, and they agreed to live in peace with the French.

Nicolet apparently ventured farther and is believed to have been the first European to see not only Wisconsin but Illinois and the site of what would become Chicago. He spent the winter of 1634–35 with Indians along the Fox River before returning in the fall of 1635 to Trois-Rivières. He announced that he had been plying a river that surely would have taken him to the Pacific—had he kept on it just three days longer. This, of course, would prove to be an illusion, but what he did bring back with him was the establishment of French influence over extensive Native populations, which gave the French a firm foothold in North America and opened a way to the vast beaver peltries of the West, a prize more than one contender would covet and be willing to spill blood to obtain.

His Sauvagesse Nipissing notwithstanding, Nicolet, on October 7, 1637, married Marguerite Couillard, Champlain's goddaughter and the daughter of William Couillard, who had come to New France back in

1613 as a carpenter and now prospered as a farmer. In 1642, the couple had a daughter, Marguerite. She barely had time to get to know her father, however. In October of that year, Nicolet was named to an important administrative post in the Compagnie des Marchands and in this capacity set off for Trois-Rivières to intervene on behalf of a captive Indian friendly to the French but allied with the Iroquois. Nicolet hoped to prevent his death at Huron hands, but en route he himself was swept into the swift currents of the St. Lawrence when his canoe capsized. The very last words this intrepid river man managed to utter were the sad news that he did not know how to swim.

Nicolet drowned seven years after his patron Samuel de Champlain died. Champlain had been the dominant driver of French colonization in North America. That process may be traced back to 1523, when the Italian Giovanni da Verrazano (1485–1528) persuaded King Francis I of France to fund an expedition to find—what else?—the Northwest Passage to China. The king said yes, but he didn't give Verrazano much. The Italian sailed from Dieppe later in the year with a crew of only fifty-three in a caravel of modest dimensions. He coasted along the Carolinas early in 1524, working his way north, probing for any inlet that promised to convey him to the Pacific. He got as far as the Narrows of New York Bay, becoming the first European to lay eyes on what is today New York, which he named Nouvelle-Angoulême to honor Francis, formerly the count of Angoulême. Although Verrazano failed to find the Northwest Passage, his discovery moved the king to establish a colony on the territory between New Spain (Mexico and the American Southwest) and Newfoundland, which England had already claimed. This vast tract Verrazano dubbed Francesca and Nova Gallia.

A full decade passed before Francis acted on his own colonizing impulse by sending Jacques Cartier to America. This navigator planted a cross in the Gaspé Peninsula and took possession of the land in the king's name, making it the first province of New France. Yet colonization efforts were desultory at best, and it was only thanks to French fishermen, who not only worked the waters off the North Atlantic coast but sailed inland via the St. Lawrence River, that trading alliances were made with the Indians. This was the start of the French beaver trade, which finally gave some impetus to colonization, though it wasn't until well into the 1580s that trading companies were set up and ships were regularly contracted to bring back beaver and other furs to the European markets.

Fishermen and traders were not writers. So all we know for certain about the last twenty years of the sixteenth century in New France is two things. First, trading relations were established between the Europeans and the Indians; although sufficiently cordial to produce profit, they evidently did nothing to promote colonization. This brings us to the second thing. What paltry gestures were made toward establishing permanent French settlements failed. A trading post was established on Sable Island, off the coast of Acadia, in 1598 but was soon abandoned. Two years later, another trading post was built at Tadoussac. By the end of the winter, only five emaciated settlers were left alive. Bad weather and intense want, not Indians, had killed their comrades. Four years passed before another attempt at settlement was made. In 1604, a little "Habitation" was set up at St. Croix Island on Baie François—today the Bay of Fundy—which was moved (not a very big job) to Port-Royal in 1605.

This time, Champlain intervened. Determined to create a community, he decided to found a jolly social club, the Ordre de Bon Temps (Order of Good Cheer), with the object of raising morale and building a sense of communal fellowship even as he fostered healthy eating, which, he reasoned, was what was most needed to get his settlers through the coming winter of 1606–07. Every few days, the Ordre organized a feast, to which colonists and their Micmac Indian neighbors were invited. Only the Indian men were welcome; the women and children, along with the poorest of the French settlers, were offered naught but leftover scraps. In addition to food, festivities included strong drink and a good show. Something called *The Theater of Neptune in New France* by one Marc Lescarbot (lawyer by vocation, explorer by circumstance, playwright by avocation) was staged on November 16, 1606, becoming the first dramatic work both written and performed in North America.

It was all a promising beginning, and high time at that. In 1607, how-ever, King Henri IV suddenly revoked the trading monopoly he had granted Port-Royal's founder, Pierre Dugua, which forced everyone to pack up and return to France that fall. Dugua left the Micmac *sakmow* (grand chief) Henri Membertou to look after the Habitation, which he did until 1610, when another Frenchman, Jean de Biencourt de Poutrin-court et de Saint-Just (1557–1615), arrived. Biencourt oversaw the con-version of Membertou and other local Micmacs to Catholicism, a move that allied him with the Jesuits and was designed to secure government finance ostensibly to promote the dissemination of the Catholic faith in New France.

As for Champlain, he turned away from Port-Royal and, with twenty-eight men, founded in 1608 the city of Quebec, the second permanent French settlement in New France. It hardly took off. The climate and disease did their usual work, so that by 1630 Quebec had grown from 28 to just 103 settlers. By the time of Nicolet's death, the population had slightly more than tripled, to 355. Despite the unimpressive numbers, Champlain was aggressive in his effort to ally himself and his settlement with the local Hurons and Montagnais, taking advantage of their en-mity with the Iroquois to make common cause with them against those tribes, as explained in chapter 1.

Champlain's persistence kept Quebec from following Port-Royal into a long indolence, but he was nevertheless unable to awaken royal enthusi-asm for the colony until the ascension of Louis XIII and his powerful adviser Richelieu. The Company of One Hundred Associates Richelieu founded to invest in New France, unlike the earlier Compagnie des Marchands, was not primarily a trading cartel but an enterprise to pro-mote colonization. Richelieu promised land to hundreds of new set-tlers in the hope of accelerating the growth of the colony. Thanks to Richelieu's influence, too, the king named Champlain governor of New France.

Financially, Richelieu wanted to use the resources of New France to add to his wealth and power. Politically, for France, he wanted to create a colony as important as those of the English. Religiously, as a man of the Church, he sought to propagate the faith and, toward that end, barred non–Roman Catholics from living in New France. Those few Protestants who already lived in the colony were given a stark choice: Convert to Catholicism or leave. Most left, and thereby the Protestant English colonies grew larger.

Not only did Richelieu's theocratic ambitions retard the political and commercial growth of New France, they also caused the driving power behind the colony to shift from motives of secular empire and commerce to religion—although religion was hardly divorced from either empire or commerce. When Champlain died in 1635, he was replaced not by another entrepreneurial explorer but by an army of Jesuit and Recollect missionaries. As if this weren't a sufficient retreat from the Enlightenment trends then beginning to sweep through Europe, Richelieu also transported New France back into the Middle Ages by instituting a quasi-feudal seigneurial system in which lords owned great tracts of land, which were farmed by a peasantry exported from France.

It was Richelieu who enthusiastically sanctioned the missionary presence in New France, but the Jesuit mission began on October 25, 1604, well before the cardinal's ascension, when Father Pierre Coton, SJ, made a request of the Jesuit superior general, Claudio Acquaviva, for a pair of missionaries to be sent to North America.

Born in Atri, Italy, in 1543, the youngest son of the Duke of Atri, Acquaviva was one of those singularly ruthless religious entrepreneurs who made the Jesuit Order universally envied, feared, and despised. In 1559, he gained appointment as papal chamberlain to Pius IV, then, after Cardinal Francisco Borja engineered the murder of Diego Laynez, the second superior general of the Jesuits, early in 1566, Acquaviva supported Borja's succession to the vacant generalship, attached himself to Borja, and, in the fullness of time, became the fifth superior general in 1581.

By all rights, Acquaviva was a servant of the pope, the earthly pontiff—the "bridge"—to God. In actuality, he served first and foremost King Philip II (1527–98) of Spain and, in the nearly thirty-four years he was the

Jesuits' superior general, was responsible for the poisonings of no fewer than six popes who proved less than wholly pliable to Philip's will. In addition to his iron alliance with the secular prince of Spain, Acquaviva transformed the Society of Jesus into a commercial powerhouse. Besides North America, he set up missions in South America, England, Germany, France, Flanders, Spain, and Japan, growing the Jesuit society from five thousand to thirteen thousand members and increasing the number of Jesuit schools from 124 to 371 and of "provinces" (as Jesuit parishes or territories were called) from twenty-one to thirty-two worldwide.

It was in Japan that Acquaviva saw his greatest opportunity for creating a mighty engine to drive the worldly expansion of his spiritual order. In 1579, he transferred the Neapolitan Jesuit Alessandro Valignano (1539–1606) from the recently established mission in Macau, China, to Nagasaki, Japan. Operating through one of his priests, Father Vilela, Acquaviva had negotiated the purchase of the port of Nagasaki from a local Japanese warlord. Valignano understood that his job was not so much to advance the Christian faith in Japan as to establish Jesuit cultural and financial power there. Accordingly, he developed a strategy of adaptation to Japanese customs, drawing up in 1581 the remarkable handbook *Il Cerimoniale per i Missionari del Giappone,* which instructed missionaries to liken their own Jesuit hierarchy to that of the Zen Buddhists and to behave like Buddhist priests of the highest class. Thus, the missionaries transformed themselves into daimyo, striding through city streets in magnificent robes and in company with bodyguards and manservants. Beyond this, Valignano encouraged his priests to become the equivalent of Japanese warrior monks in a city that was now the headquarters of a Jesuit commercial enterprise.

Under Acquaviva and Valignano, Nagasaki became one of the most profitable centers of trade in Asia. The Society of Jesus enjoyed a monopoly on taxation of all goods that came into Japan via Nagasaki while also engaging in the Japanese silver trade, using the silver to purchase Chinese silk from Canton, the Chinese port city in which its missions were also extensively established.

With his neatly trimmed beard and thin lips typically set in a benign smile, Acquaviva looked more like a prudent merchant than he did a priest, a murderer, or a rapacious entrepreneur, let alone a military commander. However when the Portuguese, responding to Jesuit encroachment on their Asian trade, armed pirates to prey on Jesuit-financed vessels—many of them Dutch—going in and out of Nagasaki, Acquaviva made an alliance in 1595 with the Dutch States General (government) to aid in the defense of their ships. Protestant England responded by chartering the powerful East India Company in 1600 as a mercantile and mercenary pirate enterprise. Two years later, Acquaviva was instrumental in negotiating a twenty-one-year exclusive charter from the States General to create the Vereenigde Oostindische Compagnie (VOC), the United East India Company—popularly known as the Dutch East India Company—to compete directly with the English firm. The VOC was history's first international corporation with shares, though the controlling interest was always Jesuit. The VOC traded in all the goods of the East but made some of its best money in opium and may be seen as creating another first: the first international drug cartel.

Given the magnitude of the Jesuits' Japanese enterprise, Father Coton's request for a modest mission presence in New France may have struck Acquaviva as small potatoes. In any case, he put off attending to the request for a long time, and it was not until 1611, seven years after the request had been made, that Acquaviva finally dispatched just two Jesuits, Pierre Biard and Enemond Massé, to Port-Royal in Acadia. Two years later, the struggling mission they erected was raided by Englishmen from Virginia and wiped out, the missionaries eventually making their way back to France. Acquaviva made no further attempts to establish missions in North America before he died in 1615.

A decade passed before the Jesuit Order sent Massé and Fathers Charles Lalemant (as superior), and Jean de Brébeuf, along with assistants François Charton and Gilbert Buret, to set up a new mission in 1625 on the banks of the St. Lawrence River. This one lasted four years, folding when the English occupied Quebec in 1629.

· · ·

Paul Le Jeune (1591–1664), a native of the French Champagne, was ordained a priest in the Jesuit Order in 1624 and named superior of the Jesuit mission in New France in 1631, arriving in Quebec the following year. It was with his arrival that the main phase of Jesuit mission work in New France began.

Le Jeune's approach in North America was very different from that of Acquaviva and Valignano in Japan. A priest first and foremost, Le Jeune did not integrate his missions seamlessly with French commercial enterprise, as was the case in Japan. Although Le Jeune insisted that his missionaries learn the languages and customs of the Indians—he himself became a linguist and ethnographer of prodigious achievement—he and the forty-six Jesuit fathers he sent out to establish missions were by no means anthropologists. Even less were they "adaptationists" in the mode of Father Valignano. They would learn the local languages and customs not for the purpose of fitting in, but the better to transform heathens into Christians—and not just Christians, but European Christians. For it was not Native religion per se that disturbed the missionaries, but the absence of hierarchical government among the Hurons and Montagnais. Perhaps this, more than a difference between the philosophy or character of Valignano and that of Le Jeune, is responsible for the very different approaches of the Jesuits in Japan and those in America. Valignano was quick to appreciate the hierarchy of Japanese society and was culturally prepared to adapt to it and co-opt it. Nothing, however, could prepare Le Jeune and his priests for the utter flatness of tribal organization, which was beyond their social experience and seemed to them simply chaotic. Confronted by chaos, compromise and adaptation were out of the question; therefore, Le Jeune instructed his priests to undermine the influence of the traditional medicine men, or shamans, whom they regarded as the sources of all this chaotic egalitarianism. Le Jeune's object was to replace them with other teachers, Jesuit teachers who would impose on the villages and tribes the proper hierarchical reality of the seminary, which embodied the true hierarchy of the Christian universe. Key to this transition out of chaos was book learning, for the Indians' oral tradition provided no central organizing authority. Indians had to be taught to read so they could read the Bible, *the* book.

Le Jeune's Jesuits took on the shamans, village by village. In contrast to the free invention of the shamans' oral traditions, the priests were able to present with an air of absolute authority the Word. Their ultimate goal was to reach the minds of the Indian children. Education had always been the chief instrument of Jesuit religious indoctrination. To get to the children, though, Le Jeune knew he had first to win over the adults. Accordingly, he and his priests fanned out to challenge and debate the shamans in the midst of every village. They staged plays in the language of the people. They overwhelmed the tribes with information and demonstration—and the better to do this, they sought to organize and consolidate the Indians into fewer and larger villages, villages in which a permanent mission, with a church and a school, could be built. To add to the cohesion and attractiveness of such villages, the Jesuits encouraged the establishment of trade. Here at last, the religious and commercial impulses that had coexisted so effectively in Japan came together in North America. However, whereas in Japan and elsewhere the Jesuits looked upon trade as a source of power and finance, working among the Indians of New France it was an aid to conversion, a means of attracting more Indians to the faith by creating a rationale for their settlement in mission towns.

As is well known, the Europeans brought with them to the New World more than their trade goods and their religion. They brought their epidemic diseases. The virulence of smallpox and the measles, two infectious agents especially devastating among Native Americans, who had never been exposed to them before contact with the outsiders, was doubtless intensified by the new order the Jesuits brought—life lived in the relatively dense population of mission towns centered on church, school, and trading post. For the missionaries, the diseases carried an unexpected dividend. Indians saw that their shamans were powerless to prevent the epidemics or to treat the sicknesses when they came. The Jesuits, who had been instrumental in bringing the diseases in the first place, had at least marginally greater success in dealing with the ailments.

. . .

Of all the Jesuit mission towns, Sainte-Marie-au-pays-des-Hurons—St. Mary Among the Hurons—at Wendake, near modern Midland, Ontario, was considered the jewel. When it was established in 1639, it was the first non-Indian settlement in what is now Ontario, and it served as the center for Jesuit missionary operations throughout the region.

The eighteen men who first arrived in November 1639 raised a roof of birch bark upon pillars of cypress, then built up interior walls with clay. Soon, other buildings went up, including a chapel, a Jesuit residence, a kitchen, a smithy, and buildings that served traders in furs and other commodities. It was a place to preach, but it was also a living lesson to the Hurons, an example of the ordered life of a European village. Here, traders and Indian fur hunters met, and here, from time to time, soldiers were quartered.

As time went on, the mission, adjacent to a Huron village called Quieunonascaranas, led by Chief Auoindaon, drove a wedge between those Hurons who, attracted to what the mission had to offer, converted to Christianity and those who clung to traditional beliefs. Among some Hurons, the outbreak of the same diseases that undermined the reputation of the shamans also led to accusations against the missionaries. From outside the tribe, however, Sainte-Marie-au-pays-des-Hurons seemed evidence of a full alliance between the French and the Hurons—the alliance Champlain had initiated in 1609. When Iroquois—first Seneca, then Mohawks—attacked with increasing frequency and intensity during the 1640s, the Hurons, divided by the missionaries, were vulnerable. So were the missionaries. Eight of them would die in warfare between the Hurons and Iroquois, and so Sainte-Marie would become something more than a mission and trading post. It would become a center of martyrdom. Eight priests headquartered in the village, Jean de Brébeuf, Noël Chabanel, Antoine Daniel, Charles Garnier, René Goupil, Isaac Jogues, Jean de Lalande, and Gabriel Lallemant, would be made saints.

Of these, one, Isaac Jogues, earned the distinction of two martyrdoms, becoming a "living martyr" before he became a dead one.

It happened like this. A native of Orléans, France, Jogues joined the

Jesuits in 1624 and in 1636 was sent to New France. In 1642, while he was en route to a Huron village, he, along with lay missionary Guillaume Couture, Father René Goupil, and some converted Hurons, was captured by Mohawk Iroquois. All suffered gruesome tortures. Goupil succumbed, earning his sainthood that very day, but Jogues, according to his own account, was treated "as a Captain—that is to say, with more fury than the rest." One of the Indians exclaimed "that the Frenchmen ought to be caressed."

> Sooner done than it is said,—one wretch, jumping on the stage, dealt three heavy blows with sticks, on each Frenchman, without touching the Hurons. Others, meanwhile drawing their knives and approaching us, . . . treated me as a captain. . . . An old man takes my left hand and commands a captive Algonquin woman to cut one of my fingers; she turns away three or four times, unable to resolve upon this cruelty; finally, she has to obey, and cuts the thumb from my left hand; the same caresses are extended to the other prisoners. This poor woman having thrown my thumb on the stage, I picked it up and offered it to you, O my God! Remembering the sacrifices that I had presented to you for seven years past, upon the Altars of your Church, I accepted this torture as a loving vengeance for the want of love and respect that I had shown, concerning your Holy Body; you heard the cries of my soul.

It was a moment as extraordinary as it was horrific. Thinking to derive religious meaning from what was happening to him—somehow to make spiritual sense of it all—Jogues picked up his amputated thumb and offered it to God as a kind of reverse Eucharist. In celebrating Mass, he had often offered his congregants the body and blood of Christ; now he offered *his* body and *his* blood to God. Then—

> One of my two French companions, having perceived me, told me that, if those Barbarians saw me keep my thumb, they would make me eat it and swallow it all raw; and that, therefore, I should throw it away somewhere. I obeyed him instantly.

The Indians would have forced Jogues into sacrilege and blasphemy, compelling him to eat *his own* body and blood; therefore, he ended up consecrating his sacrifice not to God, as he had intended, but to the dark void of the wilderness.

Jogues nevertheless survived both physically and spiritually. After living as a slave among the Mohawks for a time—during which he dutifully attempted to preach to them—he escaped and threw himself on the mercy of some Dutch traders (allies of the Iroquois, rivals of the French), who conveyed him to their settlement at Manhattan. He sailed from here back to France, where he was pronounced a living martyr and received from Pope Urban VIII extraordinary dispensation to continue saying Holy Mass, even though he could no longer handle the Eucharist as prescribed—with thumb and forefinger only.

Jogues soon returned to New France, and in 1646 he and Jean de Lalande deliberately ventured into the Mohawk country to serve as ambassadors among them during a time of tenuous peace between Iroquois and Huron.

Champlain had tried to *integrate* French traders into Indian society. The Jesuits had tried to *inject* French priests into that same society. The Iroquois had a different aim. They wanted to *absorb* other peoples. The five Iroquois tribes, especially the Mohawks, made it a practice to "adopt" those they conquered. In this way, they intended to spread their own power ever westward. By the 1640s, the Mohawks were firm trading partners with the Dutch, who had guns and other goods they wanted. What the Dutch most wanted from them was beaver. However, the beaver were all but gone from the eastern lands, the Mohawk lands, and so the Mohawks turned to the west, to the land of the Hurons, where beaver were still plentiful and were being traded by the Hurons to the French.

By the 1640s, the French were standing in the way of the Mohawks. French traders and missionaries were protecting the Hurons, keeping the Mohawks from adopting and absorbing them. The missionaries laid claim to their souls. All the Mohawks wanted was their land, but in order to hold on to the souls of the Hurons, the missionary French were unwilling to give up the bodies and the land that went with them. Isaac Jogues's ambassadorial task, in 1646, was to reinforce the peace that had been established the year before. This meant effectively splitting up the tribes of the Iroquois, so that one tribe would not permit another to use its well-worn trails as routes by which the other might attack the Hurons. In his high-handed Jesuit way—the way Le Jeune had taught: affirmative, authoritative, absolute—Jogues lectured his Mohawk hosts and thereby, little by little, irritated them.

Maybe this alone was not sufficient to provoke them to violence, but there was more.

The crop that spring was poor, but sickness was plentiful. Jogues busied himself trying to turn Mohawk clans who were inclined to stay friendly with the French against those that wanted to break the peace. The dissension this created, combined with the air of doom caused by crop failure and epidemic disease, united the Mohawk factions on one fatal point: Jogues was obviously a witch.

On October 18–19, 1646, Fathers Isaac Jogues and Jean de Lalande were beaten to death with clubs and then beheaded by their Mohawk hosts near what is today Auriesville, New York.

There was an attempt to preserve the peace, despite the assassination of these Jesuit ambassadors. Indeed, the Hurons hoped that the other Iroquois tribes would split with and turn against the Mohawks for what they had done. Father Paul Ragueneau, at Sainte-Marie, believed it possible that the Cayuga, Onondaga, and Oneida, the three Iroquois tribes that occupied the land between the easternmost Mohawks and the westernmost Seneca would break with both, leaving only those two tribes to contend with.

It was not an unreasonable hope. Ragueneau was aware that the so-called Iroquois League had cracks in it. The other tribes, especially the middle ones, coveted trade with the Dutch and greatly resented the monopoly the Mohawks exercised over it. The Mohawks arrogantly controlled access to the main trading post, Fort Orange (modern Albany, New

York). Even so, it was not French intervention that nearly succeeded in preserving the peace. Another tribe, the Susquehannocks, who occupied the areas adjacent to the Susquehanna River in what is now New York, Pennsylvania, and Maryland, had a remarkable, pan-tribal vision of reaching an agreement with the Iroquois and the Hurons to end the competition in trade and open it up equally to all the tribes of the region. The Susquehannock idea was to join into a kind of cartel that would dictate terms not just to the Dutch (trading partner of the Iroquois) or the French (trading partner of the Hurons) or the Swedes on Delaware Bay (trading partner of the Susquehannocks), but to all Europeans who sought trade.

Essentially, the Susquehannocks presented the Mohawks with an ultimatum: Open up access to Fort Orange or be excluded from the cartel and count the Susquehannocks along with the French *and* the Hurons as enemies.

The Mohawks listened. Then again, so did the Dutch.

The Geoctroyeerde Westindische Compagnie (GWIC)—the Chartered West India Company, more familiarly known as the Dutch West India Company—was founded on June 3, 1621, on the very model of the VOC, the Dutch East India Company, in which the Society of Jesus played so central a role. The GWIC, however, was independent of the Jesuits and answerable only to its investors and directors, who saw in the Susquehannock threat against the Mohawks a golden opportunity to usurp trade from the French. On April 7, 1648, the directors at Fort Orange reversed their long-standing policy against arming the Indians and suddenly traded to the Mohawks some four hundred rifles. They knew full well that the warriors would use them against the French-backed Hurons and the French themselves, and because they knew this, it would be accurate to say that the GWIC employed the Mohawks as proxy troops and instruments of terror against the French and the tribe that traded with them. By July 4, 1648, a thousand Mohawks had cut their hair for war, scalps bare save for a strip down the middle, three finger widths across, running from forehead to nape.

3

Beaver Wars

———◆·◆———

W HEN FATHER ANTOINE DANIEL, the Jesuit missionary of
the Huron village of St. Joseph (present-day Port Huron, Michigan),
heard the dull thunder of Mohawk moccasins pounding up the stockade, he sprinted for the rude wooden chapel, the biggest building in the
walled town, in which the women, children, and old men had sought the
refuge he had told them God would provide in time of need.

Daniel entered, surveyed his terrified charges, and pronounced a general absolution upon them. Upon those who had been reluctant to accept
baptism in peaceful times, he hurriedly conferred the sacrament. These
rites completed, he quietly urged all to save themselves, turned back to
the doorway, and went out to meet the warriors as they tumbled over the
stockade and into the town. Perhaps intending to create a diversion that
would buy time for "his" Hurons to escape, Daniel took down a cross
from the chapel wall, grasped it in his right hand, and ventured straight
toward the enemy, icon uplifted. The sight of the black-robed figure, un-
afraid, advancing toward them with the symbol of his faith, froze the
attackers.

For a moment only, however. Soon, several of them leveled their Dutch
guns against Father Antoine Daniel, and they fired. Shot many times, he

fell, even as other warriors killed or captured everyone they overtook. They shot, they brained, they gutted, they scalped, they made captive, pausing at intervals only to put each of the village buildings to the torch. As the chapel leaped into flame, some warriors flung Daniel's lifeless body through its open door.

The Mohawk raiding party left St. Joseph ablaze as they withdrew with about seven hundred prisoners. From this attack, they went on immediately to another, striking the nearby mission village of St. Ignace. It was a place almost exclusively of women, children, and old men, and their slaughter or capture consumed but a few minutes. It, too, was followed by all-consuming fire. Once again, with their objective burning behind them, the Mohawks moved on, this time to the mission village of St. Louis, about three miles away.

A later generation would call the Mohawk raiding tactics "blitzkrieg," and a still later one would use the phrase "shock and awe." To those on the receiving end, the attacks seemed nothing less than a force of nature, overwhelming and irresistible. Even so, there was a tactical downside. Mohawk raiding doctrine was founded on speed rather than thoroughness, and haste left survivors. Three Huron refugees from the St. Ignace raid outran the advancing Mohawks and reached St. Louis in time to alert the village. Most of its seven hundred inhabitants evacuated, leaving only about eighty warriors behind, together with those too old or too sick to move. Awaiting the onslaught with them were the two Jesuit missionaries who had also escaped from St. Ignace, Jean de Brébeuf and Gabriel Lallemant.

If speed and ferocity were the essence of Mohawk raiding tactics, the doctrine of vastly superior numbers was common to virtually all Indian war making. The rule was this: Attack only when you enjoy a great numerical advantage. In the case of St. Louis, the ratio was a thousand Mohawks to eighty Huron warriors. Yet those eighty twice turned back the Mohawk attack, killing some thirty of the enemy. This prompted the attackers to change tactics. Instead of concentrating on a single entry point through the village stockade, they mounted their third assault from several directions simultaneously, wielding their hatchets against the walls of wooden palings woven together with stout grasses. They broke through in many places, and once the Mohawks were within the confines of St. Louis, it was all quickly over.

Survivors were few but included the two Jesuits. Taken captive, they were marched off from the blazing town back to St. Ignace, which was occupied by the Iroquois. Here, all were tortured to death, the greatest brutality accorded Brébeuf and Lallemant. The pair were tied upright to stakes, scalped alive, then "baptized" with boiling water. For each a "necklace" of linked hatchets was prepared by throwing it into the fire, then withdrawing it when the metal glowed red hot. These were put around their necks.

Both men endured their martyrdom as martyrs do—stoically—and it was said that Brébeuf, fifty-five years old at the time, uttered not the slightest sound throughout all the torture and even to the moment of his death. That his tormentors cut out his heart and ate it was a tribute accorded only to the most worthy of adversaries. The Mohawks, like a number of other eastern tribes, believed that by eating the heart of a courageous enemy they would partake of his courage.

The Mohawks used the remains of St. Ignace as a forward base of operations, from which they launched raids against all the smaller villages of the region, including, on March 17, Sainte-Marie-au-pays des Hurons, a fortress-village defended by a garrison of forty well-armed Frenchmen augmented by perhaps three hundred Hurons. No commander, whether a seventeenth-century Huron warrior or a twenty-first-century military officer, wants to fight defensively, even though defenders often benefit from significant advantages of cover and supply. The Hurons left the shelter of their stockade and launched a preemptive ambush on the leading edge of the Mohawk force as it approached the town. Despite finding themselves victims of surprise, the Mohawks not only repulsed the surprise attack but forced the Hurons into retreat.

Or so the Mohawk warriors believed.

Although historians generally credit Indian warriors with bravery—sometimes mythologizing this quality in them—they rarely acknowledge demonstrations of tactical sophistication even when they are quite evident. In this case, the withdrawing Hurons drew the Mohawks into a larger attack by their main force. The Huron retreat, therefore, had not been one of simple necessity but was genuinely tactical in its nature and intent. It worked. The Mohawks were routed.

They were not annihilated, though. Despite heavy losses, they retreated intact and were able to regroup to renew the assault against Sainte-Marie. By this time, the Huron defenders had been reduced to about 150 warriors, half their original number. In the fighting that followed, the French estimated that the Hurons killed at least another hundred Mohawks, though in the process lost all but twenty of their own number. No question that the Hurons and their French allies had been defeated, but the Mohawks were so unnerved by the resistance they had met with that, instead of capitalizing on their victory, they withdrew.

On June 16, 1649, Father Paul Ragueneau and other Jesuit missionaries returned to what was left of Sainte-Marie but decided that it was better to burn the mission rather than see it fall into Iroquois hands permanently. Ragueneau wrote, "We ourselves set fire to it, and beheld burn before our eyes and in less than one hour, our work of nine or ten years." Ragueneau and the others were determined that the physical obliteration of Sainte-Marie would not erase its spiritual presence. The Jesuit Order had already decided that Brébeuf and Lalemant would be canonized, and hired a shoemaker named Christophe Regnault to find the missionaries' burial places and recover their bones. After duly exhuming the bodies, Regnault immersed them into a strong lye solution, which separated the flesh from the bones. The skeletons he wrapped in linen to be preserved as relics. The flesh he collected and reburied in a dual grave.

Although the Hurons' desperate stand at Sainte-Marie had dispirited the Mohawks, by the end of March 1649, they had forced their enemy out of fifteen principal towns. Indeed, by this time, the Huron nation ceased to exist as an organized community. Many refugees were adopted by allied tribes, large numbers finding refuge with the Tobacco—or Tionontati—tribe. As for the French Jesuits, suddenly lacking Indians to convert, they abandoned a number of their missions. The defeat of French rivals in the beaver trade greatly gratified the Dutch, who now looked on their sale to the Mohawks of four hundred guns as a very fine investment indeed.

Through November and December 1649, the Mohawks and Seneca raided Tobacco villages as punishment for harboring enemy refugees. As the Iroquois approached the Tobacco mission town of St. Jean, its warriors prepared for the inevitable onslaught—but the Iroquois did something unheard-of. They did not attack.

They were out there, the residents of St. Jean knew, but day after day passed without a raid. The Mohawks and the Seneca were infamous for their seemingly inexhaustible repertoire of torture, but this suspense was worse than any of their fiery torments. It was simply incomprehensible. Unable to endure the waiting any longer, Tobacco and Huron warriors sortied out of the St. Jean stockade to force the enemy into battle on the outside.

From their places of concealment, the Mohawks and Seneca saw the gate open and watched as the warriors moved out, but they resisted the temptation to attack *them*. Instead, at two o'clock on the afternoon of December 7, 1649, they stormed St. Jean, which was now wholly undefended. As they opened fire, one of St. Jean's missionaries, Charles Garnier, passed rapidly from Indian to Indian, baptizing and absolving, absolving and baptizing. Against the din of war cries and musketry, he continued this work until he was cut down by a succession of three musket balls. At least one round severed his spinal cord, leaving him instantly paralyzed, prone and helpless as a warrior's hatchet descended. He was found later, brains beaten out.

Again the hasty attackers failed to round up all prisoners, and a few survivors wandered westward. The Tobacco refugees mingled with the surviving Hurons and, after the passage of half a century, became known as the Wyandots of the Detroit and Sandusky region.

The raids against the Huron villages and missionary towns of French Canada were episodes in what white writers later called the Beaver Wars.

The "Five Nations" of the Iroquois League had united in what they themselves denominated "the Great Peace," essentially a mutual nonaggression pact among themselves and a defensive alliance against other tribes. Some historians have pointed out that a desire to impose this Great Peace on others led to a policy of conquest and tribal adoption in which the Iroquois made war on their neighbors with the object of either killing them or absorbing them. Indeed, the battle usually identified as the beginning of the Beaver Wars—a 1638 clash in which a war party of one hundred Iroquois was defeated by some three hundred Hurons and other Algonquian warriors—was typical of the earliest phase of the war: an intertribal conflict fought independently of any Euro-American interests. Because the Indian combatants kept no written records of such encounters, little is known about this phase of the Beaver Wars. Only when battles involved missionaries or were near missionary towns do we have significant documentation. By this time, the "Beaver Wars" moniker was pretty well justified, since the Iroquois' immediate objective was to acquire fresh beaver peltries to exploit in trade with the Euro-Americans, principally the Dutch. The Beaver Wars were fought to dispossess the French-allied Hurons of the best peltry land.

Many perished in the Iroquois raids; however, it was the long-term effect of the raids rather than their immediate, albeit terrible, impact that amounted to a program of tribal genocide. Huron society was disrupted, the people transformed from a tribe into a clutch of refugees. To live alone in the wilderness was essentially impossible. The presence of a cohesive tribe, village, or community was essential to sustenance. For this reason, an attacker need not kill every last man, woman, and child to destroy a people. Death on a genocidal scale was a consequence of exile into the wilderness.

For example, early in 1650 a band of Hurons took refuge on St. Joseph Island (now Christian Island) in frozen Lake Huron. In March, after weeks on the island, the refugees were compelled to seek food and shelter on the mainland. They struggled to walk to shore across the softening ice. In many places, the ice gave way, people fell through, and they drowned. Those who did manage to make it across survived for a time by fishing, only to fall prey, piecemeal, to marauding Iroquois war parties. That these refugees were near starvation made them soft targets and in no way modulated the ferocity of the attackers. Jesuit missionary Father Paul Ragueneau had already laid eyes on all manner of Indian torture and cruelty. The fate of the St. Joseph Island refugees, however, left him speechless. "My pen," he wrote, "has no ink black enough to describe the fury of the Iroquois. . . . Our starving Hurons were driven out of a town which had become an abode of horror. . . . These poor people fell into ambuscades of our Iroquois enemies. Some were killed on the spot; some were dragged into captivity; women and children were burned. . . . Go where they would, they met with slaughter on all sides. Famine pursued them, or they encountered an enemy more cruel than cruelty itself."

Traditionally, students of colonial American history have assessed the Iroquois as remarkably successful in their genocidal campaign. The course of the principal phase of the Beaver Wars, from 1650 through 1655, is typically portrayed as beginning late in the fall of 1650 with an Iroquois campaign against the Neutral nation, who, as their French-bestowed name implies, unlike the Tobaccos, prudently attempted to remain neutral in the ongoing combat between Iroquois and Huron. In the initial attack, a great town of some three or four thousand persons was destroyed, and an assault on another town in the spring of 1651 prompted the Neutrals to abandon all of their settlements and disperse. Many—perhaps most—were adopted by the Seneca, westernmost of the Iroquois tribes. The magnitude of this conquest can be appreciated by noting that the Neutrals had numbered about ten thousand at the beginning of the seventeenth century; by 1653 no more than eight hundred could be found.

Between 1651 and 1653 the Iroquois harried the French and their Indian allies until all of the Iroquois nations except for the Mohawks concluded a peace treaty at Montreal late in 1653. The peace proved short-lived. In the spring of 1654, an Erie who was a member of a treaty delegation visiting a Seneca town quarreled with a Seneca and killed him. In retaliation, the Seneca killed all thirty members of the Erie delegation, touching off a series of reprisals and counterreprisals that escalated into war between the Eries and all the Iroquois. Although brief, the war spelled the end of the Erie nation by 1656.

Such is the traditional view of the main phase of the Beaver Wars: a genocidal Iroquois juggernaut. Indeed, it is true that by 1655 the Five Iroquois Nations held sway from the Ottawa River in the north to the Cumberland in the south, and as far as Lake Erie in the west. Yet the success of the Iroquois push westward was so thorough that their failures elsewhere are easily overlooked.

During 1651–52, the Mohawks had attacked a people known as the Atrakwaeronons, which may have been another name for the Susquehannocks or may have denoted a tribe closely allied with the Susquehannocks. In either case, the result was a quarter century of sporadic warfare between the Susquehannocks and the Iroquois, during which the Susquehannocks more often than not prevailed.

The Susquehannocks were an eastern tribe, concentrated, as their name suggests, along the Susquehanna River and its tributaries in New York, Pennsylvania, and Maryland. Similarly, the Iroquois failed to defeat the Sokokis, another eastern tribe, who lived in the upper Connecticut Valley, and the Mahicans of the Hudson River Valley, near Albany. Thus, while the Iroquois swept westward, they were unable to defeat key eastern tribes and, therefore, committed what is a cardinal strategic sin for an advancing army. They left enemies in their rear.

Why had the Iroquois failed against these tribes?

The Hurons, Tobaccos, and Neutrals were all allied with the French, which meant that they had missionaries aplenty but few guns, for the French were reluctant to trade firearms to Indians. The Iroquois, having established trading relations with the Dutch, had guns but no missionaries. The Susquehannocks, Sokokis, and Mahicans traded with the English and therefore also had guns but no missionaries. It seems that the Iroquois and those they failed to defeat had chosen more useful allies than the Hurons, Tobaccos, and Neutrals had.

.   .   .

By the seventeenth century, trade-based alliances between Indians and Euro-Americans determined the varied destinies of the tribes. Against the western, French-allied tribes, Dutch guns gave the Iroquois a sovereign edge. Against the eastern tribes, this advantage was more than offset by trading relations between the Susquehannocks and the Swedes (with some English trade as well), and between the Sokokis and Mahicans on the one hand and the English on the other. The Sokokis successfully repulsed a large Mohawk raiding party on one occasion, wiping it out nearly to a man. Both the Susquehannocks and the Mahicans invaded Iroquois lands, putting so much pressure on the Mohawks that at one point the tribe made a formal request to the Dutch for assistance.

For the Dutch, having the Mohawks as allies gave them a terror weapon to use against the French and their Indian trading partners. Yet the Dutch neither respected nor trusted the Mohawks and always had their ears attuned to rumors of conspiracy and treachery. This may have made the Dutch amenable to peace negotiations in 1653 between the Iroquois and the French. The very nature of these negotiations gives lie to the traditional picture of the Beaver Wars as an unstoppable Iroquois juggernaut. As it turned out, the Iroquois League was not the great Indian monolith that it is often portrayed to have been. The Mohawks were both the easternmost and most militant of the Iroquois Five Nations. They enjoyed success in the west, fighting alongside the Seneca, the league's westernmost tribe, but in the east, fighting alone against the well-armed, European-connected Susquehannocks, Sokokis, and Mahicans, they suffered reverses. The Seneca, with some participation by the Onondaga and less from the Cayuga and Oneida, had reaped the rewards of the western genocide; however, as of 1653, the Eries, who lived in a territory stretching from western New York to northern Ohio on Lake Erie's southern shore, were still very much a formidable presence. Perhaps it would have been worthwhile for the western Iroquois to continue fighting the Eries were it not for the Mohawks' insistence on monopolizing access to the Dutch traders. Monopolize it they did, though, and so the Seneca led the Onondaga, Cayuga, and Oneida in peace negotiations with the French and French-allied Indians at Montreal. This left the Mohawks isolated, effectively encircled by hostiles. So they also opened up negotiations with the French, albeit separately, at Trois-Rivières rather than Montreal. High-handedly, in an effort to undercut the other four of the Five Nations, the Mohawks also tried to make Trois-Rivières the *only* legitimate location for negotiations. Just as they had made themselves the sole conduit for trade with the Dutch, so the Mohawks now attempted to become the sole means of negotiation with the French.

Perhaps, at this point, the Dutch were more fearful of their Mohawk allies than of losing ground to the French, and so they approved of the peace negotiations. Yet it is difficult to determine the Dutch strategy, which, in the end, seems more ambivalent than prudent or even purposeful. Initially, the Dutch had used the Mohawks as terror weapons against the French. Yet they were never comfortably confident that this "weapon" would not backfire on them, and so they sanctioned the Iroquois-French peace of 1653—even as they presented the Mohawks with brand-new and very ample supplies of gunpowder, presumably to be used against the French and French-allied Indians.

As the Dutch-Mohawk alliance came to be marked by increasing ambivalence, so the integrity of the Iroquois League began to crack. The Mohawks had long acted with considerable autonomy from the rest of the Five Nations. Now it seemed that those four were cutting the Mohawks loose, making that tribe the odd man out.

This division was deepened in August 1654 when the Onondaga, with the consent of the other western tribes, invited the French to set up a trading post and mission at the village of Onondaga (in present-day New York state). Father Simon Le Moyne, a Jesuit, eagerly embraced the offer, presenting each of the four western Iroquois tribes with ceremonial hatchets—to be used against the Eries, the very tribe whose fierce presence had moved the western Iroquois to make peace in the first place.

Why would an agent of the French attempt to shatter the peace in this manner? The Eries were an Iroquoian tribe, not a member of the Iroquois League, but of the same linguistic and broad cultural group; therefore, the French may have perceived them as a likely potential ally of the Five Nations, which had generally aligned themselves with the

Dutch and (at this point to a lesser extent) the English and had opposed themselves to the French and the French-allied Hurons, Tobaccos, and Neutrals. By sanctioning war between members of the Five Nations and another Iroquoian tribe, Le Moyne may well have intended to forestall the expansion westward of a potential English ally and French enemy.

His effort to foment a war was successful, and the Eries were largely destroyed. The outcome could be termed tribal genocide, although more individual Eries were absorbed into (adopted by) the western Iroquois tribes than were killed by them. Still, the result was that the Eries ceased to exist as an identifiable tribe.

Le Moyne had done even more than block an Indian alliance potentially harmful to the French. Picture the distribution of the five Iroquois tribes. The Mohawks were the easternmost, with the Oneida just to their west. The Seneca were the westernmost, with the Cayuga to their east. The Onondaga were in the middle, between the Oneida on the east and the Cayuga on the west. Each Iroquois village had a large longhouse at its center. It was a communal building and the site of village meetings. The Iroquois League referred to the entire territory of the Five Nations metaphorically as a longhouse, in which the Onondaga occupied the central place and, as such, were the tribe at whose council fire all collective Iroquois decisions were made. Yet, at the same time, Iroquois tradition designated the easternmost Mohawks as the "head" of the longhouse, effectively the leaders of the Iroquois League. Iroquois government has frequently been cited as a model for the founding fathers in the creation of the United States' constitutional government. If so, the founding fathers must have overlooked the built-in conflict within Iroquoian government between the Onondaga central council fire and Mohawk leadership. In effect, Iroquois government was founded on a flawed principle of equality, in which all tribes were equal but one was more equal than the others. Evidently, unlike the future framers of the Constitution, Le Moyne did not overlook this, and by sanctioning the western tribes to war against the Eries, he made a move toward exploiting the conflict inherent in the structure of the Iroquois League to decapitate it, severing the western tribes from their eastern head.

For years, the Mohawks had made good use of their geographical proximity to the Dutch trading capital at Fort Orange to control access to Dutch trade, using their traditional role as "head" of the Iroquois League to justify this monopoly. Le Moyne's encouragement of friendship between the western Iroquois and New France not only allowed the western tribes to bypass Mohawk control by transporting beaver and other furs through French-controlled territory rather than Dutch-Mohawk territory but also resulted in the French designating Onondaga as the only place at which French-Iroquois negotiations could take place. Thus, in a single stroke, the Mohawks lost their trade monopoly and were foiled in their attempt to monopolize treaty making with the French.

Doubtless dismayed, the Mohawks nevertheless did not passively roll over. Instead, they responded by threatening Le Moyne with war, arguing that only a thief enters the longhouse by its chimney (at the center of the building) rather than by its front door (the easternmost position occupied by the Mohawks). The implication? There is only one way to deal with a thief.

The French took the threat seriously enough to delay for more than a year acceptance of the Onondagas' invitation to erect a trading post and mission at their main village. Even when they finally did so, on July 11, 1656, they set up shop—fifty French traders accompanied by four Jesuit missionaries—five "short leagues" (a little over ten miles, assuming the *French* "short league" was the unit of measurement) distant from the village. Despite this act of prudence, violent outbreaks between the French and the Mohawks were frequent, and Louis d'Ailleboust, who became acting governor of New France in 1657, decreed a get-tough policy of what might be termed preemptive defense against the Mohawks. This, predictably, moved the Dutch to overcome their habitual ambivalence and renew their overtures of outright friendship with the tribe.

Thanks to the Dutch, the Mohawks' fortunes now looked up. In 1655, Dutch forces had overrun New Sweden, the always tenuous Swedish settlement on the Delaware. This cut off the Susquehannocks, the

Mohawks' most formidable eastern rivals, from their principal source of trade firearms and forced them to come to terms with the Dutch, which, under the circumstances, also meant coming to terms with the Mohawks.

For their own part, the Dutch, now under the stern leadership of Governor Peter Stuyvesant, found themselves menaced by bands of Lenape (Delaware) Indians—like the Hurons, an Algonquian tribe—in a conflict known as the Peach War, because it had begun when a Dutch farmer killed a Delaware Indian woman for picking peaches in his orchard. In retaliation, the slain woman's family ambushed and killed the farmer. As word of the incident spread, other Lenape bands struck. Several settlers were killed at New Amsterdam, and 150 were taken captive. Governor Stuyvesant called out the militia, which freed most of the captives and destroyed some of the Indians' villages. Following this, Dutch-Lenape violence sporadically continued, debilitating the Indians as well as settlers through about 1657. This motivated Stuyvesant to further strengthen the Dutch alliance with the Mohawks.

The Mohawks wasted little time in exploiting their renewed alliance. Having addressed major threats in the east—actual hostility from the Susquehannocks and potential hostility from the Dutch—they moved against the French at Onondaga, which meant that they also moved against a member of the Iroquois League. Yet they apparently did so in the knowledge that the presence of the French missionaries near the village of Onondaga had deeply divided the tribe. A sizable faction of Onondaga made it known that they intended to side with the Mohawks, and so the French prudently abandoned their mission/trading post *before* the arrival of the attackers. The Onondaga had come to fear the Mohawks far more than they feared the French; however, the presence of missionaries among them—even ten miles distant from their principal village—had touched off an epidemic (either of measles or smallpox; perhaps both). Presumably, this tipped the scales in the Mohawks' favor, making them appear as the lesser of evils.

. . .

Two years after the Peach War had ended, a much larger conflict erupted between the Dutch and another Lenape tribe, the Esopus, who lived along the Hudson in what is now southeastern New York. By the 1650s, Dutch farmers were settling along the Rondout and Esopus creeks, tributaries of the Hudson River. They purchased land from a group of Esopus Indians, and relations were cordial at first but deteriorated in the late 1650s, as local Esopus became increasingly dependent on alcohol, which they purchased from illicit Dutch traders operating in the vicinity of Fort Orange. In 1658, a young warrior deep in his cups killed a settler and burned his farm, prompting Governor Stuyvesant to meet with Esopus leaders to demand reparations. He also pressured them into selling more land to New Netherland. Having secured these concessions, Stuyvesant strengthened New Netherland's militia, a move that brought a short-lived measure of peace—broken when the Esopus grew impatient over the long delay in receiving payment for the land they had ceded.

The Dutch who had settled on the purchased but unpaid-for land were acutely aware of the Indians' ugly mood and, on September 21, 1659, acted preemptively. They ambushed a band of warriors who had been drinking brandy in the woods near the Dutch settlement. One Esopus was killed. On the following day, a number of young warriors exacted revenge by attacking some settlers, killing a few and capturing a few others. This triumph encouraged a major assault, as some five hundred Esopus warriors laid siege to a newly built Dutch stockade, in which local colonists sought refuge.

Traditional Indian battle tactics did not favor protracted siege warfare, and by the time Stuyvesant arrived on the scene with reinforcements—October 10—the attackers had already walked away. Nevertheless, Stuyvesant recognized that he did not command the military strength to wage an offensive against the Indians. Accordingly, he ordered the commander of Fort Orange, Johannes La Montagne, to negotiate a peace.

It lasted less than a year. In the spring of 1660, Ensign Dirck Smith, commanding the Dutch militia garrison at Wiltwyck, New York, took it upon himself to launch a number of assaults against various local Indians. Under pressure from neighboring tribes, the Esopus agreed to a new treaty on July 15, 1660. Yet, as was more often than not the case with treaties between Euro-Americans and Indians, the fighting fitfully continued. When a second Dutch settlement, Nieuwdorp (New Village), was founded near Wiltwyck, Esopus sachems complained to Stuyvesant that he had yet to deliver the promised payment for much of the Esopus land that had been ceded. At last, on June 7, 1663, the frustrated Indians attacked Wiltwyck as well as Nieuwdorp, starting the Second Esopus War.

The attackers waited until most of the men had left the two villages to work the outlying fields. The Indians, arms concealed, then entered Wiltwyck and Nieuwdorp on the familiar pretext of trade. Once inside, they attacked, immediately taking control of the streets and putting various buildings to the torch. They took numerous women and children hostage and sniped at the men as they returned to the villages. Nieuwdorp fell, but as more men returned from the fields, the tide turned in favor of the settlers. By the end of the day, the Battle of Wiltwyck was over. Wiltwyck remained in Dutch hands, but some forty-five settlers had been captured, and twenty or more slain. A band of sixty-nine settlers, including a handful of refugees from Nieuwdorp, hunkered down in Wiltyck and awaited a siege.

It did not come. Just outside the walls of the fortified town, skirmishing was sharp and frequent over the next several weeks. At length, Stuyvesant marched into Wiltwyck and, by the end of June, reinforced the settlement with a contingent of sixty militiamen. The Dutch forbore taking the offensive, however, and instead tried to negotiate for the release of prisoners. Over the next several weeks, a few captives were surrendered, but by the end of July the Dutch resolved to counterattack. For this, they turned to the Mohawks, who contributed warriors to a force that also included militiamen, civilian settlers, and slaves—210 troops in all. Their objective was the Esopus stronghold, which they reached only after a difficult trek over rough terrain. Once arrived, they found the Esopus "fort" deserted.

The Dutch occupied the fort, using it as a base from which they dispatched a smaller force, including Mohawks, to give chase to the Esopus warriors. In the meantime, those who remained at the stronghold set about destroying the Esopus' food caches. Still, the Esopus resisted, releasing only a few more hostages as they quickly fortified a new position. The Dutch commander at Wiltwyck assembled a mixed force of fifty-five men, Dutch militia and Mohawk warriors, to attack the new Esopus stockade on September 5. The Esopus were routed, and the Dutch destroyed the guns and provisions they had left behind. Thirty Esopus had been killed or captured, and twenty-three Dutch captives were recovered. Losses to the Dutch force were slight, at six wounded and three killed.

Three more Dutch expeditions were launched in the fall but resulted in few Indian casualties. Nevertheless, the military action and the demonstrated threat posed by the Dutch-Mohawk alliance prompted the Esopus to sue for peace in May 1664. They ceded much of their territory.

The victory ratified the Mohawks' monopoly on trade with the Dutch. All Indian trade to Fort Orange had to pass through them. Moreover, they had largely destroyed French-Huron commerce. Yet, beyond this, they had not gained any control over trade with the French via Montreal, and whereas the Dutch had identified no significant alternatives to trading with the Mohawks, the French saw many alternatives to doing business with either the Iroquois or the Hurons. They turned westward, to the Ojibwa family of tribes (Chippewas, Missisaugas, Ottawas, and Potawatomis) and the Miami, all peoples who occupied regions still rich with beaver. This gave French traders and trappers access to the best peltries for many years and motivated successive governors of New France to support their Ojibwa and Miami trading partners in turning the tide of the Beaver Wars against the Iroquois, whose campaigns against these Indians, especially those living along the Illinois and Mississippi rivers, resulted in heavy Iroquois defeats after some initial victories. By the 1680s Iroquois forces had also failed in confrontations with the Miami, in the present-day states of Wisconsin and Michigan.

The two Esopus Wars had taken their toll on New Netherland, which emerged from them victorious yet weakened. When English warships sailed up the Hudson on September 8, 1664, to claim New Netherland, the Dutch colonists simply declined to resist. Peter Stuyvesant had no choice but to surrender, although he managed to negotiate the retention of important trading privileges for the Dutch West India Company, including its right to trade with the Mohawks.

The English became the beneficiaries of the Dutch-Mohawk alliance, which would prove crucial in the coming wars with New France, but with the collapse of Dutch political influence came an end to much of the special power the Dutch-Mohawk alliance had conferred upon the Mohawks. This loss, combined with the long years of defeat that followed the shorter period of triumph in the Beaver Wars, initiated the long decline of the Mohawks and of the entire Iroquois League. In the long run, the Beaver Wars drained the resources of all the Indians involved in them and consequently aided the powers of Europe in their conquest and colonization of North America. Euro-American alliances with Native peoples, almost always facilitated by the fur trade, would continue to be the central feature of warfare on the continent; however, as the seventeenth century gave way to the eighteenth, the Indians lost the initiative, and the alliances served Euro-American rather than Native American ends.

4

Inland Empires

———⬦———

DRIVEN BY A DESIRE to monopolize trade with the Dutch and the French, the Iroquois fought the so-called Beaver Wars to control access to both the fur and the markets for it. By the end of the 1650s, however, war had severely disrupted the very trade for which it was being fought. Indian trade with the Dutch slowed, and that with the French came virtually to a halt. Into this climate of counterproductive violence stepped two French *coureurs de bois*—literally "forest runners"—Pierre-Esprit Radisson (1636–1710) and Médard Chouart des Groseilliers (1618–1696).

A teenager when he arrived in New France, Radisson was captured by Iroquois in 1652, at the height of the Beaver Wars, but instead of suffering torture and death, he was adopted into the tribe. This was not an unusual outcome in the instance of a young captive. The Iroquois concept of conquest was almost precisely the inverse of the European paradigm. Whereas the European conqueror invaded an area and occupied it, displacing, killing, or subjugating its original inhabitants, the Iroquois absorbed many of those they conquered. Radisson learned the woodcraft, language, and lifeways of his adoptive tribe, but while he was young enough (as the Indians judged) to merit adoption, he was old enough (in terms of his own sense of self) to stop short of fully relinquishing his Euro-

American identity. Seeing a chance to escape, he took it, only to be recaptured. His former hosts did not welcome him back as the prodigal son but punished him with harsh torture. He survived, however, and, in all, lived a little more than two years with the Indians before he made good a second escape attempt, fleeing to Trois-Rivières, where he moved in with his sister and her husband, Groseilliers.

The older man had been a trader in the Jesuit Huron missionary towns during the 1640s, the towns that had now largely been abandoned under the Iroquois onslaught. During the worst of the Beaver Wars, he took off for what was then the Far Northwest, in search of fur-trading country as yet untouched by Iroquois depredation. Between 1654 and 1656, Groseilliers probed present-day northern Ontario, becoming one of the first Euro-Americans to lay eyes on Lake Superior. Here, Cree Indians told him of abundant beaver peltries north and west of this great inland sea, in the region of Hudson Bay. He did not venture on, however, but instead returned to Trois-Rivières. Then, in 1658 or 1659, he tapped young Radisson to accompany him to Lake Superior. Yet again, the Cree spoke of the great wealth of beaver in the region. The pair erected a trading post at Chequamegon Bay on Lake Superior, around which gathered members of several tribes, all eager to trade their beaver pelts.

Suddenly, the beaver trade was not only reborn but expanded, and with this expansion came a blossoming in the West of a new kind of relationship between the French and the Indians. Although traders had always outnumbered missionaries in the Jesuit Huron mission towns, life was centered nonetheless on the missions, and the Indians were never permitted to forget that the Black Robes would not rest until they had converted them to their religion. True, Father René Menard, the first missionary in the Northwest, would visit Chequamegon Bay in 1661, about three years after the trading post had begun operations, but it would be 1665 before Father Claude Allouez built a mission house at the southwest end of the bay. Effectively, therefore, the Chequamegon Bay community was entirely or mostly secular for its first seven years of existence, and this made all the difference. Instead of a mission culture colored by trade, a rich Euro-Native microcivilization developed, which nurtured a cultural attitude and orientation that would strongly flavor French-Indian relations and make them very different from those that had developed between the Indians and the Dutch and that would develop between the Indians and the English.

Just about everyone who writes about the French and Indian Wars—that is, the seventeenth- and eighteenth-century wars between the French and French-allied Indians on the one side and the English and their (significantly fewer) Indian allies on the other—describes how the French earned the friendship of more Indians than the English did because the French freely mixed with the Indians, extensively intermarrying with them, whereas the English treated them as racial inferiors, seemingly missing no opportunity to demean and otherwise give offense.

There is some truth to this view, thanks in no small part to what Groseilliers and Radisson started in the Far Northwest, but there is also much that is misleading. The civilization that emerged out of the long encounter between Euro-Americans and Native Americans was too complex to be defined simply by how one group of Euro-Americans related to Indians versus how another group did. As citizens of a nation long influenced by race and racial politics, we are quick to assume that racism dominated "white-red" relations from October 12, 1492, on. That is, while we acknowledge the obvious fact that the warring nations of Europe—all populated by "whites"—used North America as an extension of the Old World battlefield throughout the seventeenth and eighteenth centuries, we also believe that even as English colonist fought French colonist, they both ultimately thought of themselves as "white" people menaced in common by "red."

This interpretation of history is both anachronistic and simplistic. It is anachronistic (as just suggested) because it is founded on our own assumptions about racial perception and identification rather than on the beliefs and behavior actually manifested in seventeenth- and eighteenth-century North America. It is simplistic because it does not adequately account for all the motives and all the players of that same time and place.

Consider. Groseilliers and Radisson were fabulously successful. They returned to Trois-Rivières from Chequamegon Bay in 1659 with nearly a hundred canoes laden with thousands of pelts, gunwales scant inches above the waterline. If the powers that be in Trois-Rivières had been motivated chiefly by a desire for friendship and alliance with the Indians, the pair would have been feted on their return. Or if those same powers had been motivated chiefly by a desire to revive—and spectacularly at that—the dormant and sorely missed beaver trade, Groseilliers and Radisson would have been embraced as saviors of New France.

Instead, they were jailed and fined, their furs confiscated. Their crime was having failed to obtain a royal license to trade fur before they set out on their adventure.

Was this rude welcome an act of misplaced bureaucratic zeal or, perhaps, a product of the eternal rapacity of revenue agent and taxman? No. It was more than this, and what it was proves that the motives driving civilization in North America during the mid-seventeenth century were complicated.

Indian alliance was wanted. Trade was wanted. The independence Groseilliers and Radisson had demonstrated by their unlicensed trading in the Far Northwest was, however, not only unwanted, but feared.

Because he was born on a Sunday, September 5, 1638, Louis XIV would be known as the "Sun King." After his father died when he was only four, the Sun King reigned in the shadow of his regent, Jules Cardinal Mazarin (1602–61), whose acute focus on Europe left very little room for concern about New France. When Mazarin died in 1661, Louis XIV emerged from eclipse and, among many other things, discovered that he had a North American colony and took an interest in it. Unlike his father—or, more accurately, unlike his father's powerful minister Cardinal Richelieu—the Sun King saw in New France more than a source of quick profit. He saw in it the makings of a genuine world empire. This, he believed, meant treating it as something more substantial than a hunting ground. In fact, the king believed that coureurs de bois—those "forest runners"—

were inimical to empire and quite probably destructive to civilization itself. English objections to intermarriage between white and Indian were founded on a combination of racial, cultural, and religious concepts. The French entertained no such objections, but Louis XIV nevertheless believed that any lure to life in the forest, especially a peripatetic life out there, was destructive to the roots of the empire he intended to build. He wanted to populate New France with yeoman farmers, not trappers and traders.

Radisson and Grosseilliers knew nothing of this when, chastened by their harsh homecoming, they proposed to the king's finance minister, Jean-Baptiste Colbert—a man of such icily intellectual temperament that Madame de Sévigné, indefatigably acerbic chronicler of court life, dubbed him "Le Nord," as in the *Frozen* North—a scheme to create a company to effectively monopolize the northern fur trade. To sweeten the proposal (for they unwittingly assumed that they were appealing to a man whose imagination was stocked with the customarily grandiose visions of limitless wealth), they also pledged to seek out the Northwest Passage, which (they said) would become an exclusively French route for the transportation of fur directly to Asia. In Japan and China, they explained, a little fur would buy a lot of spices.

The parsimonious Colbert and his often extravagant king were rarely of one mind, but they were agreed on this. Neither was interested in sending French subjects on such errands. As if in response to the proposal, the royal court instantly approved a plan by Jean Talon, comte d'Orsainville (1626–94), the intendant (colonial administrator) of New France, to import at least five hundred Frenchwomen from the mother country. Talon called them *filles du roi*, the king's daughters, but despite the regal name, they were all commoners, poor girls mostly, many orphaned (or, at least, having only a single living parent), and their enticement to journey to New France was the costs of transport plus a royal dowry of fifty livres each and even more if a girl married an army officer. Between 1663 and 1673, as many as nine hundred *filles du roi* emigrated (nobody knows the precise number), of whom 737 were married in New France. Talon's objective was simply to increase the population of New

France as quickly as possible. The king, however, hoped not merely to populate the colony but to entice young "runners" like Radisson to settle down and till the earth—though he did authorize a handsome bounty for all men who sired large families in New France. Women and money, those were the honey. The vinegar? Louis urged his archbishop to excommunicate any men who abandoned their farms without the government's permission.

That New France enjoyed a monopoly on the Canadian fur trade, and that the continuance of this monopoly required pushing ever farther northwest to fresh peltries, as Radisson and Groseilliers had done, meant virtually nothing to the king and his finance minister. The business did not fit their concept of empire, which was a European concept that had nothing to do with a blend of Indian and Euro-American identities motivated by commercial ends. For their part, Radisson and Groseilliers knew when a horse was just too dead to respond to further beating. Still, this did not mean they gave up. Life in the far wilderness had taught them what it had taught others of their kind. Being "French" was no more important than being "Indian" or "white"—or English. Look around. This was not the Old World but the New, a world not yet made but very much in the making, and Radisson and Groseilliers were men on the make.

They journeyed down from New France to New England, where they met with a group of investors in Boston. These Bostonians were as excited by the prospect of penetrating into new peltries as the French court had been indifferent. The so-called romantic historians of the nineteenth century, whose dean was Francis Parkman (1823–93), saw in this an English patriotism that, in reality, almost certainly played no role in the Bostonians' enthusiasm. They were interested less in extending the English empire than in building one of their own, and that meant finding profitable territory free from what had already been carved up and apportioned by royal charters, letters patent, and proprietorships. Nevertheless, investors from the mother country as well as the royal court itself would have to get involved, and the Bostonians, agreeing on the merits of what the Frenchmen proposed, took ship with the men for England to raise money for an expedition.

That is how two French coureurs des bois came to serve as seconds in command of the English vessels *Nonsuch* and *Eaglet,* which set off from Deptford, England, on June 3, 1668, to scout the opportunities for trade around Hudson Bay. Groseilliers served directly under Captain Zachariah Gillam, master of the *Nonsuch*, and Radisson was second to the *Eaglet's* Captain William Stannard. Not that this was a Franco-English expedition. It was, rather, a transnational business enterprise. The two ships had been chartered not by the crown but by Rupert, Count Palatine of the Rhine and Duke of Bavaria (1619–82), a son of the Palatinate elector Frederick V and Elizabeth Stuart, which made him the nephew of King Charles I of England. That monarch created him both Duke of Cumberland and Earl of Holderness, even though he had been born in Prague and spent much of his childhood and youth in Dutch exile before his uncle commissioned him, aged twenty-three in 1642, to lead the Royalist cavalry in the English Civil War. Exiled during the Puritan Interregnum, Rupert commanded other English exiles in the French army during the Thirty Years' War, fell out with fellow Royalists, and turned for a time to West Indian piracy, preying on English shipping in the Caribbean. After living in Germany and the Netherlands from 1654 to 1660, he returned to England upon the restoration of Charles II and undertook top naval commands during the Second and Third Anglo-Dutch Wars (1665–67 and 1672–74) while also diverting himself by copying master paintings as mezzotints, a technique in which he proved so fluent and innovative that the English letter writer John Evelyn mistakenly credited him with having invented the process.

A man of parts, a man of the world, not quite English but not quite anything else either, Rupert was more than ready to back the men of the New World in New World exploration and commercial exploitation. Yet while both ships left Deptford, only the *Nonsuch* made it across the Atlantic. Badly damaged by storms off the Irish coast, the *Eaglet* turned back. The *Nonsuch* sailed into the southern end of Hudson Bay and continued into James Bay, a vast body of water that borders present-day Quebec and Ontario. The ship anchored at the mouth of a river Groseilliers had the good sense to name after Rupert, and here he built Fort

Rupert at the present-day Cree town of Waskaganish, Quebec. It is considered the first fur-trading post of the Hudson's Bay Company.

The *Nonsuch* returned to England, its hold stuffed with furs collected over the winter of 1668–69. Duly impressed, King Charles II chartered his cousin Rupert and Rupert's investors as "the Company of Adventurers of England Trading into Hudsons Bay" on May 2, 1670, giving the Hudson's Bay Company a monopoly on trade in what came to be known as Rupert's Land, the territory whose rivers drained into the Hudson Bay. By modern calculation, this was a region of 1.5 million square miles, a lordly empire indeed, encompassing more than a third of modern Canada and extending into the north-central United States.

Of course, at the time, no one knew the extent of Rupert's Land because no one had explored all the rivers draining into the Hudson. The charter Charles II had granted was hardly unique in being so vague. All royal charters and grants in the New World were vague. As late as 1803, the Louisiana Purchase presented legal problems in part because it did not (and could not) precisely define what was being sold and what was being purchased. This was the nature of the "ownership" of vast wilderness lands in the centuries before satellite imagery and GPS devices. Charles's charter was not simply vague, however. Its definition of Rupert's Land as encompassing whatever drained into Hudson's Bay was both organic and commercial. It defined the land in terms of flowing waterways, thereby engaging the natural environment of the New World more realistically than any arbitrary land-based survey could. Not that Charles or Rupert or Radisson or Groseilliers were environmentalists. Rather, it was just that the nature of rivers, which is to flow, happened also to be of the essence in their commercial enterprise. The charter was based on the natural infrastructure of trade—primarily the trade in beaver fur. The king did not impose an empire on the land, but the hydrological realities of the land, coinciding with the plan for its commercial exploitation, dictated the extent of the empire he proposed.

Yet again, conditions in the New World had prompted unconventional political, cultural, and social alignments. France's Louis XIV had visions of a New World empire based on sedentary agriculture. His conventional, Eurocentric concept of empire was incompatible with what had thus far actually been established in New France, namely the beginnings of a hegemony based not on royal assertion but on trade via alliances with certain Indians—alliances imperiled by other Indians who had trading alliances with other European powers. In the contest between the French king's vision of empire and the rudiments of empire as it actually existed at the time, it was the rudiments that lost. As a result, Radisson and Groseilliers were thrown into jail and, on their release, turned their backs on king and country by approaching agents of Rupert, who might be described as at most half an Englishman, but who was more accurately a citizen of transnational Europe. In contrast to Louis XIV and his minister Colbert, Rupert and his partners, with the consent of a king newly restored to the English throne, were quite willing to take a New World empire on its own terms.

Although Fort Rupert at the mouth of the Rupert River was the first Hudson's Bay Company trading post, the company's first formal headquarters was built in 1682 on the western shore of Hudson Bay at the mouth of a river Sir Thomas Button, a Welsh explorer, had named the Nelson in 1612 after the captain of one of his ships, Robert Nelson, died there. The first building was dubbed Fort Nelson, but the site would soon become more famous as the York Factory. The word requires some explanation. In the seventeenth and eighteenth centuries, a "factory" was not a place of manufacture but the headquarters of a "factor," a company agent who has authority to deal on behalf of his firm.

At its inception, Fort Nelson was not much different from what Fort Orange had been in Dutch New Netherland. It was a trading post. The Hudson's Bay Company, however, would refine the trading post concept into what historians call the "coastal factory model," creating a network of factories around which Euro-American settlement grew up and at which raw pelts were not only acquired but put through the first stages of processing into usable furs. This was something that the French had never done and would never do. Their fur production model was based on a casual system of inland outposts, located on rivers, where traders lived among the Indians with whom they did business. Whereas the coastal factory model inherently segregated Euro-Americans from Native Americans, the French practice inherently integrated the two. This would have a profound effect on Anglo-Native civilization versus its Franco-Native counterpart, which, in turn, would do much to shape military alliances through the French and Indian War and the American Revolution.

Between the genocidal pressure the Iroquois were applying in the Beaver Wars and the policies of Louis XIV and Minister Colbert, there was very real doubt that New France would long continue to participate significantly in the beaver trade at all. The defection of Radisson and Groseilliers and the creation of the Hudson's Bay Company instantly ended the French monopoly on the Canadian fur trade. If the French court wasn't alarmed, the French intendant in Canada, Jean Talon, was panic-stricken and desperate to do something.

On May 25, 1961, after the Soviet Union had beaten the United States into space with *Sputnik I* in 1957 only to trump that achievement by orbiting the first human being, Yuri Gagarin, President John F. Kennedy told Congress that, because the United States had lost the first two laps of the space race, he wanted to sprint ahead, way ahead, by "achieving the goal, before this decade is out, of landing a man on the Moon and returning him safely to the Earth." Talon was desperate enough to be thinking much the same way in 1672. The English had taken the lead in exploiting the fur trade. Talon needed a way to sprint ahead of them.

A few years earlier, in 1669, Talon had approved a fateful expedition led by René-Robert Cavelier, sieur de La Salle (1643–87). Born to wealth in Rouen, he had come to New France dirt poor because he had renounced his father's legacy when he took Jesuit vows in 1660, only to renounce the vows seven years later on account of what he himself called "moral weaknesses." His release from the order did not restore his fortune, but the king did grant him a seigneury at the western tip of the island of Montreal. La Salle subdivided his newly acquired land and spent much time among the Indians who lived on parts of it. He learned Iroquoian and other languages, and he listened to their tales of a river—the Ohio—which, they said, flowed into the "Mesippi," which they called the "father of waters." La Salle assumed (correctly) that the Mississippi flowed into the Gulf of Mexico but further surmised (incorrectly) that the Gulf provided a through passage west to China. Talon and New France's governor at the time, Daniel Courcelle, approved an expedition to find the Ohio, the Mississippi, and a passage to China. It set out on July 6, 1669.

With twenty-four men in canoes, La Salle glided up the St. Lawrence River and into Lake Ontario, reaching the mouth of the Seneca River on the lake's south shore thirty-five days later. Here, Seneca warned him that he was unwelcome in the Ohio Country, and they turned down his request for a guide. Undaunted, La Salle pressed on toward the Niagara River. Encountering another party of Seneca, with a Potawatomi prisoner in tow, La Salle ransomed the captive, who agreed to lead him and his fellow explorers into the Ohio Country. On reaching Lake Erie, the party turned south and trekked overland to a branch of the Ohio, which took them to the great river's main channel. At the Falls of the Ohio near what is today Louisville, Kentucky, La Salle's men declared that they had had enough. Indignant, the voyageur released them and boldy probed farther on his own, but soon turned back. He could claim to be the first white man to have seen and navigated the Ohio River, but its connection with the "father of waters" and the gulf and "southern sea" that would take him to China remained undiscovered.

Now, in 1672, Talon was willing to gamble that La Salle might have been onto something. Find the Pacific passage, and the English foothold in the French fur trade would seem like nothing at all. Talon saw in young Louis Jolliet (1645–1700) just the man to follow up on what La Salle had begun. Louis was born in New France, and after his father died when the boy was just five, his mother married a prosperous merchant, who owned land on the Île d'Orléans in the St. Lawrence River. It was among the Indians who lived on this island that Louis Jolliet learned a variety of Native languages and became closely acquainted with Indian lifeways. He also heard a great many stories from the mixed-blood fur traders who passed in and out of Quebec. He was, however, no wild man himself. Educated at a Jesuit school, he was literate and even cultivated— a natural musician who mastered several instruments. Yet while Jolliet, comfortable in the world of the Indian and the Frenchman, was the ideal candidate for the expedition, Talon knew he could not simply pack him off on his own authority but would have to await the arrival of a new royal governor from France. He had every reason to believe that the man, dispatched by the king, knowing how the king felt about coureurs des bois, would summarily nip the expedition in the bud.

Louis de Buade, comte de Frontenac et de Palluau (1622–98), arrived in New France on September 12, 1672. At fifty, he was a stocky bulldog presence, an army hero, wounded nobly many times, whose unhappy marriage to the ravishingly beautiful Anne de la Grange-Trianon had sent him in search of escape into an oblivion of high living at his estate on the Indre River. In short order, he was financially ruined, and his penurious state made the prospect of life in New France very inviting. Talon, who expected to find himself saddled with a king's man through and through, discovered instead that Frontenac was a shrewdly pragmatic visionary. Without a word of protest, he approved the expedition, reasoning that even if Jolliet failed to find a passage to China, he would nevertheless succeed in pushing the claims of France westward, an end of great strategic importance in itself.

By the time Jolliet was ready to set off, a Jesuit priest by the name of Jacques Marquette (1637–75) had returned to New France after having founded missions at Sault Ste. Marie and at La Pointe, on Lake Superior (near modern Ashland, Wisconsin). At La Pointe, he heard from visiting Illinois Indians the kind of stories La Salle had heard from those closer to home, of a "father of waters," the Mississippi River. The Illinois men even asked Marquette to come south and live among them, closer to the river, but when the Dakota, or Sioux, commenced a war against the Hurons and Ottawas throughout the western Great Lakes region, Marquette prudently withdrew to the Mackinac Straits, where he told his Jesuit superiors about the Mississippi and secured from them leave to search for it. Through Talon, Marquette and Jolliet were united at St. Ignace, from which place, on May 17, 1673, they set off in just two canoes with five voyageurs of mixed French and Indian blood.

The results of the expedition are very well known. The pair did not find a shortcut to the "southern sea" and thence to the Pacific and China, of course, but they did find the Mississippi River, thereby establishing France's claim to a vast portion of what one day would be the United States. In honor of their monarch, they called the territory Louisiana, which they defined far more vaguely than the English had defined Rupert's Land. There was no rationalization of lands drained by rivers, but blunt blanket assertion that "Louisiana" was whatever lay between the Appalachian and Rocky mountains.

Not that Louis XIV really knew what to do with all that had been claimed in his name, even after another Frenchman, Daniel Greysolon, sieur Du Lhut (or Duluth) brought Louis's name into the interior of Minnesota in 1679. Nothing, it seemed, could alter the king's vision of an immense agricultural kingdom that would reflect in the New World the glories of the Old. Mere possession—or the even more tenuous assertion of possession—of a vast territory moved almost no one to settle in it, and by 1715, the year that ended the Sun King's life and long reign, New France still consisted of nothing more than a scattering of precarious settlements in Nova Scotia, along the St. Lawrence, and one or two isolated outposts in Louisiana.

If the French crown did little except assert claims, however, coureurs de bois and voyageurs remained active trading furs as best they could in the overtrapped and depleted peltries of the East while doing business with the Hudson's Bay Company in the West. For its part, the company (product, after all, of two French entrepreneurs scorned by their government and of Rupert's transnational sponsorship) did very little to extend England's claims beyond the original tract represented by Rupert's Land. One way or another, the beaver of the richest peltries was tumbling into Bay Company factories, either directly from Indians or via coureurs de bois and voyageurs of French or mixed French-Native blood. With business highly profitable from the end of the seventeenth century until into the late 1740s, and in possession of a monopoly on the fur trade, Hudson's Bay officials were well pleased with their coastal factory system. Let everyone come to them. Why not? There was no reason to go in search of new sources of fur. Why should they?

So the money rolled in, enriching investors in England and New England, yet doing very little to build an Anglo-Indian community beyond the immediate neighborhood of the factories. The flow of fur-trade money to investors in New France was diminished in proportion to the growth of the Hudson's Bay Company, but those who actually practiced the trade, the likes of Radisson and Groseilliers, a type for whom the French king had professed no use, found in the Hudson's Bay Company deep appreciation in the form of a fresh market. While New France stagnated and the English counted their cash, these men created an intersocietal Franco-Indian civilization based on a trading model that had them living among the Indians, not separating themselves from them. There would be war, both in Europe and America, between the French and the English. In the American theater of these wars, the French would find themselves bound to various tribes by ties political, social, and commericial as well as familial, whereas the English, whose trading model kept the Native Americans at arm's length and more, reaped a mixture of enmity and resentment leavened by tentative alliances that were scarred by cultural animosity and strictly limited by the bounds of prudent business and military necessity. The impact of these essential differences on early American civilization was dramatic and profound, shaping the course of white-Indian warfare through the American Revolution and beyond.

5

"This New Man"

———◆◆◆———

As THE BEAVER WARS died out, Radisson and Groseilliers explored the upper Mississippi River, and La Salle, in 1682, traveled down the lower Mississippi, all the way south to its delta. Whereas Radisson and Groseilliers laid claim on behalf of Louis XIV to everything between the river and the Rocky Mountains, La Salle followed the example of the Hudson's Bay Company up north and claimed all of the lands drained by the Mississippi and its multiple tributaries. Both sets of claims provoked a series of wars between France and England, wars related to parallel conflicts that erupted in Europe. These fires in the North American wilderness are the subject of this and the next chapter. The fighting for control of the land and all it produced—the quickest money was always in fur—disrupted trade with Indians as far west as Minnesota and ripped through Euro-American settlement as far north as Newfoundland and south into Florida.

Yet it was not war with the English that ended French dominance of the fur trade, the most immediate and reliable source of colonial revenue. As we saw in chapter 4, the primary cause was the French king himself. He considered New France a profound disappointment. Thanks to the coureurs de bois and voyageurs, it represented a vast territory, but its vastness, even toward the end of the seventeenth century, was populated by fewer than two thousand French inhabitants. As Louis saw it, a true empire consisted of people more than land, and he wanted a colony of farmers, not fur trappers and traders. He wanted men who would settle down, marry, raise families, and create enduring communities, like those of the English along the seaboard that extended from the Massachusetts Bay Colony in the north to the Carolinas in the south.

Far from seeing the traders and trappers as the pioneers of civilization, Louis XIV considered them the enemies of civilization, of government, of good order, and certainly of empire. His impulse was to suppress this class of men and replace them with farmers, men he understood because they were long familiar in the Old World. Louis was far from appreciating what an expatriate countryman would famously appreciate some seven decades after the end of the king's life and reign. In his 1782 *Letters from an American Farmer*, J. Hector St. John de Crèvecoeur asked, "What then is the American, this new man?" and he answered, "He is an American, who, leaving behind him all his ancient prejudices and manners, receives new ones from the new mode of life he has embraced, the new government he obeys, and the new rank he holds. He has become an American by being received in the broad lap of our great Alma Mater. Here individuals of all races are melted into a new race of man, whose labors and posterity will one day cause great changes in the world. Americans are the western pilgrims."

Crèvecoeur would have looked back some seventy years at a Radisson or a Groseilliers and recognized a "new man," neither French nor Indian but a product of life lived in the frontier interface of two worlds. In the tiny human community of vast New France, these new men were accepted, apparently without censure or prejudice. Indeed, they were valued for their profitable ability to navigate the cultural and economic space between the races. Outside of that community, however, they were feared and scorned—whether by the French king at Versailles or the English with their "coastal factory system," which enforced so strict a division between Indian and Euro-American.

Even Crèvecoeur recognized that the transformation into an American, a "new man," was not without cost. He described those we call pioneers—a class we can extend to include the coureurs de bois and voyageurs—as "a kind of forlorn hope, preceding by ten or twelve years the most respectable army of veterans which come after them." "Forlorn hope" is military jargon for the advance guard or shock troops who, in an assault operation, are calculatedly sacrificed to secure a position for the main force—the "respectable army of veterans" that come after them. *Forlorn hope*—lost souls. In this respect, Crèvecoeur saw the frontiersman much as Louis XIV saw the coureurs de bois and voyageurs. They were shiftless, rootless, wandering, amoral. Forlorn indeed.

Always keen to analyze, Crèvecoeur ascribed this state in part to the brutish practice of hunting instead of farming. "Eating of wild meat," he wrote, "tends to alter their temper." It was due as well to long periods of separation from Euro-American civilization. Yet, unlike the king, Crèvecoeur interpreted the painful status of the frontiersman as a necessary step toward the establishment of a more permanent civilization of the type Louis himself wanted to create in New France. In effect, the coureurs de bois and voyageurs were not to be disparaged but honored as necessary casualties in a war for civilization.

They were casualties the government of King Louis XIV was not willing to accept. The monarch's failure, unwillingness, or inability to embrace the "new man" prompted him to issue a royal edict in 1696 summarily closing all western fur posts. Incredibly, the French fur trade was officially abandoned for twenty years—although illegal traders abounded, most of them doing business with the Hudson's Bay Company.

From the French king's perspective, New France was a malfunctioning component of empire. He had sent women, he had provided bounties, he had threatened excommunication, all with the object of transforming hunters and wanderers into stay-at-home farmers. Beyond this, he gave New France little support, sending to it governors who had failed to make a go of it elsewhere and, beyond scolds and reprimands, mostly leaving the small population to fend for itself. The Indians became increasingly important to the people of New France almost in direct proportion to the increase of royal neglect. The Indians extended the commercial and military reach of the Franco-Americans, especially in the frontier between the colonies.

The Abenaki were a loosely confederated group of Algonquian tribes (including the Penobscots, Kennebecs, Wawenocks, and Androscoggins of New England's eastern frontier; the Pigwackets, Ossipees, and Winnipesaukes of the White Mountains; the Pennacooks of the Merrimack Valley; the Sokokis and Cowasucks of the upper Connecticut Valley; and the Missisquois and other groups in Vermont) who were broadcast throughout the region of present-day Maine, New Hampshire, Vermont, and southern Quebec. The English often referred to these tribes collectively as "the eastern Indians," and, to the English, they represented the hostile line demarcating the border region between New England and New France. Like other Algonquian groups, the Abenaki gravitated toward alliance with the French, in part for reasons of trade—though the beaver peltries in these parts had been largely depleted by the end of the sixteenth century—but mostly because thinly populated New France represented less of a threat to their traditional lands than the English, whose outlying settlements continually pushed into country the Abenaki counted as theirs. Supplied by the French, the Abenaki harried and raided New England's eastern frontier from 1675 to 1678, when the English, weakened by the intense and sustained combat of King Philip's War of 1675–76 (which pitted the loosely united New England colonies against the Wampanoag, Narragansett, and Nipmuck Indians), concluded a frankly abject treaty with the Abenaki, promising them an annual tribute payment.

Despite the treaty and the tribute, the First Abenaki War (as it is often called) proved but the prelude to other conflicts in which Abenaki warriors fought, both on their own and under the direct command of French officers. These conflicts included the first two of what are generally called the French and Indian Wars (note the plural): King William's War of 1689–97 and Queen Anne's War of 1702–13.

The Abenaki role in Queen Anne's War is often referred to as the Second Abenaki War. The change in nomenclature is significant because it underscores the dual nature of these "French and Indian Wars." On the one hand, they were extensions of European conflicts—King William's War was the North American theater of the War of the League of Augsburg, while Queen Anne's War corresponded to the War of the Spanish Succession in Europe—yet they were also American wars in which Indians fought to gain advantage through their relationship to the Euro-Americans, and the Euro-Americans fought variously to dominate certain Indian tribes or to use them to defeat their Euro-American rivals for North American empire. The alliances were often tenuous at best. Indian "auxiliaries" (as European-trained officers called them) were typically employed less as allies than as weapons—and weapons of terror at that. Yet the connections between Indian warriors and French or English militiamen were more intimate than the remote link between those fighting on the frontier and the kings, queens, officers, and soldiers conducting warfare in far-off Europe. More often than not, war in the wilderness did not reflect a vision of imperial hegemony but, rather, motives ranging from advantage in trade to basic survival.

The Old World basis for the New World war named after England's King William III was that monarch's decision, on May 12, 1689, to join the League of Augsburg and the Netherlands, creating the "Grand Alliance" in opposition to Louis XIV, who had invaded the Rhenish Palatinate on September 24 of the previous year. The fighting between the league and Louis spanned eight years and, in Europe, is remembered as the War of the League of Augsburg or the War of the Grand Alliance. In North America, the war served to exacerbate the chronic hostility between New France and New England. The French aligned themselves once more with the Abenaki, whose location on the English frontier made them the tip of the French spear. The English relied on the Iroquois, especially the Mohawks, whose trade they had taken up from the Dutch when they transformed New Netherland into New York.

Louis de Buade, comte de Frontenac, the latest governor of New France, wanted nothing more desperately than to reach into the English colonial realm by invading New York, but he knew only too well that he lacked the troops for the job. Instead, he proposed to fight what he called *"la petite guerre,"* a little war, using a phrase that would eventually metamorphose into "guerrilla war." Whereas the crown found little or no use for woodland runners, the men who were neither quite French nor quite Indian, Frontenac was ready to exploit them and their special relationship with the Indian warriors to fight the small-unit war he envisioned, a war that would consist not of great "set battles" but of ruthless murders, committed without warning or mercy and, most important, without distinguishing between combatants and civilians.

Frontenac used the Abenaki first, encouraging them to terrorize English settlements throughout Maine and New Hampshire. Through the summer of 1689, the raiding was so intense that the English abandoned all of their outposts east of Falmouth, Maine. Authorities in Boston mustered and fielded a militia army of six hundred, but this conventional military force was outmatched by the Abenaki guerrillas. For his part, Frontenac was thinking far outside of the box. Everyone knew that armies suspended combat in the winter. Frontenac knew this, too—and for that very reason used the onset of the season to assemble a mixed force of 160 New France militiamen and about one hundred Abenaki to hit the English when they least expected it.

He planned a three-pronged assault out of Montreal into New York, New Hampshire, and Maine; however, after they had reached the Hudson River by way of a harrowing frozen trek down Lake Champlain to the southern tip of Lake George, the French Canadian commanders of the assault force decided to attack Schenectady, which was closer than Albany. On the afternoon of February 8, 1690, after marching across bitterly cold, frozen swampland, they reached the vicinity of the settlement, concealed themselves, and awaited nightfall.

It was moon bright, the silver light outlining a pair of sentries before the rude stockade surrounding the village. The French and their "auxiliaries" waited and watched, looking for a moment in which the guards would become distracted or tired or step away. The sentries never moved. At length, the attackers, cold and tired, advanced. Still the guards remained motionless. On further advance, the French and their Indian auxiliaries saw that these "sentinels" were nothing more fearsome—or more effective—than a brace of snowmen.

A whoop arose, and for the next two hours the French and Indians raked Schenectady, killing sixty men, women, and children, most of them in their beds.

On March 27, another detachment of Frontenac's forces attacked Salmon Falls, New Hampshire, where they killed thirty-four settlers, and in May, Fort Loyal (modern Falmouth, Maine) was attacked by a mixed Canadian and Abenaki force. Nearly a hundred English settlers perished.

By this time—on May 1, 1690—delegates from Massachusetts, Plymouth, Connecticut, and New York had convened at Albany, where they determined to seize the offensive by invading Canada with two land forces, one from New York and one from New England, joined by a flotilla sailing up the St. Lawrence River. The combined assault was led by Sir William Phips (1651–95), whose grudge against the Indians was personal. He had set up a shipyard on his wife's land on Maine's Sheepscot River, only to be forced from it under Indian attack. Fortunately, he had built one substantial ship before the attack and was able to load it with everyone in the surrounding settlement, whom he conveyed to safety before the shipyard and the village were burned to the ground. Now, on May 11, 1690, with fourteen vessels, he attacked French-held Port-Royal, Acadia (present-day Annapolis Royal, Nova Scotia) and easily captured it. In July, he hoped to follow up this triumph by taking Quebec.

As his regulars and militiamen, plus sixty Indians, huddled in some thirty-four ships, Phips sent ashore his envoy, Major Thomas Savage, to deliver to Frontenac a surrender demand. The governor blindfolded the emissary and led him through the streets of the city. A mob roared. In truth, Quebec was sparsely populated, but the few who were present yelled loudly and without intermission, following Savage's blindfolded progress to give the sightless man the impression of a great multitude out for blood. When Savage presented Phips's demand, Frontenac responded haughtily, "I have no reply to make to your general other than from the mouths of my cannons and muskets."

The English siege, accordingly, was mounted, and the siege failed. Thirty of Phips's twenty-three hundred men were killed in battle and another fifty were wounded, but the far deadlier enemy was smallpox, which sickened about half of his force, compelling the English to withdraw. It was the beginning of a series of reversals, and before 1690 was out, French forces had evicted the English from their Hudson Bay outpost at the mouth of the Severn River. The next year, the French even retook Port-Royal. Yet Frontenac's "little war" produced nothing but relatively little victories that achieved nothing of enduring strategic value, and while the Abenaki guerrilla raids excited much terror, New England's Iroquois allies remained loyal—though they suffered the heaviest losses in the war.

In September 1691, Benjamin Church led three hundred militiamen to Saco, Maine, an English outpost that had been the target of repeated attacks. Like the French, Church won no single decisive engagement, but he did sufficiently wear down the Abenaki to motivate a number of sachems to travel to peace talks in October. The result was a treaty on November 29, 1691, by which the Abenaki agreed to release captives, to inform the English of any future French designs against them, and to refrain from hostilities until May 1, 1692.

It was promising—especially the part about ratting out the French, which, Church was confident, would drive a wedge between the allies—but, promising though it was, the treaty produced the result most treaties between the colonies and the Indians produced: complete failure. The dreary pattern of raid and counterraid resumed. No sooner had they agreed to the peace than the Abenaki joined with French Canadian militiamen to attack York, Maine, on February 5, 1692. In June, Wells, Maine, fell under the hatchet. On June 6, the raiders penetrated farther south, hitting Deerfield, Massachusetts. It was one of a handful of frontier settlements against which raids repeatedly crashed like waves against the rocks of the New England shore. The town would be struck in war after frontier war.

Most raids were small and targeted English settlements; however, a French-led expedition in January 1693 hit Mohawk villages in New York, capturing some three hundred Mohawks, most of them women, children, and old men. Others fled to the Caughnawaga Mission in Canada. This was particularly significant in that the Caughnawagas, although Iroquois, were Catholic converts allied not with the English but with the French. The colonial wars between Euro-Americans were beginning to tear apart the old Indian alliances and solidarities.

In September 1697, the Treaty of Ryswick ended the War of the League of Augsburg. With this treaty, the conflict officially concluded in America as well, although violence continued spasmodically on the frontier and, in 1702, blew up into what was destined to be a decade of renewed warfare between the French-supplied Abenaki and the people on the northeastern fringes of English settlement. Some historians call this conflict spanning 1702 to 1712 the Second Abenaki War, while others consider it a part of the more general Queen Anne's War of this same period. In either case, the Maine frontier suffered attacks from Wells to Casco, in which about three hundred settlers were killed in the course of a decade.

The Abenaki raids ended only after the French withdrew their support at the conclusion of Queen Anne's War. Like King William's War, Queen Anne's War was the American theater of a European conflagration. England, the Netherlands, and Austria, fearful of an alliance between France and Spain, formed a new anti-French Grand Alliance in 1701 after King Charles II of Spain, a Hapsburg, died in 1700—though not before he had chosen a Bourbon as his successor. The French supported Charles II's nominee, Philip of Anjou, a grandson of Louis XIV, as his successor; England, Holland, and Austria gave their support to the second son of Hapsburg emperor Leopold I, the obscure Bavarian archduke Charles. So the War of the Spanish Succession, as it was called, was declared in Europe on May 4, 1702, and, under the name of Queen Anne's War, spread to the colonies on September 10, 1702, when the South Carolina legislature authorized an expedition to seize the Spanish-held fort and surrounding town of St. Augustine, Florida. In the initial attack, a British naval expedition plundered the town; then, in December, a mixed force of five hundred South Carolina colonists and English-allied Chickasaw assailed the fort itself. Failing to breach it, they turned to further pillaging of the town before putting the settlement to the torch.

Predictably, South Carolina's actions brought a series of French- and

Spanish-allied Indian raids in retaliation, to which James Moore, former South Carolina governor, responded by leading a force of South Carolina militiamen and Chickasaw through the territory of the Spanish-allied Appalachees of western Florida during most of July 1704. Moore and his men killed or captured the inhabitants of seven Appalachee villages, virtually wiping out the tribe.

Moore's expedition also burned down thirteen of fourteen Spanish missions in the country. It is important to note that these attacks were not the work of Indians but of South Carolina militiamen. They reflect the fact that the Protestant English feared the Roman Catholic French and Spanish almost as much as they feared the Indians. Indeed, what a Pennsylvania farmer wrote to his colony's provincial secretary in 1756, during the French and Indian War, applies equally to the late seventeenth century and early eighteenth: "Must we in Very Deed become a province of France? . . . If so, . . . farewell Religion." He next evoked something like the Spanish Inquisition—an institution many Protestant colonists believed the French and their Spanish allies intended to bring to North America: "Must we have Persecution? Images Crucifixes &ca. &ca. Alas! Alas!" There was a widespread belief that the French were using Indian terror just as the Grand Inquisitors had used their red-hot instruments of torture—and for the same purpose: to forcibly convert the Protestant masses to the Roman Catholic faith.

Whatever Moore's motive for burning the Spanish missions, his ruthless actions in Florida did not result in the usual pattern of raid and reprisal but instead had profound strategic effect, opening a path directly into the heart of French Louisiana territory and the sparse French settlements along the Gulf of Mexico.

For their part during the war, emissaries of New France had been active in recruiting alliances among the southern tribes. By means of cajolery and bribery, French colonial officials courted the Choctaw, Cherokee, Creeks, and Chickasaw. The last-mentioned tribe remained loyal to the English, and the Cherokee managed to maintain a neutral stance. A few bands of Creek Indians sided with the French, but, by far, France's most powerful ally proved to be the Choctaw, who marched to intercept

Moore's relentless advance and successfully blocked him, preventing his passage into Louisiana.

Up north, the French-Indian alliances were both more extensive and of longer standing. English colonial authorities persisted in treating the Indians with contempt, heedlessly provoking them even as French authorities courted and recruited them. On August 10, 1703, a party of English settlers broke into and plundered the Maine house belonging to the son of Jean Vincent de l'Abadie, baron de Saint-Castin. Because his mother was the daughter of an Abenaki chief, Saint-Castin was considered likewise a chief, and the attack on his house touched off Abenaki reprisal raids along two hundred miles of the northern New England frontier. On February 29, 1704, a mixed force of French troops and Indian warriors raided Deerfield, Massachusetts, where the Reverend John Williams was the local pastor. He, his wife, five of their children, and most of his congregation were among the 111 captives carried off to French Canada. His immensely popular narrative, *The Redeemed Captive Returning to Zion*, was published shortly after he was ransomed and returned to Deerfield. It provides an extraordinary picture of an Indian raid.

"They came," Williams wrote,

to my house in the beginning of the onset [onslaught], and by their violent endeavors to break open doors and windows, with axes and hatchets, awaked me out of sleep; on which I leaped out of bed, and, running towards the door, perceived the enemy making their entrance into the house. I called to awaken two soldiers in the chamber, and returning toward my bedside for my arms, the enemy immediately broke into the room, I judge to the number of twenty, with painted faces, and hideous acclamations. I reached up my hands to the bed-tester for my pistol, uttering a short petition to God, for everlasting mercies for me and mine, on account of the merits of our glorified Redeemer; expecting a present passage through the valley of the shadow of death. . . . Taking down my pistol, I cocked it, and put it to the breast of the first Indian that came up; but my pistol missing fire, I was seized by three Indians, who disarmed me, and bound me naked, as I was in my shirt, and so I stood for near the space of an hour. Binding me, they told me they would carry me to Quebeck. My pistol missing fire was an occasion of my life's being preserved; since which I have also found it profitable to be crossed in my own will. The judgment of God did not long slumber against one of the three which took me, who was a captain, for by sunrising he received a mortal shot from my next neighbor's house; who opposed so great a number of French and Indians as three hundred, and yet were no more than seven men in an un-garrisoned house.

I cannot relate the distressing care I had for my dear wife, who had lain in but a few weeks before; and for my poor children, family, and Christian neighbors. The enemy fell to rifling the house, and entered in great numbers into every room. I begged of God to remember mercy in the midst of judgment; that he would so far restrain their wrath, as to prevent their murdering of us; that we might have grace to glorify his name, whether in life or death; and, as I was able, committed our state to God. The enemies who entered the house, were all of them Indians and Macquas, insulted over me awhile, holding up hatchets over my head, threatening to burn all I had; but yet God, beyond expectation, made us in a great measure to be pitied; for though some were so cruel and barbarous as to take and carry to the door two of my children and murder them, as also a negro woman; yet they gave me liberty to put on my clothes, keeping me bound with a cord on one arm, till I put on my clothes to the other; and then changing my cord, they let me dress myself, and then pinioned me again. Gave liberty to my dear wife to dress herself and our remaining children. About sun an hour high, we were all carried out of the house, for a march, and saw many of the houses of my neighbors in flames, perceiving the whole fort, one house excepted, to be taken. Who can tell what sorrows pierced our souls, when we saw ourselves carried away from God's sanctuary, to go into a strange land, exposed to so many trials; the journey being at least three hundred miles we were to travel; the snow up to the knees, and we never inured to such hardships and fatigues; the place we were to be carried to, a Popish country. Upon my parting from the town, they fired my house and barn. We were carried over the river, to the foot of the mountain, about a mile from my house, where we found a great number of our Christian neighbors, men, women, and children, to the number of an hundred, nineteen of which were afterward murdered by the way, and two starved to death, near Cowass, in a time of great scarcity, or famine, the savages underwent there. When we came to the foot of the mountain, they took away our shoes, and gave us in the room of them Indian shoes, to prepare us for our travel. Whilst we were there, the English beat out a company that remained in the town, and pursued them to the river, killing and wounding many of them; but the body of the army being alarmed, they repulsed those few English that pursued them.

Williams and the other captives were marched toward Quebec.

When we came to our lodging place, the first night, they dug away the snow, and made some wigwams, cut down some small branches of the spruce-tree to lie down on, and gave the prisoners somewhat to eat; but we had but little appetite. I was pinioned and bound down that night, and so I was every night whilst I was with the army. . . . In the night an Englishman made his escape; in the morning (March 1), I was called for, and ordered by the general to tell the English, that if any more made their escape, they would burn the rest of the prisoners.

At length, Williams was separated from his wife, who was left behind, under guard, with others too weak to keep up with the main body of prisoners.

I sat pitying those who were behind, and entreated my master to let me go down and help my wife; but he refused, and would not let me stir from him. I asked each of the prisoners (as they passed by me) after her, and heard that, passing through [a] river, she fell down, and was plunged over head and ears in the water; after which she travelled not far, for at the foot of that mountain, the cruel and bloodthirsty savage who took her slew her with his hatchet at one stroke, the tidings of which were very awful. And yet such was the hard-heartedness of the adversary, that my tears were reckoned to me as a reproach. . . . I begged of God to overrule, in his providence, that the corpse of one so dear to me, and of one whose spirit he had taken to dwell with him in glory, might meet with a Christian burial, and not be left for meat to the fowls of the air and beasts of the earth; a mercy that God graciously vouchsafed to grant. For God put it into the hearts of my neighbors, to come out as far as she lay, to take up her corpse, carry it to the town, and decently to bury it soon after. In our march they killed a sucking infant of one of my neighbors; and before night a girl of about eleven years of age. I was made to mourn, at the consideration of my flock being, so far, a flock of slaughter, many being slain in the town, and so many murdered in so few miles from the town; and from fears what we must yet expect, from such who delightfully imbrued their hands in the blood of so many of His people.

Farther north, in Nova Scotia, Benjamin Church, now so old that he had to be helped over fallen logs in his path, marched 550 men into Acadian French territory, visiting terror upon two settlements, Minas and Beaubassin, in July 1704. Above Nova Scotia, in Newfoundland, between August 18 and 29, a mixed force of French and Indians operating out of Placentia destroyed the English settlement at Bonavista in a series of raids in retaliation for Minas and Beaubassin.

Along the entire stretch of English and French settlement, the war dragged on in a dreary succession of murders, raids, and counterraids. In 1710, hoping to bring about a breakthrough victory, English colonial officials sent a contingent of English-allied Mohawk chiefs to England and the court of Queen Anne. The visit was carefully orchestrated to win sympathy and support for the plight of the colonies. The Mohawks' English handlers took their charges to a London theatrical costumer, who meticulously arrayed them in "savage" attire before their appearance at the court. The effect was electric, and Queen Anne immediately authorized a substantial contingent of regular English troops to be sent to the colonies, the land forces under the command of Colonel Francis Nicholson and the naval transports and warships under Sir Francis Hobby. Acting in concert, the land and sea forces reduced Port-Royal, Nova Scotia, by October 16, 1710. The following summer, all of French Acadia fell to the British.

Flushed with victory, Hobby's subordinate, Sir Hovenden Walker, led another naval expedition, this one aimed at Quebec, only to suffer shipwreck at the mouth of the St. Lawrence River with the staggering loss of nearly 900 of 1,390 soldiers and 150 sailors who had been crowded into troop transports. The next year, another move against the French Canadian capital was badly mismanaged and had to be aborted. Yet by this time Louis XIV, war weary and burdened by debt, was ready for peace. Besides, the original source of the conflict in Europe, the issue of who would succeed to the Spanish throne, had become moot. In the course of the eleven-year struggle, Archduke Charles, the Bavarian candidate supported by the Grand Alliance, succeeded his elder brother as Holy Roman Emperor, and thus was no longer a viable challenger to Louis's grandson Philip of Anjou. Fate having taken his side in the matter of Spain, Louis XIV signed the Treaty of Utrecht on July 13, 1713, ceding to the English Hudson Bay and Acadia but retaining Cape Breton Island and other small islands in the St. Lawrence. The Canadian boundaries, however, remained unsettled and, of course, would continue to prove a source of conflict. The Abenaki and other French-allied Indians signed a treaty with the New Englanders, pledging to become loyal subjects of Queen Anne.

Trade had produced what Crèvecoeur would call a "new man," and yet this new man remained tightly bound to the Old World. Wars in the wilderness that looked like no wars the Europeans had ever known—wars that were little more than serial murders of the most brutal kind perpetrated in the darkest recesses of the North American forest—were nevertheless linked to large-scale, multinational campaigns fought on European battlefields to resolve obscure but momentous questions of royal succession. What was panoramic combat on the fields of Europe emerged in North America as so many fires in the wilderness, one upon another, blazing fitfully from Newfoundland in the north to Florida in the south.

6

Fires in the Wilderness

———◆———

THE "INDIANS" IN THE first two of the so-called French and Indian Wars, King William's War and Queen Anne's War, were regarded, from the perspective of the English, French, and Spanish, as allies or as enemies. ("Hired guns" or "agents of terror" was often a more accurate term than "ally.") That Euro-Americans were fully capable of what today might euphemistically be called "unconventional warfare"—especially brutal hand-to-hand combat and the torture of captives—is undeniable; however, there was a general perception that the Indians were simply better at it. Besides, no "Christian" nation liked to admit to using, much less sanctioning, such tactics.

Consider the infamous issue of scalping. No feature of Indian warfare is more familiar or subject to more folklore based on Euro-American propaganda. Non-Indian commentators have pointed to scalping as evidence either of the inherent and gratuitous cruelty of Indian war practices or have attributed to it significance as a kind of religious favor granted to one's enemy, claiming that the act of taking a scalp was intended to release the "spirit" or "soul" of the slain. Others, more recently, have made the revisionist claim that scalping was actually unknown among Native American tribes before the arrival of Europeans.

As usual in matters of early American civilization, the truth is a more complex interaction of Euro-American and Indian traditions, neither of which is uniform, let alone monolithic in its nature. Revisionist claims notwithstanding, there is ample evidence that scalping was practiced among North American Indians before the advent of the Europeans. Jacques Cartier reported it in 1535, Hernando de Soto in 1540, Tristán de Luna in 1559, and others subsequently. It was not universally practiced among Indian tribes, however, but was spread generally from east to west with the movement, migration, or invasion of eastern tribes *and* also as a result of contact with Euro-Americans, who adopted the custom from eastern Indians. Thus, while Euro-Americans did not introduce scalping to the Indians of North America, they did contribute to the proliferation of the custom. In part, this was due to Euro-Americans displacing some Indian groups from the east to the west or encouraging such westward movement to facilitate trade. The Iroquois sought the rich beaver peltries of the western tribes because they wanted to increase and monopolize trade with the Euro-Americans. It is also evident that the practice was sometimes transmitted by Euro-Americans to Indians.

As for the claim, made chiefly by nineteenth-century romantic historians, that scalping was meant to be of spiritual benefit to the victim, quite the contrary was the case. The act of scalping seems to have been intended as an insult, and the scalp served as neither more nor less than a battle trophy. Euro-Americans added an additional incentive during portions of the colonial period by offering "scalp bounties," rewards paid to "friendly" Indians for the delivery of scalps taken from hostiles.

Colonists also influenced the methods employed in taking a scalp. Some Indians took the whole skin of the upper head, ears included; others removed only the crown. After Euro-Americas introduced as trade goods among the Indians sharper, sturdier steel knives and hatchets, many tribes began employing a faster method of scalping, grasping the forelock, making a single gash in the front of the head, and forcibly popping out the "scalp lock" trophy with a sharp tug. Anthropologists generally believe that, as the "scalp lock" method was an abbreviated technique for taking scalps, so the practice of scalping itself served as a "metonymic"—using a part to stand for the whole—substitute for decapitation. Indeed, the scalp trophy symbolized the entire head even as the head represented the whole person of the victim. A few tribes, particularly among those in the Plains, persisted in decapitating their enemies well into the nineteenth century. Among them, a severed head was considered an even greater trophy than a scalp or scalp lock. This practice, certainly more atavistic than scalping, was, if anything, also more familiar to Euro-Americans. Decapitation was, of course, long a familiar form of judicial execution in Europe, but it also featured in clashes between Euro-Americans and Indians, most horrifically in 1643 when New Netherland governor Willem Kieft sent a party of Mohawk warriors up the Hudson from New Amsterdam to extort an exorbitant tribute payment from the Wappinger Indians. Terrorized by the Mohawks, and ignorant of Kieft's role in what amounted to a violent shakedown scheme, the Wappingers responded to the Mohawks by fleeing to Pavonia (the environs of present-day Jersey City, New Jersey) and, across the Hudson, to New Amsterdam (present-day New York City), where they appealed to Kieft for protection. The governor responded by turning the Mohawks loose upon them. In an orgy of violence, Mohawk warriors killed seventy Wappingers and enslaved others; then, during the night of February 25–26, Kieft dispatched bands of Dutch soldiers to Pavonia with orders to finish off any refugees from the Mohawk assault. The night of horror in that settlement would become infamous as the "Slaughter of the Innocents." The Dutch troops returned to New Amsterdam bearing the severed heads of some eighty Indians, which soldiers and civilians alike used as footballs on the streets of New Amsterdam. Thirty prisoners taken alive were tortured to death in the city for the public amusement. As Captain David Pietersz (or Pietersen) de Vries, a local patroon (landholder), wrote in 1655:

> I remained that night at the governor's, sitting up. I went and sat in the kitchen, when, about midnight, I heard a great shrieking, and I ran to the ramparts of the fort, and looked over to Pavonia. Saw nothing but firing, and heard the shrieks of the Indians murdered in their sleep. . . . When it

was day the soldiers returned to the fort, having massacred or murdered eighty Indians, and considering that they had done a deed of Roman valour, in murdering so many in their sleep; where infants were torn from their mother's breasts, and hacked to pieces in the presence of the parents, and the pieces thrown into the fire and in the water, and other sucklings were bound to small boards, and then cut, stuck, and pierced, and miserably massacred in a manner to move a heart of stone. Some were thrown into the river, and when the fathers and mothers endeavoured to save them, the soldiers would not let them come on land, but made both parents and children drown, children from five to six years of age, and also some decrepit persons. Many fled from this scene, and concealed themselves in the neighbouring sedge, and when it was morning, came out to beg a piece of bread, and to be permitted to warm themselves; but they were murdered in cold blood and tossed into the water. Some came by our lands in the country with their hands, some with their legs cut off, and some holding their entrails in their arms, and others had such horrible cuts, and gashes, that worse than they were could never happen.

De Vries implies that Kieft intended the brutality of the massacre to look like the work of Indians. That is, the Dutch soldiers purposely emulated the bloodiness of an Indian raid: "And these poor simple creatures, as also many of our own people, did not know any better than that they had been attacked by a party of other Indians,—the Maquas [Mohawks]."

Thus relations among the Euro-Americans and between the Euro-Americans and the Indians were complex, compounded of trade, politics, military utility, and culture, further complicated by competitive relations among colonies of the same nationality (in the case of the English) and relations between the colonies and the mother country, which, for both the French and the English, were often contentious.

As if the royal closure of the fur trade were not bad enough for the geopolitical position of New France in North America, beginning in 1712, French settlers in the southern reaches of the colony engaged in a ruinous war with the Fox Indians, who were far western allies of the Iroquois. This closed the key trading route via the Fox and Wisconsin rivers, and all through the upper Mississippi region even the unlicensed French fur trade stopped and would not resume until the Fox War ended in 1730, after the French and their Indian allies, now eager to reopen the fur trade, had virtually exterminated the Fox in what was a determined and carefully plotted Franco-Native war of genocide.

The war, which historians call the Fox Resistance, seems to have been incited by the Iroquois in a desperate bid to reverse the decline of their monopoly on the inland beaver trade. Since at least the late seventeenth century, the Fox had been sporadically at war with the Ojibwa, who were concentrated in present-day northwestern Wisconsin. Unlicensed French traders, who had maintained profitable relations with the Ojibwa, supported these Indians in their ongoing conflict with the Fox. In turn, Fox raiders harassed French frontier outposts and in 1712 attacked the French fort at Detroit but were driven off.

During this period, only the Mohawks remained steadfast military allies of the English. The rest of the Iroquois League struggled to remain neutral in the ongoing Euro-American conflict, and the Seneca in particular traded freely with the French. By the 1720s, the western Iroquois, still purportedly neutral, repeatedly sought to play the English off against the French, presumably hoping to achieve a balance of power they thought would be beneficial. In 1729, however, when a combination of French and Indians, chiefly Ojibwa, attacked the Fox, the Iroquois League came together in a move toward outright alliance with the English.

The attack had been motivated by the growing intensity of Fox raiding, which not only reduced trade between the French and the Ojibwa but threatened the very lifeline connecting New France in the north with Louisiana in the south: Lake Michigan, the upper Mississippi, and the portages linking them. To counter the threat, French officers held a number of councils with the Ojibwa to formulate an overall war strategy. The most ambitious solution proposed was the outright extermination of the Fox tribe. Appealing as this was, French authorities thought it impractical and decided instead to round up the Fox and "relocate" them to Detroit, where the well-armed garrison of the fort could monitor and control their activities. Several French-Ojibwa campaigns toward this end were mounted with little success, and in 1729, when the Fox raids became more destructive, French-Ojibwa policy turned from concentration to extermination. A large combined French and Indian force swept through the Fox territory during 1729–30 and wiped out much of the tribe, dispersing the survivors.

The loss of their Fox allies was a blow to the English, yet it also served to strengthen their alliance with the Iroquois, even though English colonial leaders repeatedly showed themselves to be treacherous "friends." Throughout the seventeenth century—the period of early contact between them and the English—the Tuscaroras, who lived along the coastal rivers of North Carolina, were inclined to maintain friendly relations with their colonist neighbors. By the second decade of the eighteenth century, however, their peaceful ways had been rewarded by nothing but abuse, especially at the hands of local English traders. This seemed to signal English-allied Mohawks to make it their practice to routinely ambush Tuscarora hunters. Nevertheless, with apparently limitless patience, the Tuscaroras endured, always acting to avoid out-and-out war.

At last, they came to believe that their best hope lay in leaving North Carolina for Pennsylvania. The Pennsylvanians were willing to take in the Tuscaroras, but only if the tribe received formal permission to emigrate. The colonial government of North Carolina, loath to lose trading partners, refused to grant the required permission, and in 1710 came a new provocation, when a band of Swiss immigrant colonists organized by a wily entrepreneur named Baron Cristoph von Graffenried settled on a tract of North Carolina land at the confluence of the Neuse and Trent rivers. They christened the settlement New Bern. That the land was already occupied by a Tuscarora village disturbed Graffenried not at all, and instead of even making a show of negotiation with the Indians, the count lodged a complaint with North Carolina's surveyor general, eliciting from him an affirmation that, as far as the government was concerned, the Graffenried settlers held clear title to the land. Fortified legally, Graffenried drove the Tuscaroras off.

Or so he believed. On September 22, 1711, a large Tuscarora raiding party attacked New Bern and other settlements in the area, killing two hundred settlers, eighty of them children. Graffenried himself was captured but secured his release, along with the Indians' pledge not to attack New Bern again, in exchange for his solemn promise to live in peaceful harmony with the Tuscaroras from then on.

It is unlikely that Graffenried intended to keep his promise, but, even if he did, he had so little control over his settlers that when one of them, William Brice, led an attack on members of the local Coree tribe, allies of the Tuscaroras, there was nothing he could do—even after Brice roasted a captured Coree chief alive.

The Tuscaroras, the Corees, and other, smaller tribes united in retaliatory raids. North Carolina officials called on South Carolina for aid, eliciting a response from Colonel John Barnwell, an Irish immigrant, who led thirty militiamen and five hundred Indians, mostly Yamassees, in a lighting sweep of the Tuscarora settlements as well as those of their allies. Their objective was simple: destruction. They achieved it.

Elated by victory, Barnwell added North Carolina militiamen to his force and, in March 1712, attacked the stronghold of the Tuscarora "king" known to the English as Hancock. When the North Carolinians encountered fiercer opposition than they had anticipated, they broke ranks, spoiling the assault. Barnwell had no choice but to fall back, whereupon the Tuscaroras offered to parley. When Barnwell indignantly refused to talk, the Tuscaroras began to torture their captives to death—in full view of Barnwell and his men. The colonel noted with dismay that his ranks were losing their collective nerve, and he accordingly agreed to withdraw from the area in exchange for the release of the surviving captives. The Tuscaroras complied, and Barnwell returned to New Bern.

He was not greeted graciously. The North Carolina colonial assembly pronounced his expedition an abortive failure and ordered him and his men back to the front. After recruiting more soldiers, Barnwell marched back to Hancock's stronghold and managed to intimidate the chief sufficiently to extort his signature on a treaty. On his way back to New Bern, Barnwell promptly broke his own treaty by seizing a party of Tuscaroras and selling them as slaves, presumably seeking to placate the North Carolina legislature by presenting them with cash to defray the cost of the failed expedition. Thus war was renewed in the summer of 1712, and North Carolina again appealed to South Carolina for help.

This time, the neighboring colony sent Colonel James Moore with a force of thirty-three militiamen and about a thousand Yamassees. Arriving in November 1712, they took on the North Carolina troops as reinforcements and, in March 1713, struck at the principal concentration of Tuscarora warriors. Hundreds of Tuscaroras died in this battle, and perhaps four hundred more were captured. The proceeds from their sale into slavery in the West Indies, at £10 each, helped defray the cost of this campaign as well. Most of the Tuscaroras who managed to escape death or enslavement fled north, not stopping until they reached New York, where they sought and were given asylum among the Iroquois and, in 1722, were formally admitted into the Iroquois League as its "sixth nation." Thus, even as the Iroquois were playing off the English against the French, they admitted into their "longhouse" a tribe hostile to the English.

A smaller Tuscarora faction, led by a chief the English called Tom Blount (or Blunt), remained in North Carolina and signed on February 11, 1715, the peace treaty that formally ended the war. No sooner was this done, however, than the Yamasees, so recently allied with the English, went to war against South Carolina. Like the Tuscaroras, the Yamasees had suffered many wrongs at the hands of traders and squatters, ranging from land fraud to kidnapping and enslavement. On Good Friday, April 15, 1715, the Yamasees, Catawba, and other smaller tribes, probably at the instigation of French provocateurs, attacked English settlements north of present-day Savannah, Georgia, which was then under the jurisdiction of South Carolina. Settler cabins were burned, and more than a hundred persons were killed. Panic-stricken survivors fled to Charleston, where South Carolina's governor, Charles Craven, quickly mustered his militia. By June, he had managed to drive the Yamasees from their villages. In the fall of 1715, Craven pressed the pursuit of the Yamasees, chasing them down into Spanish Florida. His militia, merciless, harried the tribe to the point of extinction.

In 1716, Craven employed Cherokee allies to drive out the small remainder of Yamasees from Georgia, as well as members of the Lower Creek tribe. Although resistance was surprisingly stiff, the Cherokee-English alliance carried the day in this, the final battle of the brief and bloody Yamassee War.

In addition to the Cherokee, with whom they traded extensively, the English of the Carolinas found allies among the Chickasaw, who, like the Cherokee, warred against the French and the French-allied Creeks and Choctaw. In 1720, the Chickasaw rose up in defiance of local French colonial authorities, who demanded an end to their trade relations with the English. To make the defiance all the more aggravating, the Chickasaw *invited* English traders into the territory France had long claimed along the Mississippi River. In an attempt to reassert control, the French incited their Choctaw allies to raid Chickasaw settlements, which provoked Chickasaw retaliatory raids, not only against Choctaw villages but against French shipping on the Mississippi. For the next four years, the Chickasaw and Choctaw engaged in an ongoing exchange of raids, disrupting Mississippi trade traffic until an armistice was concluded in 1724.

This brought respite for the French in the Middle South but no lasting peace, as, on November 28, 1729, the Natchez Indians, centered a little east of the present Mississippi city that bears their name, rose up against Fort Rosalie, a French settlement, military fort, and trading outpost, in which nearly two hundred French colonists were killed. The raid was followed by scattered assaults on French interests throughout the lower Mississippi Valley.

In the past, relations between the French and the Natchez had been marked by animosity, even violence, but open warfare had been averted largely through the efforts of Tattooed Serpent, brother of the Natchez principal chief, known as the Great Sun. After Tattooed Serpent died, however, the commandant of Fort Rosalie, the sieur de Chépart (or

Chopart or Etcheparre or Chépar) acted in a manner more imperiously English than accommodatingly French by summarily ordering the removal of the Natchez from their sacred Great Village, opposite the fort on the bluffs of the Mississippi. This offense to religious belief trumped considerations of trade, and in defiance of the pacific counsel of the tribal "queen mother," Tattooed Arm, the Natchez took up the hatchet. Among those taken captive in the attack on Fort Rosalie was the commandant himself, who was clubbed to death.

The killing of Chépart was not about to go unavenged. French colonial authorities dispatched several invasion forces out of New Orleans, and the Natchez, together with the Yazoo Indians, who had joined in the uprising, found themselves overwhelmed. Those captured were sold into West Indian slavery, while survivors sought refuge among the Chickasaw.

While the Louisiana French were having a rough time with their Indian neighbors, in the northern colonies, it was, as usual, the English who found themselves most frequently under assault. The Treaty of Portsmouth (New Hampshire), which followed the Treaty of Utrecht, ending Queen Anne's War in 1713, proclaimed an end to war with the French-allied, French-supplied Abenaki. However, the treaty did not address, let alone resolve, the fundamental land issues that had incited conflict between the Abenaki and the English in the first place. In contrast to the population of New France, that of the English colonies was growing rapidly. Despite new treaties concluded in 1717 and 1719, the Abenaki were enraged by repeated territorial encroachment and the presence of well-garrisoned English forts on their lands, not to mention the abusive and crooked practices of English traders. The friction became so intense that Governor Samuel Shute of Massachusetts, anticipating an "uprising," decided to declare a kind of preemptive war on the Abenaki, whom he branded as "Robbers, Traitors and Enemies to his Majesty King George."

In contrast to King William's War and Queen Anne's War, the Third Abenaki War (which would also be known as Dummer's War, Grey Lock's War, Father Rasles's War, and Lovewell's War) never became more than a local conflict, in which only troops from Massachusetts and New Hampshire were pitted against the Abenaki. Both the New York colony and the Iroquois League looked on without participating. This does not mean that the English avoided attacking French interests. While much of the war consisted of the customary routine of raid and counterraid, the English also targeted the French Jesuit missionary Sebastian Rasles, who they believed (with good reason) devoted himself to provoking the Abenaki to continual warfare. Significantly, the English regarded Rasles not as an agent of the government of New France but as a Jesuit terrorist, who was willing to use the Abenaki in a war of religion with the objective of either converting to Roman Catholicism or killing the Protestants of the New England frontier.

Militia captain Jeremiah Moulton led a force of eighty militiamen against Norridgewock, Maine, at three o'clock on the afternoon of August 12, 1724. They engaged a force of Abenaki—about sixty men and a hundred women and children—whom they sent fleeing across the river, after killing many. Breaking off the pursuit, Moulton's men returned to Norridgewock, where they discovered Rasles (according to a history published in the nineteenth century) "firing upon a few of our men, who had not pursued after the enemy. . . . Moulton had given orders not to kill the jesuit, but, by his firing from the wigwam, one of our men being wounded, a lieutenant [Richard] Jaques stove open the door and shot him through the head. Jaques excused himself to his commanding officer, alleging that Rallé was loading his gun when he entered the wigwam, and declared that he would neither give nor take quarter."

After Jaques killed Rasles, Moulton's men burned the village. The death of Rasles and the destruction of Norridgewock greatly dispirited the Abenaki, who were further demoralized the following spring when Captain John Lovewell defeated the Pigwackets (Abenaki allies) in the White Mountains of New Hampshire and then burned the Indian town at Penobscot. Instead of mounting a reprisal, many of the Abenaki withdrew into Canada, seeking refuge among the French missionaries there.

West of this action, in the Green Mountains of present-day Vermont, the English did not enjoy similar success. The war chief Grey Lock led his Missisquoi Abenaki from the Champlain Valley in one highly destructive raid after another all along the Massachusetts frontier. Hoping to contain the attacks, the English built Fort Dummer near present-day Brattleboro, Vermont. Fort building was the typical English military response to frontier violence and would persist through the French and Indian War, despite the fact that the tactic was repeatedly discredited. Even after Fort Dummer had been built and garrisoned, Chief Grey Lock continued to harass the frontier. Nor did the signing of Dummer's Treaty in 1727 (by some tribes signed as early as 1725), which officially ended the war, do much to abate the actual fighting on the northeastern frontier between New England and New France.

Combat on the fringes of the English colonial frontier during and following the Third Abenaki War became the background noise of the unsettled years in which the French and Indian *Wars* brewed the French and Indian *War*. In Europe, during this period, the end of the War of the Spanish Succession—Queen Anne's War in America—brought about a commercial agreement between England and Spain called the *asiento,* a cross between a treaty and a contract, which gave the English license to trade with the Spanish colonies in goods and slaves. It was a good idea, but English traders almost immediately abused the privileges granted by the *asiento,* provoking Spanish officials to respond with uncharacteristic energy. One English sea captain, Robert Jenkins by name, claimed that Spanish coast guards boarded his ship and cut off his ear during a brutal interrogation. No one believes this tale today. Jenkins lost an ear—that no one disputes—but almost certainly in a barroom brawl. At the time, however, his countrymen wanted to believe him, and believe him they did, to the extent of provoking a war between England and Spain in 1739, dubbed the War of Jenkins's Ear. After a year, this curious conflict melted into a much larger war.

In Europe, it was called the War of the Austrian Succession (1740–48), and it began when the death of the Holy Roman Emperor Charles VI in 1740 provoked several challenges to the succession of his daughter

Maria Theresa to the Hapsburg throne. The most serious challenge came from King Frederick the Great of Prussia, who, eager to preempt Maria Theresa's prerogatives, invaded Silesia, one of the traditional Hapsburg territories. Immediately, France, Spain, Bavaria, and Saxony aligned themselves with Frederick's Prussia, while Britain came to the aid of Maria Theresa. Combat spread to the colonies, where the conflict was called King George's War, after King George II of England.

James Oglethorpe, who had founded the colony of Georgia on utopian principles, was the first in the colonies to take the decidedly un-utopian action of making war. He led an invasion into Spanish-held Florida in January 1740. Aided in the west by the Creeks, Cherokee, and Chickasaw, none of whom had any love for the French-allied Spanish, Oglethorpe captured Fort San Francisco de Pupo and Fort Picolata, both on the San Juan River. He laid siege to St. Augustine from May through July but was compelled to break off when Spanish forces threatened him from behind. His troops successfully repulsed a Spanish counterattack on St. Simons Island, Georgia, in the Battle of Bloody Marsh, on July 7, 1742, but after Oglethorpe's second attempt to capture St. Augustine failed in 1743, the Georgia governor withdrew from Florida.

In the north, neither side vigorously prosecuted the American phase of the war until the French made an unsuccessful assault on Annapolis Royal (formerly Port-Royal), Nova Scotia, late in 1744. This was followed by the war's only major European-style battle, the British siege of Louisbourg on Cape Breton Island, Nova Scotia. On June 16, 1745, after a siege of forty-nine days, the fort at Louisbourg fell to William Pepperell at the head of 4,200 Massachusetts militiamen.

Boasting the biggest concentration of cannon in North America and guarding the approach to the vital St. Lawrence River, Louisbourg was indeed a great prize. For the most part, however, King George's War, like the other colonial wars prior to the French and Indian War, consisted not of sieges and formal battles but of guerrilla warfare, much of it using Indian "auxiliaries" to do the fighting. For the English, the Indian auxiliaries were managed by a remarkable man named William Johnson.

He had been born in County Meath, Ireland, about 1715, not to

Protestant parents but to Catholics, who, though of the gentry, had suffered much at the hands of Protestant English interlopers. William might well have been an outcast were it not for his uncle Peter Warren, who, having been raised as a Protestant, was able to gain advancement in the Royal Navy, ultimately achieving the rank of admiral and a knighthood to boot. William Johnson converted to Protestantism in order to seize the opportunity to join his uncle in America. Admiral Warren had bought a great tract along the Mohawk River and enticed his nephew to establish Warrensburgh there. From Ireland, Johnson brought in 1738 twelve Protestant families. Together, they began clearing the land—aided by African slaves.

While the clearing work was under way, Johnson noted that the principal trade routes with the Indians lay on the opposite bank of the Mohawk. Using money his uncle had advanced him, he purchased—on his own and in his own name—a house and farm on the north side of the river, where he immediately erected a store and a sawmill. Calling his little satellite settlement Mount Johnson, the wily Irishman set about siphoning off some of Albany's Indian trade. He furnished Fort Oswego–bound traders with merchandise to trade for beaver pelts, which he acquired from them when they returned downriver. Then he sold the furs directly to the rising class of merchants in New York City, bypassing the Albany middlemen altogether. Not surprisingly, Johnson's high-handedness angered the Albany merchants and greatly displeased Warren as well. Having alienated both New York's biggest, most established, and most important center of trade and his uncle, Johnson gravitated toward the Mohawks who were his nearest neighbors.

Like Johnson, they needed a friend. Throughout the previous century, the Mohawks had been the "head" of the Iroquois League, universally feared, harboring imperial ambitions that did not balk at genocide. By the 1740s, however, there were fewer than six hundred Mohawks still living in their traditional eastern lands. If they were to revive their fortunes, it would be by attaching themselves to the British Empire, and William Johnson seemed to them the gatekeeper to this realm. About 1742, they made him an honorary sachem, bestowing on him the honorific name of Warraghiyagey: "Man who undertakes great things."

The "great thing" English colonial officials wanted was strong, reliable Indian allies to use against the French, and in 1746 they named Johnson New York's agent to the Iroquois. It was a position he eagerly embraced because it leaped over the traditional Indian commissioners who were based in Albany. Having already usurped a large segment of Albany trade, Johnson now took over that town's privileged position in Indian politics and diplomacy as well. With his appointment came a colonial commission as "Colonel of the Warriors of the Six Nations." He was tasked with recruiting and equipping a force of settlers and Iroquois for the war against the French. The Mohawks were no problem, but the other tribes of the Iroquois League had once again committed to neutrality. Still, Johnson made the most of what he could get, transforming Mount Johnson into a guerrilla headquarters from which he equipped and organized raiding parties that penetrated the settlements of the French and their Indian allies. The colony's Scalp Act of 1747 funded scalp bounties, which Johnson liberally administered and disbursed. Whereas most colonial authorities with similar powers made some show of distinguishing between the scalps of warriors and those of old men, women, and children—admittedly a hopeless task—Johnson simply paid the bounty on whatever was brought to him. He intended to wage total war on combatants and noncombatants alike.

While Johnson's relations with colonial officials were often strained, he enjoyed an extraordinary rapport with the Mohawks. His strategy of continually mounting small-scale raids, mostly against French supply lines, had a significantly disruptive impact that amounted to a wilderness war of attrition. For their part, the French-allied Indians responded not by targeting military supply lines but by using the familiar tactics of terror, raiding New England settlements almost at random. By the end of 1745, the terror was at its most intense. During November 28–29, French and Indians captured and burned Fort Saratoga, New York, and throughout the next year, French-supported Indians—mostly Abenaki—raided one New England town after another.

Although the majority of Indians involved in King George's War allied themselves with the French, the English could rely on the Mohawks in the Northeast. Officially, the other Iroquois tribes struggled through-out the conflict to maintain neutrality, but they, too, inclined generally toward the English. Iroquois neutrality nominally extended to Iroquois-dependent tribes (preeminent among which were the Shawnee) in the Ohio Country beyond the Alleghenies; nevertheless, a delegation of Ohio warriors came to Philadelphia in November 1747 asking for arms to fight the French. They had been won over not by official agents of any colonial government but by fur traders, including the wily, rapacious, and resourceful George Croghan, like Johnson, Irish born and, perhaps for this reason, unburdened by English Protestant prejudices. In sharp contrast to the coastal factory system practice of the Hudson's Bay Company, Croghan established his trading posts among the Indians and was fluent in the language of the Delaware as well as the Mohawks. Recognizing the value of men like Croghan, in August 1748, Pennsylvania and Virginia collaborated in commissioning another prominent trader, Conrad Weiser, to treat officially with the Ohio tribes. Weiser followed through on what Croghan and others of his kind had begun. As a result, the Wyandots, whose territory lay just above that of the Shawnee, joined Pennsylvania's celebrated Chain of Friendship, a unique alliance between the Pennsylvania colony and a number of Indian tribes, including the Miami (also called Twightwees, a name derived from the cry of the crane), from present-day Indiana and western Ohio.

From the standpoint of schoolbook history, King George's War defies easy summary. In terms of territory lost or acquired, it accomplished little for any of the colonial powers before October 18, 1748, when the Treaty of Aix-la-Chapelle ended the War of the Austrian Succession and therefore abruptly ended King George's War as well. Beneath the little-changed surface of the colonial map, however, civilization in North America had crystallized. In the course of the war, the Iroquois tribes, especially the Mohawks, grew closer to the English, while many of the Algonquian tribes attached themselves—usually with considerable en-thusiasm—to the French. In the East, this alignment would determine the course of the coming French and Indian War, which, in turn, would establish the environment in which the American Revolution would be fought. In the West, the alignment remained in flux. The violent tumult that began in the late seventeenth century and extended through the 1740s frequently disrupted the fur trade, especially between the French and the Indians. When it resumed following the conclusion of King George's War, it was profoundly changed. Indian middlemen traders, who had profited from consolidating the products of many independent Indian trappers, had been taken entirely out of the loop. Licensed and unlicensed white traders now carried goods west and bought furs directly from the Indians. The elimination of the Indian middlemen contributed to the outbreak of a new war between the Ojibwa and the Dakotas, who, in the course of a half century or more, were driven out of their eastern woodlands and far to the west, where they would adopt new lives on the Plains and in the Black Hills of the territory that would be named for them. This was the origin of the great Dakota Sioux "Plains" tribes with which white Americans are most familiar. *Native* Americans, the Sioux were nevertheless internal immigrants within the continent, displaced by an epoch of intense regional warfare previously unknown in Indian experience.

7

Colonel Washington's Mission

—➤•➤—

IF NEW FRANCE HAD been populated by families like the Washingtons of Virginia, King Louis XIV would have been delighted with his New World empire. The Washingtons and their ilk were interested in land not for hunting, trapping, and trading but for settling. When young George Washington cast about for a profession, he took to surveying as if he had been born to it and was barely seventeen in July 1749 when he began tramping through Culpeper County and beyond, measuring off lots for settlement. He would pursue this profitable enterprise through October 1752, not only collecting handsome fees but scouting out and acquiring promising tracts for himself.

Just as George was embarking on his surveying career, his half brother Lawrence set out for London on a double mission. Long afflicted with what would soon prove to be a terminal case of tuberculosis, he hoped to find a physician who might cure him, even as he pursued an extraordinary business opportunity with a syndicate of British and American traders and speculators who were calling themselves the Ohio Company. On March 16, 1749, King George II granted 200,000 acres to the syndicate—with, however, the kind of stipulation Louis XIV would have enthusiastically endorsed. Within seven years, the Ohio Company had to plant a settlement of one hundred families and build a fort for their protection on the grant or forfeit the land. If Lawrence and his partners managed to attract the required number of settlers, the company would not only keep its 200,000 acres but would be granted an additional 300,000.

For more than two centuries now, the history of colonial America has been explained as a grand narrative of evolving national, ethnic, and racial allegiances, alliances, and enmities. Yet, as we have seen, more pragmatic motives of business often had effects that were both more immediate and at least equally far-reaching. The Ohio Company project, on which his family's fortune depended, would shape George Washington's early military career and, through that career, by bringing Anglo-American fortunes into direct conflict with Franco-American fortunes, would in large measure determine the destiny of North America.

Lawrence Washington found no cure in London, but he was so excited by the prospects of the Ohio Company that his health generally improved when he returned to his northern Virginia estate, Mount Vernon, in 1750. Yet as he found himself wrestling with threats from the French, who laid claim to lands King George II had granted him and his fellow investors, and laboring in vain to find firm allies among the Indians at the fringes of the land grant, his health once again slipped into decline. At the time, the salubrious sea air of Barbados was widely regarded as a sovereign cure for those afflicted in the lungs. He persuaded George to suspend his surveying career and accompany him to the islands. The pair took ship on September 28, 1751, and settled near Carlisle Bay.

By the end of 1751, Lawrence, his condition unimproved, decided to give the Bermudas a try. He sent his half brother home to Virginia, recognizing that the young man's surveying career had been interrupted long enough. George Washington landed at Yorktown on January 28, 1752, and, en route to Mount Vernon, to bring Lawrence's wife, Nancy, tidings of her husband, he detoured to Williamsburg to introduce himself to Robert Dinwiddie, Virginia's energetic lieutenant governor. Little is known of this visit, but the young man must have made a good impression on

Dinwiddie, who was also a principal Ohio Company investor. Within less than two years, Dinwiddie would send George Washington on a hazardous diplomatic mission, the outcome of which was critical to the future of Virginia and the significant portions of both the Dinwiddie and Washington fortunes that were tied to the Ohio Company.

In the meantime, Lawrence Washington's letters from Bermuda grew increasingly dark. He confessed that his illness made him feel "like a criminal condemned," and, giving up on Bermuda, he returned to Mount Vernon in June, scribbled his will within days of his arrival, and, on July 26, 1752, died. He was thirty-four. His half brother, grief-stricken, executed the hastily composed will, most of the estate, including Lawrence's stock in the Ohio Company, going to Nancy and their infant daughter, Sarah. George would share equally in real estate that would go to Lawrence's brothers in the event that daughter Sarah should die childless. Further, upon Nancy's death—and if Sarah died without issue—George would inherit Mount Vernon, together with all of his half brother's other Fairfax County holdings. The young man's more immediate inheritance was Lawrence's speculative faith in the future of the Ohio Company.

Upon Lawrence Washington's death, the presidency of the Ohio Company passed to his fellow investor Lieutenant Governor Dinwiddie. Lawrence had also held another important office, adjutant general of the Virginia colony, with the rank of major and the responsibility for raising, organizing, and training the colonial militia. In view of the business relationship between Lawrence and the lieutenant governor, George believed himself entitled to inherit his half brother's position as adjutant general, even though he had no experience as a soldier, let alone as a commander of soldiers. On November 6, 1752, the Council of Virginia decided to divide the colonial adjutancy into four districts but, at Dinwiddie's urging, did offer the Southern District to the callow Washington, who eagerly took the oath of office on February 1, 1753, three weeks before turning twenty-one.

By law, all Virginia men over twenty-one were obliged to render militia service if called, but, like so much other British colonial legislation, the law had long languished unenforced. Feeling a growing threat from the French, Dinwiddie called for the first general muster of the Virginia militias to commence in September 1753. As adjutant, it fell to Washington to instruct his subordinate officers sufficiently so that they could instill in the men under their command some level of discipline and combat effectiveness. Yet no record survives of young Major Washington's ever meeting with the militia officers under his supervision or even of his visiting any of the counties under his jurisdiction during 1753. None of his letters or diary entries during this period so much as mentions military matters or his military responsibilities. Did he take the French threat seriously?

On June 26, 1749, less than a year after the end of King George's War, Roland-Michel Galissonière, marquis de La Galissonière, governor of New France, sent Captain Pierre-Joseph Céleron de Blainville with 213 men on an expedition into the Ohio Country—the very tracts King George II had awarded the Ohio Company. Céleron de Blainville traveled as far west as Logstown, site of modern-day Ambridge, Pennsylvania, on the east bank of the Ohio River, eighteen miles northwest of Pittsburgh. He carried with him a message to all of the Indians he encountered: *The English want to rob you of your country. I am warning them to stay away.* He also lugged a load of lead plates, each inscribed with the French emperor's claim to sovereignty, which he buried at intervals along his round-trip of some three thousand miles.

In August 1749, La Galissonière was replaced as governor by Jacques-Pierre de Jonquière, who decided to enforce French claims with something more than a few words to the Indians and bundle of lead plates. He built Fort Rouillé at the location of modern Toronto with the purpose of reclaiming the fur trade for French traders while severing British trade between the northern Great Lakes and Oswego, the British stronghold on the south shore of Lake Ontario in New York. Jonquière also built up and augmented the French fortifications at Detroit, a fur-trading headquarters that rivaled that of the Hudson's Bay Company, then launched a raid against the Shawnee, who were the most powerful of the tribes doing business with the few English traders working the Ohio Country.

Jonquière's move against the Shawnee was not big enough to inflict decisive damage or even to intimidate them. If anything, it was a strategic error, which served only to drive the Shawnee more deeply into the English fold; however, the French fur traders, licensed and unlicensed, were, on their own, steadily edging out English traders and, in the process, cementing good French relations with Indian hunters and trappers. The Washingtons and the Dinwiddies were far more interested in land than in beaver pelts. They wanted to build settlements and great plantations. Nevertheless, they understood that skins were the currency of the far frontier, and by the mid-eighteenth century, the richest harvest of pelts was to be had in the Ohio Country, the more easterly environments having been hunted and trapped to virtual extinction. Thus, whoever controlled the region of the Ohio laid claim not only to the future—of the country and of the family fortune—but to the present as well. With the peltries of the Ohio Country came cash liquidity as well as influence over the Indians, who, much as they resented any Euro-American incursions into their homeland, also craved the profitable trade they brought.

In response to Jonquière's aggressive expansion into the region, British colonial authorities encouraged English traders to be more aggressive. They authorized the purchase of more western land from the Indians and, during May–July 1752, negotiated the Treaty of Logstown between what was now the Six Iroquois Nations (Oneida, Onondaga, Seneca, Cayuga, Mohawk, *and* Tuscarora) and the Delaware, the Shawnee, and the Wyandot Indians on the one side, and Virginia as well as the Ohio Company on the other. By the Treaty of Logstown, the colony and the company secured an Indian "quitclaim" to the entire Ohio Country.

Quitclaim. The word, redolent as it was of old English common law, was highly significant. Typically, the French sought to create productive relations with various Indian tribes through religious conversion or through even more intimate contact; French traders brought their business to the Indians, lived among them, intermarried with them. Whether the agents of New France were missionaries or traders, their effect was to create a blended Franco-Native community. In the case of the English colonies, in contrast, even "friendly" Indian relations were based not on creating a blended community but on trade and monetary exchange grounded in *English* law. The

English assumption underlying the acquisition of land was that the Indians owned the land they occupied by virtue of what the law called "primitive right." Ownership, as the English saw it, was inherently transferable. Such transfer could legitimately be made by seizure—conquest through battle— or by purchase. In either case, the acquisition of property from those who held it by primitive right gave the transferee an exclusive *legal* claim. As the English understood it, the Logstown Treaty "quitclaim" legally excluded the French from the Ohio Country; therefore, ownership of what was then the American West had been settled.

The French, naturally, did not see it this way.

To the legalistic approach of the English they responded with violence. While delegates from the Miami tribe were negotiating at Logstown, news reached them that French-led Indian forces had raided and destroyed Pickawillany (present-day Piqua, Ohio), the Miami "capital," on June 21, 1752. Tanaghrisson, a much-venerated Seneca chief known to the English as the Half-King, asked the Virginia delegates at Logstown to tell their government to build a fort at the "Forks of the Ohio" (the confluence of the Allegheny and Monongahela rivers, site of present-day Pittsburgh), the better to defend the Seneca and other western tribes (including the Miami) against the French and their Indian allies.

We do not know what answer the colonial delegates gave the Half-King, but the Virginia authorities hardly rushed to build the requested fort, nor did they take retaliatory action for the attack on Pickawillany. These failures quickly led to the unraveling of the Logstown Treaty, which presented a golden opportunity to Ange Duquesne de Menneville, marquis Duquesne, who had replaced La Jonquière as governor of New France on July 1, 1752. Duquesne immediately ordered the construction not just of a single fort, but a fortress chain running from Montreal in the north to New Orleans in the south. It was nothing less than a chain gate drawn across the Ohio Country, physically closing that territory to the English. Worse, the action thoroughly intimidated the western Iroquois, thereby neutralizing the most important Indian ally the English had. Duquesne understood the exquisite interdependence of the colonial-tribal alliance system. With the Iroquois taken out of the picture, most of the lesser tribes that had professed friendship with the English folded as well throughout the whole Ohio Country. As for the few that expressed their desire to remain loyal to the English, their appeals for aid in resisting the French were met with haughty indifference and, in some cases, outright refusal.

By the summer of 1753, the prospects for the Ohio Company—and all those heavily invested in it—were at low ebb. Seeking a remedy, in August 1753, in London, Lord Halifax, principal booster of Britain's North American empire and himself an Ohio Company investor, prodded the royal cabinet to declare war against France. Was a cause needed? He cited the 1713 Treaty of Utrecht (ending both the War of the Spanish Succession and Queen Anne's War), which stipulated the status of the Iroquois as *British* subjects. (That no one had asked the Iroquois about this hardly mattered. The agreement, made in the Netherlands and not in North America, was between European governments, not Euro-Americans and Indians.) In conjunction with this provision, Halifax also unearthed allusions to certain deeds drawn up between the English and Iroquois during 1701–26. Based on this fistful of deeds and the treaty-decreed status of the Iroquois, Halifax indignantly proclaimed the English *legal* right to a vast expanse of Iroquois lands, including those the Iroquois themselves had acquired by conquest. In other words, Halifax explained to the cabinet that all of the Ohio Country was *by law* part of the British Empire and had been invaded by French thieves. Declare war? France was *already* at war. It was now time to fight. Cabinet and crown immediately authorized Dinwiddie to take whatever action he deemed necessary to evict the French from the British Empire in the Ohio Country.

Young Major Washington waited neither for word nor action from the British crown or the lieutenant governor. He had read the colonial newspaper accounts, including those in the *Virginia Gazette,* announcing the arrival of some fifteen hundred French regulars—the *king's* soldiers, not Canadian militiamen—in the spring of 1753, and he certainly knew of the construction of French forts. Without being summoned, he rode off to Williamsburg, arriving on or about October 26, 1753. There he found the customarily sleepy capital uncharacteristically bustling as the burgesses gathered for an extraordinary early session of the assembly to debate how best to counter the French "invasion." In August, Dinwiddie had written to England for help. King George II promised men and matériel, ordering Dinwiddie in the meantime to make every possible effort to safeguard the Ohio Country. The king—or a minister over the king's signature—also directed Dinwiddie to convey a warning to the French that amounted to a landlord's notice of eviction.

In Europe, such a direction and such a note seemed quite reasonable, but on the edge of a vast wilderness, delivering eviction papers was far from a matter of routine. As early as May 1753, Dinwiddie had asked Governor George Clinton of New York, whose colony bordered the main territory of New France, to make discreet inquiries as to why the French were sending regular troops into English territory. Receiving no answer, he then sent the fur traders William Trent and William Russell to locate the key French outposts and to warn their commanders that they were trespassing. Neither Trent nor Russell proved very venturesome, however, and they never traveled west of Logstown. So by the time he received the king's orders, Dinwiddie was blind. He knew the French were out there, but he had no idea of where. Even more important, he did not know how many. While it was true that the newspapers had reported the arrival of fifteen hundred regulars on the southern shore of Lake Erie in the spring, Dinwiddie understood the reality of armies operating in the wilderness. They got sick. Paper strength was always one thing, effective strength quite another. It was the effective numbers that counted, and it was the effective numbers that remained unknown to him.

Just when Dinwiddie needed both reliable reconnaissance and a messenger, in walked George Washington.

"The Governor acquainted the Board that George Washington Esqr. Adjutant General for the Southern District had offered himself to go properly commissioned to the Commandant of the French Forces, to learn by what Authority he presumes to make Incroachments on his Majesty's Lands of the Ohio," the journal of the Council of Virginia recorded on October 27, 1753. The council approved Washington's appointment swiftly and drew up a letter for him to put into the hands of the "Commandant of the French Forces on the Ohio."

Dinwiddie's commission, dated October 30, the day before it was handed to the major, appointed Washington as the governor's "express Messenger," empowering him "to proceed hence with all convenient & possible Dispatch, to that Part, or Place, on the River Ohio, where the French have lately erected a Fort, or Forts, or where the Commandant of the French Forces resides, in order to deliver my Letter & Message to Him; & after waiting not exceeding one Week for an Answer, You are to take Your Leave & return immediately back."

Accompanying this commission were detailed instructions directing the major to proceed first to Logstown and there "address Yourself to the Half King, to Monacatoocha & other the Sachems of the Six Nations; acquainting them with Your Orders to visit & deliver my Letter to the French commanding Officer; & desiring the said Chiefs to appoint You a sufficient Number of their Warriors to be Your Safeguard, as near the French as You may desire, & to wait Your further Direction."

Dinwiddie and Washington well knew that the Half-King had already warned the French that they were trespassing on *Indian* lands in the Ohio Country. Monacatoocha, more familiarly known to the English as Scarouady, was an Oneida chief who ranked in prestige just below the Half-King and who, like him, had played an important role in the Logstown Treaty. In directing Washington to make contact with these two men, Dinwiddie sought to provide protection for his messenger while also demonstrating to the Indian leaders that he was looking out for *their* interests against the French. What he left entirely to Washington's discretion was the decision as to how close he should bring the chiefs to the French commandant. This suggests that the lieutenant governor was unsure whether their presence would enhance or diminish Washington's apparent authority. Was it better for the French to see that the English had powerful sachems on their side? Or was it better to make the mission appear to be that of a *royal* British envoy communicating with a French official?

Although Dinwiddie left the status of the Indians vague, he made it very clear that Washington's mission was not strictly diplomatic:

You are to take Care to be truly inform'd what Forts the French have erected, & where; How they are Garrison'd [manned] & appointed [fortified], & what is their Distance from each other, & from Logstown: And from the best Intelligence You can procure, You are to learn what gave Occasion to this Expedition of the French. How they are like to be supported, & what their Pretentions are.

Not to put too fine a point on the matter, Washington was a spy. Yet Dinwiddie took care to instruct him not to behave like one. After "the French Commandant has given You the requir'd & necessary Dispatches" in response to the notice of eviction, Dinwiddie wrote, Washington was to "desire of him that, agreeable to the Law of Nations," he would provide "a proper Guard, to protect You as far on Your Return, as You may judge for Your safety, against any stragling Indians or Hunters that may be ignorant of Yr Character & molest You." In other words, the spy was instructed to request bodyguards—and to request them from the very people on whom he spied.

To his written instructions Dinwiddie added a verbal order. He instructed Washington to demand that the French commandant explain why the French were holding two British traders and in particular why they had driven John Frazier (or Fraser), a Pennsylvania gunsmith and Indian trader, from his trading post at Venango, which was now occupied by the French. The lieutenant governor also directed Washington to call on Christopher Gist at Wills Creek, which was on the way to Logstown. He was to formally request Gist to serve as his guide, for Gist knew the Ohio frontier better than just about any other white man. An explorer and surveyor, he had been commissioned by the Ohio Company in 1750 to explore the Ohio region as far as the mouth of the Scioto River, and in 1751 he had pushed as far south as the Great Kanawha River. At the Logstown treaty negotiations in 1752, he had served as the representative of the Ohio Company.

Gist was an example of the frontier trader at his best—intrepid explorer, shrewd businessman, and natural diplomat—and Washington was pleased to bring him on board. In addition to his other skills and knowledge, Gist would also serve as an Indian interpreter. Washington also needed a man with a good working knowledge of French, but, given the nature of his mission, hiring a Frenchman was out of the question. Although he knew of no British colonist fluent in French, he was aware that living near Fredericksburg was a young Dutchman named Jacob Van Braam, who spoke his native Dutch as well as enough French to have emboldened him to advertise himself, in Annapolis in 1752, as a teacher of it. English was his third language, but it would have to do. When he reached Fredericksburg on November 1, Washington located Jacob Van Braam and hired him on the spot.

From Fredericksburg, Washington and Van Braam set off for Alexandria, where they purchased some of the supplies and equipment necessary for the expedition. This done, they headed through Vestal's Gap to Winchester, where Washington purchased horses and more supplies, including a tent. From here, the pair headed northwest and across the Potomac to Wills Creek, which they reached on November 14, and located the cabin of Christopher Gist, who readily agreed to be part of the expedition. Washington next recruited four "servitors": men to do the grunt work of hauling weapons, powder, ammunition, a tent, food, wampum (strings of shell beads used as a kind of currency in dealing with Indians), and trade goods. He chose Barnaby Currin, a Pennsylvania Indian trader; John MacQuire (or McGuire or McGuier), an Indian trader and former Fairfax County militiaman; William Jenkins, who often served Dinwiddie as a courier; and Henry Steward, an all-round frontier hand.

The party of seven men set out from Wills Creek on November 15 and camped at the end of the first day at George's Creek, having made just over eight miles. A breathless runner caught up with them here, delivering to Gist a letter from one of his sons. The young man had fallen ill on his way home from Cherokee country and was camped, laid up, at the mouth of the Conegocheague River, some six miles southwest of present-day Hagerstown, Maryland. Among Gist's many skills was frontier medicine, and that is what his son now sought from him. For his part, Washington did not order Gist to stay, but he did remind him that he was a critical member of an important embassy. Gist hurriedly compounded a remedy from materials he had on hand, wrote out instructions to his son, and, difficult as it must have been for him, handed the medicine and the letter to the messenger, asking him to carry them to the Conego-cheague. The boy would have to treat himself.

Clearly, Gist was a man committed to doing what he understood as his duty, and in this Washington was most fortunate. Gist enjoyed the kind of thoroughly comfortable relations with Indians—they called him Annosanah—more typical of French than of English traders. At the same time, he was educated well beyond the level of most men who plied the frontier. Years after the mission, in a letter to Speaker of the Virginia House of Burgesses John Robinson, on May 30, 1757, Washington praised Gist as one who "has had extensive dealings with the Indians, is in great esteem among them, well acquainted with their manners and customs, indefatigable and patient. . . . As for his capacity, honesty, and zeal, I dare venture to engage."

By November 17, the embassy had reached Laurel Hill and had climbed its 2,400-foot height, then descended about 700 feet to a wide and boggy plateau, which was distinguished from the surrounding country by the comparative thinness of its forest growth. Gist told Washington that the clearing was known as Great Meadows. From here, they would have to trek over another set of mountains, known as Chestnut Ridge, west and northwest of Great Meadows, then continue to the Monongahela River, which would take them to the Ohio River and the French commandant. Even the experienced Christopher Gist did not know if the Monongahela at the point due west of Chestnut Ridge was navigable by canoe. He therefore advised a more arduous but more prudent overland march to the north and directly to the Ohio River. On November 18, before they could set out, they were met by the first large snowfall of the season. Gist advised riding out the storm at what he called his "new settlement," a rude outpost consisting of a twenty-by-thirty-foot house and a few small outbuildings between the Youghiogheny and Monongahela rivers.

They were now about seventy miles from Wills Creek, and even though the snow had not let up by the twentieth, Washington insisted on making the twenty miles to Jacobs Cabins, an abandoned settlement believed to have been named after Captain Jacobs, a Delaware Indian chief. They rested through a night that turned from snow to freezing rain, and first light revealed that a number of the expedition's horses had wandered off. There was nothing for it but to lean into the weather and find the horses.

By eleven o'clock, all of the animals had been recovered, and on November 22, the expedition reached the Monongahela at the mouth of Turtle Creek, near the settlement of John Frazier, the gunsmith and Indian trader whom the French had driven out of Venango. Doubtless, Washington asked him Dinwiddie's question: *Why had the French forces evicted him?* We do not know his reply, but Washington did record that Frazier presented him with a string of wampum from the Half-King together with a message for Dinwiddie from the sachem. It warned that three tribes of French-allied Indians had "taken up the hatchet" (declared war) against the English. That was a sobering tidbit; however, Frazier also noted that the French troops had been advancing from Lake Erie toward the Ohio River, but were overtaken by messengers who delivered the news that the so-called general of French forces, Pierre Paul de la Malgue, sieur de Marin, had died suddenly. This prompted most of the Ohio-bound French army to turn around. Things were looking up after all. Perhaps Washington would find the French commandant more receptive to Dinwiddie's message than he might otherwise have been.

Of course, he still had to *find* the Frenchman—and each day brought worsening weather. "The Waters," Washington observed in his diary, "were quite impassable, without Swimming our Horses." Therefore, he secured the "loan of a Canoe from Mr. Frazer" and sent "Barnaby Currin & Henry Steward down Monongahela, with our Baggage" while he and the rest of his party rode through icy rain unencumbered to "the Forks of Ohio," where they would meet up with Currin, Steward, and the expedition's baggage.

This rendezvous successfully accomplished, Washington contemplated completing the journey to Logstown, where he would meet the Half-

King. First, apparently acting on Gist's advice, he decided to call upon Shingas, principal chief of the Turkey, or Unalachtigo, tribe of Delaware Indians. At this time, Shingas was a friend of the English and lived on the site of a fort planned for the Ohio Company. Gist persuaded Washington that it would be good politics to invite him to accompany the expedition to meet with the Half-King. Shingas accepted, and the party pressed on to Logstown, only to find that the Half-King had gone hunting. Washington sent Monacatoocha to find him.

On the next day, November 25, while awaiting the Half-King's arrival, Washington was visited by four or five men in faded and stained French uniforms, led by a British trader named Brown, who announced the Frenchmen as deserters from the army of regulars. Washington summoned his interpreter, Van Braam, and opened an interrogation, which confirmed the darkest rumors of French activity in the Ohio Country. The men said that they had been members of a hundred-man company sent up the Mississippi to rendezvous at Logstown with another hundred French troops. United, they were to advance farther up the Ohio and deeper into Ohio Company territory. Washington could only conclude that the two hundred were being sent to build and garrison a fort on the Forks of the Ohio, the most strategically commanding point in the whole Ohio Company grant—the gateway to the West.

The situation was looking serious indeed, and Washington's questions became commensurately more urgent. *How many men did the French have on the Mississippi? How many forts?*

Through the halting English of Van Braam, Washington understood that there were four small forts, with cannon, each garrisoned with thirty to forty men. They were distributed between a larger fort at New Orleans and another at what Van Braam translated as the "Black Islands," explaining that the Frenchmen said "Îles Noires." Presumably, what they meant was "Illinois," at the time an obscure reference to a western Indian tribe entirely unknown to Washington. He was, however, able to make out the names of two other western tribes: Obiash (Wabash) and Chawanon (Shawnee). From this information, it seemed clear to Washington that the French were assembling an extensive Indian alliance that included at least two tribes, the Illinois and the Wabash, hitherto unknown to the English, and one, the Shawnee, that had been an English ally in King George's War. It was as if the French were poisoning the whole western wilderness against the English, recruiting two fresh allies while trying to turn an old friend of the English into a new friend of New France.

Washington may at least have taken comfort in hearing of the small numbers of Frenchmen garrisoning each fort, but his relief could not have lasted long. The deserters went on to report that, while the forts *between* New Orleans and the "Black Islands" were thinly manned, there were "35 Companies of 40 Men each, with a pretty strong Fort, mounting 8 large Carriage Guns" at New Orleans and, at the other end of the chain of fortifications, the "Black Islands," there were "several Companies, & a Fort with 6 Guns."

Apparently, Washington completed his interrogation by three in the afternoon, because he recorded in his diary at this hour the long-anticipated arrival of the Half-King. The sachem greeted him with the welcome information that the commandant was to be found at Fort LeBoeuf but observed that "the nearest & levelest Way" to it "was now impassable, by reason of the many large miry Savannas" and that the only route now lay through Venango, some fifty miles northeast of Logstown, at the confluence of French Creek and the Allegheny River. From Venango, it would be a march of another thirty miles. Once arrived at Fort LeBoeuf, the Half-King warned, Washington could not expect a warm welcome. He had met with Pierre-Paul de la Malgue, sieur de Marin. That commandant had recently died, but, the Half-King implied, there was no reason to expect more cordial treatment from his replacement. He then recited for Washington the speech he himself had made to the sieur de Marin, how he had reminded him that "in former Days [the French had] set a Silver Bason before us wherein there was the Leg of a Beaver, and desir'd of all Nations to come & eat of it; to eat in Peace & Plenty, & not to be Churlish to one another; & that if any such Person shou'd be found to be a Disturber; I here lay down by the Edge of the Dish a rod, which you must Scourge them with." Then the Half-King related how he told the Frenchman that it was now "you that is the Disturber in this Land, by coming & building your Towns, and taking it [our land] away unknown to us & by Force."

> FATHERS [Half-King told the Frenchman] We kindled a Fire a long Time ago at a Place call'd Morail, where we desir'd you to stay, & not to come & intrude upon our Land. I now desire you may dispatch to that Place; for be it known to you Fathers, this is our Land, & not yours. FATHERS I desire you may hear me in Civilness; if not, We must handle that rod which was laid down for the Use of the obstropulous. If you had come in a peaceable Manner like our Brothers the English, We shou'd not have been against your trading with us as they do, but to come Fathers, & build great Houses upon our Land, & to take it by Force, is what we cannot submit to.

Doubtless, Washington took comfort in this narrative, which proved that the Half-King saw the French as invaders and the English as trading partners. We cannot even guess whether he also recognized the degree of political sophistication the account demonstrated: how the Iroquois skillfully exploited divisions between the Euro-Americans with the purpose of using one faction to help drive another from their land. While the Half-King wanted to exhibit his loyalty to Washington, his speech also suggested that this loyalty was distinctly conditional:

> FATHERS Both you & the English are White. We live in a Country between, therefore the Land does not belong either to one or the other; but the GREAT BEING above allow'd it to be a Place of residence for us; so Fathers, I desire you to withdraw, as I have done our Brothers the English, for I will keep you at Arm's length. I lay this down as a Tryal for both, to see which will have the greatest regard to it, & that Side we will stand by, & make equal Sharers with us: Our Brothers the English have heard this, & I come now to tell it to you, for I am not affraid to discharge you off this Land.

Whichever side, French or English, came closest to abiding by the permanent, proper, God-given state of things, the Iroquois would befriend.

Whether or not Washington appreciated the conditional nature of the alliance, the Frenchman had clearly and rudely rejected it. "NOW MY CHILD," he had begun his reply—his form of address making a sharp contrast to the "FATHERS" formula the Half-King had employed—

> I have heard your Speech . . . but you need not put yourself to the Trouble of Speaking for I will not hear you: I am not affraid of Flies or Musqui-to's; for Indians are such as those; I tell you down that River I will go, & will build upon it according to my Command: If the River was ever so block'd up, I have Forces sufficient to burst it open, & tread under my Feet all that stand in Opposition together with their Alliances; for my Force is as the Sand upon the Sea Shoar. . . . Child, you talk foolish; you say this Land belongs to you, but there is not the Black of my Nail yours, I saw that Land sooner than you did, before the Shawnesse & you were at War: Lead was the Man that went down, & took Possession of that River; it is my Land, & I will have it let who will stand up for, or say against it. I'll buy & sell with the English (mockingly). If People will be rul'd by me they may expect Kindness but not else.

There was yet more affront. Dinwiddie had instructed Washington to find out what had happened to the two English traders taken prisoner by the French. The Half-King had already asked about it "& receiv'd this Answer": "CHILD You think it is a very great Hardship that I made Pris-oners of those two People at Venango, don't you concern yourself with it we took & carried them to Canada to get Intelligence of what the English were doing in Virginia."

Washington now had pictures of his ally and of his enemy. More prac-tically, he also had some more concrete intelligence. The Half-King in-formed him that the French had built "two Forts, one on Lake Erie, & another on French Creek," and even gave Washington "a Plan of them of his own drawing." The next day, a grateful Washington addressed the as-sembled sachems. Rejecting the appellation Half-King had used with the French—"Fathers"—as well as that the commandant had used to dispar-age Half-King—"Child"—he called the assembled chiefs "Brothers":

142

I have call'd you together in Council, by Order of your Brother the Governor of Virginia, to acquaint you that I am sent with all possible Dispatch to visit & deliver a Letter to the French Commandant of very great Importance to your Brothers the English: & I dare say to you their Friends & Allies. I was desir'd Brothers, by your Brother the Governor, to call upon you, the Sachems of the Six Nations, to inform you of it, & to ask your Advice & Assistance to proceed the nearest & best Road to the French. You see Brothers I have got thus far on my Journey. His Honour likewise desir'd me to apply to you for some of your young Men to conduct and provide Provisions for us on our Way: & to be a Safeguard against those French Indians, that have taken up the Hatchet against us. I have spoke this particularly to you Brothers, because His Hon. our Governor, treats you as good Friends & Allies, & holds you in great Esteem. To confirm what I have said I give you this String of Wampum.

After conferring with the other sachems for some time, the Half-King gave Washington a message to deliver to Dinwiddie: "I rely upon you as a Brother ought to do, as you say we are Brothers, & one People. We shall put Heart in Hand, & speak to our Fathers the French, concerning the Speech they made to me, & you may depend that we will endeavour to be your Guard." The Half-King then addressed Washington directly: "BROTHER, as you have ask'd my Advice, I hope you will be ruled by it, & stay 'til I can provide a Company to go with you. . . . I intend to send a Guard of Mingoes, Shawnesse, & Delawar's, that our Brothers may see the Love and Loyalty We bear them." Washington recorded his response: "As I had Orders to make all possible Dispatch, & waiting here very contrary to my Inclinations; I thank'd him in the most suitable Manner I cou'd, & told that my Business requir'd the greatest Expedition, & wou'd not admit of that Delay." The Half-King persisted and insisted— "this is a Matter of no small Moment, & must not be enter'd into without due consideration"—and Washington relented, deciding to await the arrival of the "Guard," more (he recorded) out of unwillingness to offend the Half-King than to benefit from any protection the escort might provide.

. . .

A day passed. Then, on November 28, the Half-King, Monacatoocha, and two other sachems entered Washington's tent "& beg'd . . . to know what Business we were going to the French about."

Did this query suggest to Washington an underlying reason for the delay the Half-King had requested? The fact was that Washington had behaved like a salesman who was eager to close the sale. He had omitted from his speech all detail concerning what Dinwiddie and the other English hoped to get from the French. Clearly, the Half-King had not wanted to be rushed into a bargain. It was, Washington wrote in his diary, "a Question I all along expected, & [I] provided as satisfactory Answers as I cou'd, which alay'd their Curiosity a little."

Did it allay their curiosity, though? Washington's response, still quite vague, elicited not an expression of satisfaction but, from Monacatoocha, a report of sinister news. A "few Days ago," he said, an Indian from Venango had brought word that a Captain Joncaire, the French "Interpreter in Chief, living at Venango, & a Man of Note in the Army," had "call'd all the Mingo's, Delawar's &ca. together . . . & told them that [the French] intended to have been down the River this Fall" but postponed their advance until spring, when they would come into the country "with a far greater Number." When they did come, Joncaire cautioned, the Indians had better be "quite Passive, & not intermeddle, unless they had a mind to draw all [the French] force upon them; for that they expected to fight the English three Years . . . in which Time they shou'd Conquer."

So far, this was a disturbing though familiar threat; but Monacatoocha continued, explaining that Joncaire told the Indians that "shou'd [the English] prove equally strong [as the French], that they [the French] & the English wou'd join to cut [the Indians] off, & divide the Land between [the English and the French]: that . . . there was Men enough to . . . make them Masters of the Ohio."

This was an extraordinary thing for the Frenchman to have said— assuming that Monacatoocha was telling the truth. Washington operated on the assumption that the Half-King and his fellow sachems believed that the French were the common enemies of the English and the Indians. Now Monacatoocha was telling him that the Indians did not take this for granted. The question the Half-King had was about racial loyalty—whether the enmity between the French and the English was stronger than that between the Indians and Euro-Americans.

That Washington failed to answer this sophisticatedly skeptical question to his satisfaction is suggested by what happened the next day, November 29. Early in the morning, the Half-King and Monacootcha "beg'd me to stay one Day more," Washington wrote. Anxious as he was to leave, Washington accepted the Half-King's explanation that the Shawnee chiefs had not yet sent him their wampum and that Chief Shingas (who was to form part of the escort) had not yet assembled his warriors and had also been detained by the sickness of his wife. Washington understood that possession of the wampum was important, because returning it to the French would signify that whatever agreements existed between the tribes and the French were officially terminated. Giving back the wampum, Washington wrote, "was shaking of[f] all Dependence upon the French"; therefore, "I consented to stay, as I believ'd an Offence offer'd at this Crisis, might have been attended with greater ill Consequence than another Day's Delay."

So yet another day passed, and when Washington awoke on November 30, he was finally introduced to the promised escort. It consisted not of Shingas and a host of warriors but of one ancient chief named Jeska-kake, another old man called by the English White Thunder, and one young hunter (whose job would be to kill game for the expedition), in addition to the Half-King. Four men. *This* was all the escort the Half-King had been able to recruit. He had an explanation. "A greater Number," he said, "might give the French Suspicion of some bad Design, & cause them to be treated rudely." To his credit, Washington didn't swallow this whole. "I rather think they cou'd not get their Hunters in," he wrote in his diary. Nevertheless, at nine o'clock, he and Gist set off with their meager escort—two old men, one important chief, and a callow young hunter—on a mission intended to intimidate a French commander, who was ensconced with men and cannon in one of a chain of forts, and persuade him to meekly slink out of the Ohio Country.

8

"Property of the Crown"

———⊰•⊱———

THE MARCH FROM LOGSTOWN to Venango was about seventy miles, and when the weary party reached it on December 4, Washington noted "the French Colours hoisted at a House where they drove Mr. John Frazer an English Subject from." It was the young major's first encounter with the enemy. It would not be his last.

Washington, as he noted in his diary, "immediately repair'd to [the house] to know where the Commander resided: There was three Officers, one of which, Capt. Joncaire, inform'd me, that he had the Command of the Ohio, but that there was a General Officer at the next Fort, which he advis'd me to for an Answer." It was a strange, almost teasing reply. Captain Philippe-Thomas de Joncaire, sieur de Chabert, identified himself as being in "Command of the Ohio"—the great river by which any pretender to power, the Ohio Company, the English colonies, the French North American empire, would either prosper or die—yet he nevertheless deferred to an officer of higher rank. The fact was that Joncaire, though a soldier, made his living as a fur trader and was typical of the latest generation of French trader-trappers in that he was of mixed blood, the son of a Seneca mother and a French officer. In the government of New France, he held the office of chief interpreter for the Six

Nations and was a principal conduit between the French and the Indians. Almost certainly, he was authorized to accept the communication from Dinwiddie, but whereas the house he occupied was barely fortified, Fort LeBoeuf, to which he referred Washington, was a full-scale frontier fortification. Observing the paltry makeup of this "embassy" from Virginia, Joncaire may well have intended to overawe Washington and his party with an exhibition of French might on the frontier both countries claimed. The hard environment of the wilderness dwarfed or foiled most human enterprise, and, for this reason, appearances and posturing played a big part in wilderness diplomacy.

What happened next provides a vivid picture of the elaborate dance by which relations between the Euro-Americans and the Indians were shaped. Having directed Washington to deliver Dinwiddie's letter to Fort Le-Boeuf, Joncaire offered Washington a French escort, which, in accordance with Dinwiddie's instructions, Washington accepted. In doing so, he fell right into the Frenchman's hands.

On December 5, the weather turned bad again, and an icy rain poured down. As we have seen, Washington thought nothing of traveling in bad weather, but now that his small expedition was encumbered with the horses and supply wagons of his French escort, he would have to wait for drier conditions before setting out. Although Joncaire certainly could not conjure up the rain, he knew how to turn it to his advantage. He was aware that the forces in and around Fort LeBoeuf were still assembling. The longer he could delay Washington's arrival there, the more impressive that force would be. Even more important, the longer Washington and his Indian companions were delayed at Venango, the more time Joncaire had to undermine relations between these allies.

As it turned out, Joncaire's machinations were not the only cause of delay, a fact that says much about the fragile and fluid nature of alliances on the frontier. While at Venango, the Half-King and his two fellow chiefs met in council with their allies the Delaware. To the Delaware chief Kustaloga, the Half-King handed the wampum belt that Shingas had presented to him to return to the French as a token of renunciation of any alliance with them. Kustaloga, however, turned the belt back to the Half-King, explaining that because Shingas had sent no speech along with the belt, he could not accept it to present to the French. How, he asked, could he presume to make a speech on behalf of another chief?

It was a reasonable position for Kustaloga to take, but the Half-King had to wonder whether the real reason for Kustaloga's refusal was his unwillingness to be the messenger of a severed alliance. In any case, the refusal meant that if the belt was to be returned, the Half-King would have to do it himself. While this was not the simple equivalent of renouncing the alliance between the Iroquois and the Delaware, it unmistakably put distance between the two allies, at least so far as their relations with the French were concerned. For the Virginians, this development hardly boded well.

While the Half-King and Kustaloga were meeting over the issue of the wampum belt, Joncaire had hosted Washington and the other white men at dinner. That dinner done, he asked Washington—disingenuously feigning innocence—why he had not brought the chiefs to the meal. Washington could think of no other reply than that he had been unsure whether Joncaire wanted them there. With scarcely a pause, Joncaire ordered one of his soldiers to invite the chiefs to visit with him right away.

Joncaire greeted the sachems as warmly and respectfully as the late sieur de Marin had been rude and offensive. Most of all, he plied his guests with generous drafts of brandy while Washington looked on helplessly as the Half-King, deeper and deeper into his cups, passed the time in pleasantries. Not only did he fail to tell Joncaire that he and his fellow chiefs wanted the French out of the Ohio Country, he made not the slightest gesture of returning the wampum belt to him. Had the Half-King done so, Joncaire would doubtless have demurred, telling him what he had told Washington, that such business was a matter for his superior at Fort LeBeouf, but the mere attempt would have spoken volumes nevertheless. To Washington, the message was clear: He could not take Iroquois loyalty for granted and, from now on, would have to exert himself mightily to outmaneuver Frenchmen like Joncaire.

Early the next morning, December 6, the Half-King sheepishly presented himself at the entrance to Washington's tent. Washington noted in his diary that he was now "quite Sober" and apparently suffering deeply from morning-after remorse. He "insisted very much that I shou'd stay & hear what he had to say to the French," promising that he would repeat to Joncaire exactly what he had said to de Marin. Instead of welcoming this, however, Washington confided to his diary that he "fain wou'd have prevented his speaking any Thing 'til he came to the Commandant" at Fort LeBoeuf. All it might take was one more flask of brandy to reverse this newfound tide of resolution. Over Washington's objections, the Half-King insisted that "at this Place Council Fire was kindled . . . & that the Management of the Indian Affairs was left solely to Monsieur Joncaire."

In any time or place, Old World or New, diplomacy consists of creating bonds and driving wedges. Clearly, Joncaire was driving a wedge. To Washington, he had disclaimed ultimate authority over French forces in the region, directing him to the commandant at Fort LeBoeuf. To the Half-King, he introduced himself as the *sole* authority on "Indian affairs." Joncaire could not prevent the Half-King and Washington from marching together, but he could divide them in their understanding of the purpose of that march. Whereas Washington saw his objective miles away, the Half-King and the others were made to believe they had already arrived at the place they needed to be. Still, Washington agreed to yet another day's delay before starting for Fort LeBoeuf, explaining in his diary that the added hours would enable him to know the result of the Half-King's meeting with Joncaire.

The result proved, predictably, anticlimactic. Although, to Washington's relief, "the [Half-]King spoke much the same as he had done to the General [de Marin], & offer'd the [wampum belt]," Joncaire refused to accept it, now telling the Half-King what he had told Washington: Only the commandant at Fort LeBoeuf could accept the belt.

Washington might well have taken some satisfaction in having forced Joncaire to admit to the Half-King that he did not possess as much authority as he had claimed, but the fact remains that he did not accept the return of the wampum belt and that, therefore, the connection between the French and the Six Iroquois Nations, along with the Delaware, remained in force, at least technically. Moreover, Joncaire dragged out the council with the Indians (interminably, it seemed to Washington), presumably so that he could renew his seductions. At the approach of nightfall, Washington, his patience at an end, sent for the Indians. To his consternation, they returned reply that they could not come to him just now because they needed to call on Chief Kustaloga to discover more fully his reasons for not agreeing personally to give up the belt to the French. Seeking to put a stop to what he concluded was more of Joncaire's interference, Washington sent his Indian interpreter, John Davison, to go to the Half-King and the others and ensure that he was never "out of their Company."

So passed another tedious day and restless night.

On the morning of December 7, Major Washington was greeted at his tent by a man he had probably already met at Joncaire's dinner table, Michel Pépin, universally known among the French as Commissary La Force because he held the French colonial office of commissary of stores on the upper Ohio River. This made him a pivotal figure in French-Indian relations. He peremptorily informed the major that he and the three French regulars standing with him would now have the honor of serving as his escorts to Fort LeBoeuf. They were, he said, ready to leave without delay.

Without delay! Was La Force trying to get Washington to leave without the chiefs, who (he almost certainly well knew) were conferring with Kustaloga? If so, Washington was having none of it. Explaining that the Indians were not present, he asked La Force to wait while he sent Christopher Gist to fetch them. It was eleven o'clock before Gist returned with the three chiefs and the hunter. In an aside, he explained to Major Washington that he had had a very hard time prying them loose from Joncaire, who "did everything he could to prevail on our Indians to stay behind us."

Underway at last, on December 11, after four days on the trail, the eight Englishmen, four Indians, and four Frenchmen glimpsed the stockade of

Fort LeBoeuf through the failing light of the forest twilight. Washington sent Jacob Van Braam across the intervening creek to announce his arrival. Soon, a party of French officers paddled over to invite Washington and the others into the fort. With night upon them, all agreed that official business would wait until morning.

On December 12, "I prepar'd early to wait upon the Commander, & was receiv'd & conducted to him by the 2d. Officer in Command." Jacques Legardeur de Saint-Pierre was, Washington noted, "a Knight of the Military Order of St: Lewis, & . . . an elderly Gentleman," who nevertheless had "much the Air of a Soldier." It was an "Air" hard earned. Legardeur de Saint-Pierre had served as a lieutenant in warfare against the Chickasaw during 1739 and, over the years, had tramped far through the wilderness claimed by his king. Battle had cost him an eye, over which he wore a patch. "I acquainted him with my Business," Washington wrote, "& offer'd my Commission & Letter."

Legardeur de Saint-Pierre politely declined to accept any of the proffered documents, pending, he explained, "the Arrival of Monsieur Riparti, Capt. at the next Fort, who was sent for & expected every Hour." (This "Captain Riparti" was almost certainly Captain de Repetigny, a relative of Legardeur de Saint-Pierre.) We can imagine Washington's renewed consternation at this latest evidence of the French genius for polite delay, yet the young major did not spend the time idly. Instead, he methodically studied the fort until shortly after two in the afternoon, when he was told that Riparti (or de Repetigny) had finally arrived and that the two commanders were now prepared to receive Washington's commission and letters. After taking them, they once again retired to undertake the task of translation.

Dinwiddie's direct language, downright curt by the ornamental diplomatic standards of the day, could not have presented much of a problem for the translators. "Sir," it began:

The lands upon the River Ohio in the western parts of the colony of Virginia are so notoriously known to be the property of the Crown of Great Britain that it is a matter of equal concern and surprise to me to hear that a body of French forces are erecting fortresses and making settlements upon that river within H. M.'s Dominions.

The many and repeated Complaints I have received of these acts of hostility, lay me under the necessity of sending in the name of the King my Master, the bearer hereof, George Washington Esq., one of the Adjutants-General of the Forces of this Dominion; to complain to you of the encroachments thus made, and of the injuries done to the subjects of Great Britain in open violation of the law of nations now existing between the two Crowns.

If these facts are true and you shall think fit to justify your proceedings I must desire you to acquaint me by whose authority and instructions you have lately marched from Canada, with an armed force, and invaded the King of Great Britain's territories in the manner complained of, that according to the purport and resolution of your answer I may act agreeably to the commission I am honoured with from the King my Master.

However, Sir, in obedience to my instructions it becomes my duty to require your peaceful departure; and that you would forbear prosecuting a purpose so interruptive of the harmony and good understanding which His Majesty is desirous of cultivating with the most Christian King.

I persuade myself you will receive and entertain Major Washington with the candour and politeness natural to your Nation; and it will give me the greatest satisfaction if you return him with an answer suitable to my wishes for a very long and lasting Peace between us.

Washington asked Van Braam to review and approve the translation the Frenchmen had produced, after which he asked for the commandant's answer. Legardeur de Saint-Pierre replied that he would call a council—which Washington pointedly called a "Council of War"—to formulate his response.

While Washington yet again waited throughout much of December 13, he resumed his study of the fort and enlisted the assistance of his companions, directing them "to take an exact Account of the Canoes that were haled up, to convey their Forces down in the Spring"; they counted "50 of Birch Bark, & 170 of Pine; besides many others that were block'd out, in Readiness to make." Washington concluded that, unmistakably, an invasion fleet was being assembled.

On December 14, instead of responding to the documents as promised, Legardeur de Saint-Pierre suddenly suggested to Washington that he journey on to Quebec to present Dinwiddie's letter directly to the governor of Canada. The trek, sixteen hundred miles round-trip, would certainly have delayed any response to Dinwiddie and, perhaps more important, would have separated Washington from the Half-King and the other chiefs for a long time, if not forever. Washington replied to the suggestion by explaining that his orders were to deliver the letter to the French commandant and to no one else.

"I found many Plots concerted to retard the Indians Business, & prevent their returning with me," Washington later wrote in his diary. Determined to do "all in my Power to frustrate [the French] Schemes," he urged the Half-King to get on with the return of the wampum belt. Obliging him, the Half-King and his comrades "pressed for admittance this Evening, which at length was granted them privately with the Commander, & one or two other Officers." Later, the Half-King reported to Washington "that he offr'd the Wampum to the Commander, who evaded taking it, & made many fair Promises of Love & Friendship; said he wanted to live in Peace & trade amicably with them." As a proof of this, Legardeur de Saint-Pierre said "he wou'd send some Goods immediately down to the Logstown for them." This confirmed Washington's worst fears about the intention of the French to seduce the Indians away from him, and when he subsequently asked Riparti/de Repentigny "by what Authority he had taken & made Prisoners of several of our English Subjects," the captain replied blandly that "the Country belong'd to them, that no English Man had a right to trade upon them Waters; & that he had Orders to make every Person Prisoner that attempted it on the Ohio or the Waters of it."

After nightfall on December 14, the commandant finally handed Washington his answer to Dinwiddie's letter. It announced his intention "to send your letter to the Marquis Duquesne [the governor of Canada]. His reply will be a law to me, and, if he should order me to communicate it to you, Sir, I can assure you that I shall neglect nothing to have it reach you very promptly." For now, however, "as to the summons you send me to retire, I do not think myself obliged to obey it. Whatever may be your instructions, I am here by virtue of the orders of my General, and I entreat you, Sir, not to doubt for a moment that I have a firm resolution to follow them with all the exactness and determination which can be expected of the best officer."

Having given Washington his long-delayed reply, Legardeur de Saint-Pierre suddenly seemed very eager to send him off—even as he redoubled his efforts to retain the Indians in his embrace. Washington understood that while this Knight of St. Louis "appear'd to be extremely complaisant, . . . he was plotting every Scheme that the Devil & Man cou'd invent, to set our Indians at Variance with us, to prevent their going 'till after our Departure. Presents, rewards & every Thing that cou'd be suggested by him or his Officers was not neglected to do. . . . I saw that every Stratagem that the most fruitful Brain cou'd invent: was practis'd to get the Half King won to their Interest. . . . I went to the Half King and press'd him in the strongest Terms to go. He told me the Commander wou'd not discharge him 'till the Morning."

Here was a new crisis in the relationship between Washington and the Half-King. Either Legardeur de Saint-Pierre had dropped the pretense of seduction and was now straightforwardly asserting authority over the Indians, or the Half-King himself was fabricating a new reason for delay. Neither possibility boded well, but Washington decided it best to behave as if the Half-King's account were sincere. He therefore approached Legardeur de Saint-Pierre "& complain'd of ill Treatment; for keeping them, as they were Part of my Company was detaining me, which he promis'd not to do." As if shocked, the commandant "protested he did not keep them [the Indians] but was innocent of the Cause of their Stay"; however, Washington soon discovered that "he had promis'd them a Present of Guns, &ca. if they wou'd wait 'till the Morning." Outmaneuvered, Washington consented to wait just one more day "on a Promise that Nothing shou'd hinder them in the Morning."

December 16: "The French were not slack in their Inventions to keep the Indians this Day also," and they once again "endeavour'd to try the Power of Liquor; which I doubt not wou'd have prevail'd at any other Time than this, but I tax'd the [Half-]King so close upon his Word that he refrain'd, & set off with us as he had engag'd." At last, they were on their way.

After a perilous, exhausting, half-frozen trek, Washington arrived in Williamsburg on January 16, 1754, and put into the hands of Lieutenant Governor Robert Dinwiddie the letter from Legardeur de Saint-Pierre. The governor read it, then listened, apparently rapt, to Washington's full report. He asked the major to put it in writing and then sent the manuscript to be printed as *The Journal of Major George Washington, Sent by the Hon. Robert Dinwiddie, Esq; His Majesty's Lieutenant-Governor, and Commander in Chief of Virginia, to the Commandant of the French Forces on Ohio. To Which Are Added, the Governor's Letter, and a Translation of the French Officer's Answer.* Dinwiddie understood that, of the many commodities hard to come by on the eighteenth-century American frontier, unity and the concerted action born of unity were among the scarcest of all. He believed that he needed Washington's eyewitness account to squeeze military funding out of the always parsimonious and fractious Virginia House of Burgesses.

On the North American frontier, Indians did not think of themselves as Indians but as members of a tribe or members of a particular band or clan within a tribe. The so-called Iroquois League was regarded as a marvel because of the unprecedented degree of Native unity it represented; even at that, it was characterized as much by rivalry among the constituent tribes as by collaboration. In much the same way, colonists did not think of themselves as Englishmen or Frenchmen but as citizens of their particular colony. Much less did they consider themselves *Americans*, people who shared not only a continent but a common "national" fate. Even within a particular colony, there was always much self-interest and dissension. Without doubt, George Washington had the gratitude of the lieutenant governor when he returned from his mission to the French commandant, but there were also a great many politically powerful people in Williamsburg who did not like Robert Dinwiddie and, by extension, distrusted his protégé, the young major. Among this group were those involved in land speculation schemes that competed with the Ohio Company. They interpreted Washington's mission as a propaganda stunt intended to exaggerate the supposed French threat to *Virginia* for the purpose of persuading Parliament to assist the *Ohio Company* in settling the vast territory it had been granted.

To his credit, Dinwiddie did not wait for the burgesses to act but, even before Washington's return, dispatched an expedition to build a fort at the Forks of the Ohio. To assist and guard these men, Dinwiddie first thought to enlist a regiment of volunteers but soon discovered that the Virginia militia law prevented him from paying soldiers raised in this way. His only recourse, therefore, was to round up the two hundred men he believed he needed, drawing on a mix of frontier traders and frontier militia, send them out, then hope that the burgesses would fund this troop once it was a fait accompli. In fact, once the two hundred were in the field, he planned to ask the burgesses to authorize an additional four hundred. At the same time, he would appeal to the governors of the other colonies to provide even more men and supplies. The colonies were so intensively competitive with one another that he had no great expectation of success, but it was worth a try.

On January 21, 1754, just five days after Washington returned from the expedition to Fort LeBoeuf, Dinwiddie ordered him, as adjutant of the Northern Neck, to enlist into active militia service one hundred men from Augusta and Frederick counties. At the same time, he directed Captain William Trent to raise an additional hundred men. A native of Lancaster, Pennsylvania, Trent was the partner of the prosperous fur trader George Croghan and also functioned as an agent for the Ohio Company. Other traders looked to him for leadership, and Dinwiddie had shown considerable acumen in choosing him to recruit men from among the trading community, even though he had failed in his earlier assignment to reconnoiter French outposts. Both he and Trent well knew that traders would be highly motivated, since they understood that nothing less than their present and future livelihoods were at stake. None of them could afford to yield their Indian trading partners to the French.

Dinwiddie's awareness of the trust that existed between the traders and Trent moved him to divide command of the force between Trent and Washington. The decision was understandable, but arbitrarily dividing military authority almost guarantees strategic and tactical chaos. Of course, even the creation of chaos requires people to create it, and although raising a hundred militiamen seemed simple enough in theory, it proved very hard to do in fact. Virginia colonial law was clear: Every free white male resident of Virginia twenty-one years of age or older was obligated to answer the call to military service. Despite the law, the militia was without infrastructure, and almost no one was prepared to enlist. Virginia had a militia law but no militia. In Frederick County, for instance, the legally required registration of adult males had never taken place, and no volunteers came forth. As for a draft—also provided for by law—the county lieutenant feared it would provoke defiance, if not outright rebellion. In Augusta County, the result was the same. No volunteers were forthcoming, even though the area had been hit by a devastating Indian raid during the summer, which should have motivated the people to act if only on the simple instinct of self-defense.

A flummoxed Dinwiddie convened his council and gruffly announced his intention to throw the book at anyone who persisted in defying the militia act. The council members responded that Virginia law certainly gave the lieutenant governor extraordinary powers in the event of invasion, but the law, they pointed out, restricted any militia raised to repel invasion from acting beyond the bounds of Virginia. The problem was that no one knew whether the Forks of the Ohio lay within Virginia. Many insisted that the junction of the Monongahela, Allegheny, and Ohio rivers was within Pennsylvania. There was the very real possibility that Dinwiddie might raise his militia in the eastern Virginia counties and march it westward, only to have the men demand their rights by turning back as they neared the Forks. The French and the Indians were not the only threat to Virginia and the other English colonies. Recalcitrant colonists, intercolonial competition (even within the same empire), and the vagaries of the law all presented formidable obstacles.

In the meantime, after receiving their copies of the published version of Washington's journal on February 14, the House of Burgesses convened a committee of the whole to discuss the governor's request for defense funds. Journal or no journal, no committee member seemed unduly alarmed, and a few even voiced their opinion that Washington's account was a fiction intended only to promote the Ohio Company. One burgess even declared that the Ohio Country really *did* belong to the French after all! Only after much anguished effort was Dinwiddie able to cajole the burgesses into voting £10,000 for the defense of the entire frontier. It was a paltry sum, and paltry as it was, the burgesses attached to the appropriation a rider that hobbled Dinwiddie even further. They stipulated that fourteen leading men of Virginia (or any nine of that number), with the consent of the lieutenant governor, were to be tasked with deciding how the money should be spent.

Historians have long interpreted the French and Indian War as in some measure a prelude to the American Revolution. Perhaps the burgesses' onerous legislative rider may be seen as a prelude to the prelude. The lieutenant governor was an unelected royal officer, whereas the burgesses (who were chief among the colony's "leading men") were elected by the colonists. No one argued that appropriations were the province of the burgesses, but the lieutenant governor had always been the commander in chief of the armed forces. Now, however, the elected men were voting themselves a strong voice in the allocation of money appropriated for military purposes, thereby encroaching on what had been the unchallenged authority of a crown officer. Dinwiddie raged against the rider as "very much in a republican way of thinking" and contemplated exercising his royal authority to dissolve the Burgesses right then and there.

It would have been a satisfying step, but he needed the money. So he yielded to the Burgesses' "republican way."

. . .

Dinwiddie used the money to bypass the dysfunctional militia system and start from scratch by raising three hundred volunteers to be paid fifteen pounds of tobacco each. In eastern Virginia, tobacco served the same purpose as beaver served on the northern frontier. It was currency. To provide further motivation, Dinwiddie announced that 100,000 acres were being reserved adjacent to the proposed fort at the Forks of the Ohio and another 100,000 were reserved elsewhere along the river. After the volunteers successfully concluded their service, the entire 200,000 acres would be divided among them.

Always it came down to gain—tobacco, pelts, land, money. Washington understood that he was a major of militia, whereas the force Dinwiddie was assembling was something different. He proposed to Dinwiddie that he be appointed a *lieutenant colonel* of volunteers, and he inquired straightaway what such an officer would be paid. When Dinwiddie responded that it would be fifteen shillings a day, Washington, knowing that British regular officers of this rank made more, responded that the sum was insufficient. Dinwiddie countered that colonial officers would also receive provisions in addition to their salary, whereupon Washington allowed himself to be mollified and set about recruiting volunteers from a headquarters he set up in Alexandria.

By the end of his first week of recruiting, Washington had managed to enroll what he described as twenty-five "loose, Idle Persons that are quite destitute of House, and Home, and I may truly say many of them of Cloaths." The feckless dregs of colonial society, they were shoeless and shirtless, and what they wanted most out of their enlistment was (Washington wrote to Dinwiddie) "to be put into a Uniform dress."

Operating at the edge of the Ohio Country, William Trent fared better than Washington. He quickly filled his hundred-man quota but nevertheless wrote to Washington that even this was a force inadequate to assist in the construction and guarding of the fort at the Ohio Forks. He had just learned that Commissary La Force was being very free with threats and that some four hundred French soldiers were on the march, bound for the Forks. Trent urged Washington to get under way—fast. As for Dinwiddie, he seemed blithely unconcerned by the virtual nonexistence of his army, confidently proclaiming that three hundred volunteers were better than eight hundred militiamen—when, in fact, he had at most 125 volunteers, many of whom wanted to be soldiers for the sole purpose of securing a uniform, which would be their first and only suit of clothes. Dinwiddie took additional, and perhaps more justifiable, comfort in assurances that a thousand Cherokee and Catawba warriors would rush to the aid of Virginia, and he was also pleased to learn that an "independent company" of British regulars was being sent from South Carolina, as were two independent companies from New York.

Dinwiddie passed over Washington for overall command of the projected three hundred Virginia volunteers and chose instead Joshua Fry, who, like Washington, had no military experience but, unlike him, had been master of the grammar school at the College of William and Mary, as well as a professor of mathematics and natural philosophy, and was the author of the ambitious 1751 "Map of the Most Inhabited Part of Virginia." Promoted to lieutenant colonel, Washington would serve as Colonel Fry's number two, at a salary of twelve shillings and sixpence a day, which, Washington noted, was two shillings and sixpence less than the paltry fifteen shillings he'd been promised. He rapidly calculated that, at the prevailing rate of exchange, the daily pay was a full ten shillings less than that of a British regular of the same rank. To compound this disparity, Washington learned that he and his volunteer officers would be serving alongside officers of independent companies, who would be paid at the rate of British regulars. Moreover, despite the governor's earlier assurance that the volunteer officers would be supplied with provisions in addition to their pay, those provisions, it now turned out, would be not officer's fare but the grim rations of a common soldier. Washington made noises about resigning in protest, but the fact was that he was too excited by the prospect of leading the vanguard of the expedition to the Forks of the Ohio to quit.

Dinwiddie resolved to waste no more time. He instructed Washington to march immediately with "what soldiers you have," telling him that Fry would follow with the rest of the three hundred as soon as they were assembled. "Act on the defensive," Dinwiddie stipulated, but if "any attempts are made to obstruct the works [the building of the fort] or interrupt our settlements, . . . you are to restrain all such offenders, and in case of resistance to make prisoners of or kill and destroy them."

Washington departed with the 120 men he had managed to accumulate. His first objective was Wills Creek, but he left with supplies sufficient to get his men only as far as Winchester, ninety-seven miles from Alexandria and about forty miles short of Wills Creek. He gambled on finding additional provisions at Winchester. Such was the great lesson of wilderness warfare: Take a chance on finding what you need, and in the meantime do with less. Dinwiddie was also learning this lesson. Although North Carolina had responded to his call for aid by recruiting a force of volunteers expected to number 750, Maryland decided to send no troops at all, and Pennsylvania's intentions remained unrevealed. (The status of the independent companies from other colonies also remained uncertain.) Instead of creating hesitancy in Dinwiddie's mind, these shortages made him all the more anxious to get the expedition going. He reasoned that the faster the troops reached the Ohio, the fewer French and Indians there would be to deal with. Washington and his command marched out of Alexandria on April 2, 1754.

After five days, they had put fifty-seven miles between them and Alexandria, but now they had to crest the Blue Ridge at Vestal's Gap, then descend to the Shenandoah River, which they would cross by ferry. Two full days were required to make these seventeen miles; however, considering the long, hard climb to Vestal's Gap, Washington was pleased with the progress, and once they had been ferried across the Shenandoah, he and his men were on the road to Winchester, familiar country to Washington, who had surveyed here in 1748.

On April 10, they reached Winchester, where a company recruited by Captain Adam Stephen was waiting for them, bringing the total strength of Washington's command to 159. Nothing, however, had been done to acquire the wagons needed to carry supplies for the rest of the journey. Washington therefore personally set about "impressing" (drafting into government service) the minimum sixty wagons he calculated were needed. The lieutenant colonel strode through the town, pointing out which vehicles he wanted. It was an impressive display of command presence, but when no more than eight or nine of the conveyances were actually delivered, the lieutenant colonel had to make the weary rounds again. The situation quickly became all too typical of logistics on the colonial frontier. Each day Washington would select wagons, of which only a small fraction would be delivered. "Out of seventy-four wagons impressed at Winchester," he wrote to Governor Dinwiddie, "we got but ten after waiting a week." Moreover, "some of those [were] so badly provided with teams [of horses] that the soldiers were obliged to assist them up the hills." Washington sneered that "it was known [the people of Winchester] had better teams at home" and withheld them; but, on the other hand, he also acknowledged that he had liberally fudged the impressment law, since in Frederick County he had no official authority at all.

In the end, on April 18, Washington left Winchester with far fewer wagons than he needed—just twelve—but set off for Wills Creek, forty miles off, anyway. As for his final objective, the Forks of the Ohio, they lay some 160 miles beyond Wills, and time was wasting. An entire week had been consumed in trying to impress those wagons. To make up for it, Washington rode ahead of the column to select campsites and survey fords and crossings. At the Cacapon River, he was intercepted by an express rider carrying dispatches from Captain Trent. *Eight hundred*—not four—French soldiers were closing in on the Forks of the Ohio. Trent and his hundred men were expecting to be attacked at any hour.

Washington dutifully forwarded Trent's communiqués to Colonel Fry, who was still in Alexandria dredging up troops. Next, Washington rode to the cabin of Job Pearsall on the South Branch of the Potomac to await the arrival of his command, which now seemed very small indeed. After they caught up with him on April 20, he rode ahead again, calling at the trading post of Colonel Thomas Cresap at Old Town, Maryland. Just before he reached Cresap's, however, he was met by Edward Ward, ensign to Captain William Trent. Ward carried the news that Trent (as Washington recorded in his diary) "had been obliged to surrender to a

Body of One Thousand *French* and upwards, under the Command of Captain [Claude-Pierre Pécaudy, sieur de] *Contrecoeur,* who was come from *Venango* . . . with Sixty Battoes [bateaux], and Three Hundred Canoes, and who having planted eighteen Pieces of Cannon against the Fort, afterwards had sent him a Summons to depart."

After delivering his news, Ward pulled from his sodden coat two documents. One was the "Summons" from the French commander; the other was the transcription of a speech by the Half-King, who had been counting on the military presence of the fort at the Forks of the Ohio to keep at bay the numerous French-allied tribes that were longtime enemies of the Iroquois. Now that the fort had surrendered, the Half-King called on the governors of Pennsylvania and Virginia to be of "good courage and come as soon as possible." He promised, "You will find us as ready to fight as you are yourselves." Ward himself noted that "the *Indians* kept steadfastly attached to our Interest"; however, the Half-King concluded his speech on a note of highest pathos: "If you do not come to our assistance now, we are entirely undone, and I think we shall never meet together again. I speak with a heart full of grief."

9

"Set the World on Fire"

———◆———

LIEUTENANT COLONEL GEORGE WASHINGTON let three days pass before he held a "Council of War" on April 23 "to consult upon what must be done on Account of the News brought by Mr. *Wart*," as he spelled Ensign Ward's name. The lieutenant colonel noted the grim facts: Captain Trent's garrison "consisted only of Thirty-three effective Men"; Washington himself led 159; against this total, the French had more than a thousand. The council of war prudently concluded that it was "a Thing impracticable to march towards the Fort without sufficient Strength." Yet Washington appreciated that the Half-King, whose loyalty was so important, was pleading for help. Accordingly, he emerged from the council having decided to "advance as far as *Red-Stone-Creek,* on *Monaunga-hela,* about Thirty-seven Miles on this Side of the Fort, and there to raise a Fortification, clearing a Road broad enough to [accommodate] all our Artillery and our Baggage, and there to wait for Fresh Orders."

The next day, Washington wrote to Maryland governor Horatio Sharpe of his "glowing zeal" to serve king and country. He did not mention anything about his zeal to protect his family's investment in the Ohio Company, nor did he refer to his eagerness to come to the aid of the Half-King. For his part, the Half-King was sincerely anxious for English help. Although he might have opened up negotiations with the French—certainly Legardeur de Saint-Pierre had shown himself eager to pry him from Washington's embrace—he had a strong personal reason for doing no such thing. Years earlier, Frenchmen had killed, boiled, and eaten his father. Why they did this, we do not know, but the event (understandably) colored the Half-King's opinion of the French and surely played a role in motivating his alliance with the English. Washington believed that the Half-King was absolutely under his control, and wrote as much to Dinwiddie. In fact, the sachem, twice Washington's age, described the younger man to the colonial Indian agent and interpreter Conrad Weiser as "good-natured" but without "experience." It is doubtful that he blithely trusted his fate to Washington, but he was nevertheless pleased to have persuaded him to help the Iroquois fight the French. For that is how he saw the relationship: Washington had not won *him* over; *he* had triumphed over the Virginian. Viewed more objectively, it is clear that the two men simultaneously overestimated and underestimated one another. Washington assumed he could count on the Half-King's ability and willingness to muster all the Iroquois warriors required to evict a thousand Frenchmen from Ohio Company territory, whereas the sachem believed that, through Washington, he could summon all the Englishmen *he* needed to chase the French from *his* people's land.

Washington did appreciate that he could not take for granted the loyalty of the anticipated Indian cohort. He believed that if he did not act soon, his Indian allies would drift away (of course, they had yet to materialize). Dinwiddie had promised him reinforcements, but, like the Half-King's warriors, these men also had yet to arrive. Zealous though he was, Washington was unwilling to do battle with fewer than two hundred men against more than a thousand, but he hoped the bold march to Redstone Creek, a position sufficiently forward to put him within striking distance of Fort Duquesne, yet (in his inexperienced judgment) far enough away from the fort to safely await the arrival of sufficient reinforcements to make an attack feasible, would keep the alliance alive without risking too much.

The forty-mile march to Redstone would not be easy. Chestnut Ridge was a steep upthrust of the Allegheny Mountains, and it ran like a three-thousand-foot-high wall right across Washington's proposed route. His small band of men would have to hew through Chestnut Ridge, yard by yard, a road passable by supply wagons and artillery. Putting that prospect in the back of his mind, he scribbled out a message and handed it to the Indian youth who had accompanied Ensign Ward. It was a suitably high-flown reply to the Half-King: "This young man will inform you where he found a small part of our army," Washington wrote, "making towards you, clearing the roads for a great number of our warriors, who are ready to follow us, with our great guns, our ammunition and provisions." In the message, Washington asked the Half-King to meet the advancing force "on the road . . . to assist us in council," and then, grandiosely, signed his speech "Caunotaucarius." It was the Mingo name the Half-King himself had bestowed on him the winter before. The name, as Washington well knew, meant "Town-taker."

In his missive to the Half-King, George Washington created in words what he did not have in physical fact—at least not yet. His 159-man detachment he described as "part of our army," the whole of which (he wrote) consisted of a "great number" of men accompanied by "great guns." Shortly after he sent the messenger off with this message, the forty or so men Captain Trent had managed to enlist wandered into camp. Without consulting the lieutenant colonel or anyone else, Trent had lured them into service with the promise of two shillings a day; Dinwiddie, however, had given Washington sufficient money to pay a mere eight pence per soldier. When Washington frankly explained this to his new arrivals, they did not gripe, but they flatly refused to work. This provoked Washington to announce that he would feed no idlers, and, with that, he ordered the newcomers to get to work alongside his own detachment to clear the road to Redstone Creek. Work they would, they replied, calmly and respectfully—at the rate of two shillings per day.

The Anglo-Iroquois alliance was on the line. Indeed, the English empire in North America hung in the balance—and, with it, the fortunes of

Washington and virtually every other prominent family in Virginia. Despite the stakes, Washington didn't even have the petty cash to pay what Trent had promised. Even if he simply agreed to pay the new men two shillings on the dubious assumption that he could talk Dinwiddie into making good on the funds, he would be risking a mutiny among the eight-pence majority. Continuing to threaten the volunteers was not an option because, as volunteers, they were not subject to the strict provisions of Virginia's militia law. Washington had no authority either to compel or to punish them. In the end, he announced that he would settle the question of payment pending instructions from Lieutenant Governor Dinwiddie; in the meantime, he ordered Captain Trent to look after "his" men and to strictly segregate them from the other troops, lest they infect the loyal majority with their discontent. Trent, however, found himself unable either to segregate or, for that matter, aggregate them. Within a matter of hours, his forty recruits drifted away, deserted, leaving Washington with his original 159 men, all of whom he pressed into the labor of widening a man-narrow trail to accommodate wagons and artillery.

On good days, the column advanced four miles, but most days were not good. The rain-drenched troops-cum-laborers were lucky to make two miles. On May 7, some twenty miles from Wills Creek, they reached the upper reaches of Casselman's River, which Washington remembered from his surveying days as a shallow, placid stream. Rain had transformed it into a raging torrent, which no army could ford. Over the next two days, he and his men labored mightily to build a bridge strong enough to support heavy wagons and "great guns."

Once it had finally crossed Casselman's River, the expedition was confronted by a different kind of stream—a succession of English traders, who, like Casselman's River, had also suffered drastic transformation. These were men who, in their uncouth way, had made a point of keeping up appearances. In better days, the beaver robes they wore shone in the sun. The men wore their beards long but clean, a pipe clenched at a jaunty angle between the teeth. Now, however, they tramped by, dirty, garments soiled, tattered, and faces—usually rosy with wind and drink—ashen. They were beaten men, trudging east from the Ohio. To

Washington, they spoke numbly of their flight from the French. With a weary nod toward his meager "army," they advised him to turn around and do the same.

While most of the traders reported seeing large numbers of Frenchmen, eight hundred or more freshly arrived to further reinforce the thousand men already at the Forks of the Ohio, one, Robert Callender, owner of three prosperous trading houses, said he'd seen no more than five Frenchmen, all at one of Christopher Gist's trading posts. One of the five, Callender noted, was Michel Pépin, the man everyone called Commissary La Force.

The presence of that one man concerned George Washington far more than the eight hundred. Callender reported to Washington that one of the Frenchmen explained that La Force was rounding up deserters, but neither Callender nor Washington believed it. They knew that a man of La Force's importance would not be wasting his time hunting a few AWOLs. What he *would* be doing is leading reconnaissance for an invasion. There are some situations in which a small number of men can do more than an army. Modern military commanders call this "asymmetric warfare"; Washington had no such phrase, but he understood the concept, and he now believed that if he could quickly overtake La Force and capture him, he might thwart—or at least delay—an entire army in its drive to invade the Ohio Country.

Callender had one more piece of news. He had spoken with the Half-King, who had received Washington's message, had greeted it enthusiastically, and was even now marching with fifty warriors to meet Washington's advancing column. Pleased and relieved as he was, the lieutenant colonel decided to take no chances. Having seen how the French "worked" Indians—showering them with gifts, plying them with liquor, promising them anything to draw them from the English embrace (perfunctory though that might be)—Washington detached twenty-five of his already puny number to intercept the Half-King and his fifty warriors before the French got to them first. Washington also charged the leader of this "flying column," Captain Adam Stephen, to look for possible water routes to Redstone Creek and to keep all eyes peeled for La Force. In the meantime, Washington pressed the rest of his men to push the road through.

It was muddy, rainy work, but the slowness of it made it easy for dispatch riders to deliver the news that Colonel Fry had at last arrived at Winchester, Virginia, with a hundred men and would soon begin his march to join Washington. There was also a message from North Carolina's governor, who promised three hundred fifty men, and from Maryland's chief executive, who pledged two hundred. Pennsylvania decided to send no militiamen, but its assembly did vote £10,000 in aid. From Dinwiddie, Washington heard that Massachusetts governor William Shirley promised to open up an offensive against Canada with six hundred troops. It was a strategic move that would pin down French soldiers who would otherwise have been sent to garrison the captured Ohio Forks fort the French were now calling Fort Duquesne.

Perhaps it was this spate of hopeful news that motivated Washington's bold response to the distinctly discouraging news he received on May 16, when a pair of refugee traders he encountered shook their bowed heads at the very thought of cutting a road through Chestnut Ridge. They assured Washington that they were very familiar with the ridge— and it could never be crossed by wagons, let alone artillery.

What about a water route? Washington asked.

When the men replied that they didn't know the water routes as they knew Chestnut Ridge, Washington found reason for optimism and immediately ordered some canoes to be built so that he could explore the Youghiogheny River, which ran through Chestnut Ridge all the way to the Monongahela at Turtle Creek. He knew very well that the Youghiogheny was too shallow for heavily loaded canoes, but he had been tramping across mile after mile of rain-soaked ground, and his hunch— his hope—was that all the rain had made the Youghiogheny deep enough.

Washington was supervising canoe construction when, on May 17, he received a letter from Dinwiddie announcing the arrival in Virginia of an "independent company" from South Carolina and the anticipated arrival of two more such companies from New York. This should have been very welcome news indeed, but Washington knew that these companies were made up of British regulars commanded by officers of the regular British army. He also knew that regulars had nothing but contempt for "provincials," as they called lieutenant colonels such as himself. That he, a provincial lieutenant colonel, would now be treated as subordinate to the lowliest regular army ensign was as hard a blow as any Washington had suffered so far. What made it worse was the additional news from Dinwiddie that a legislative committee had capped Washington's compensation at twelve shillings and sixpence, without any allowance for officers to supplement their rations. Not only would Washington be outranked by the independent company officers, he would be outpaid by them.

We do not know whether Washington purposely shared the bad news with his subordinate officers, but at the very least he did a bad job of keeping it from them. They threatened en masse to resign their commissions upon the arrival of the higher-paid independent company officers and presented Washington with a letter to pass on to Dinwiddie. Washington could have refused to accept it but instead, on May 18, sent it, accompanied by a letter of his own. "I am heartily concerned," he wrote, "that the officers have such real cause to complain of the Committee's resolves; and still more to find my inclinations prone to second their just grievances." He pointed out that "nothing prevents their throwing down their commissions . . . but the approaching danger, which has too far engaged their honor to recede till other officers are sent in their room, or an alteration made regarding their pay." For himself, he asked Dinwiddie to let him serve "voluntarily . . . without any other reward, than the satisfaction of serving my country"; this, he wrote, was preferable to "slaving dangerously for the shadow of pay." He closed by observing that he could not "see why the lives of his Majesty's subjects in Virginia should be of less value, than of those in other parts of his American dominions." Here were the stirrings of revolution in the heart of George Washington.

Writing the letter seems to have given Washington renewed enthusiasm for what was increasingly coming to seem a hopeless task. While he was willing to await reinforcement by the independent companies before making an all-out assault on Fort Duquesne, he wanted to bag La Force and his party before any regulars could horn in. Hoping to hasten the arrival of the Half-King and his party, he sent an Indian messenger to tell the Half-King that he had at headquarters a speech from Dinwiddie intended for his ears alone. The messenger sent, Washington, on May 20, climbed into a canoe with a lieutenant, three soldiers, and an Indian guide to probe the Youghiogeny.

They had progressed no more than a half mile when they encountered yet another bedraggled trader, who told them that he knew the Youghiogheny well. There was no point in going any farther, he said. Even rain swollen, the river was not consistently navigable.

Hedging his bets, Washington ordered the canoe building suspended but decided to see if the trek to Redstone Creek and the Monongahela could be made by a combination of water travel and overland portage, a process that would still be easier than hacking a road over an impassable crest. Ten miles into the journey, the Indian guide peremptorily rose to his feet and proclaimed he would go no farther. Any regular army officer would have responded with rage. Instead, militia commander Washington offered presents, which he believed to be the sovereign lubricant of Anglo-Indian relations. In return for one of his own fancy ruffled shirts and a homely match coat, the guide consented to remain. The next day, however, the voyagers encountered something Washington could not buy off. It was "a fall, which continued rough, rocky and scarcely passable, for two miles, and then fell, within the space of fifty yards, nearly forty feet perpendicular." The conclusion was inescapable. Even combined with portages, there was no way to reach the Monongahela via the Youghiogheny.

Washington and his men turned back and by May 23 were where they had started, at the Great Crossing of the Youghiogheny. There they found that Captain Adam Stephen and the detachment of twenty-five men who had been on the scout for the past two weeks had returned. Stephen reported that they had reached the Monongahela near Redstone Creek, where they questioned a clutch of Indian traders, who reported having met "some" French troops along the Monongahela commanded by an officer calling himself Jumonville. Stephen promised one of the Indians the spectacular sum of £5 if he would journey back down to the Monongahela to spy on the French in "their" fort. The investment produced a flood of intelligence, including an "account of everything at Fort Duquesne, the number of French at that post, the number employed daily on the works [fortifications], the number sick in the hospital and what accidents had happened since their arrival at that place, the dimensions of the fort, the breadth and depth of the ditch [the moat surrounding the fort], the thickness of the ramparts, in what places it was only stockaded, with the length of the stockades."

What a bargain!

Or was it? Neither Stephen nor Washington believed the Indian was lying, but they agreed that the only way to have secured so much detailed information was for the informant to have told the French exactly what he was about. Five English pounds had bought a double agent, and this meant that they, the hunters, were now the hunted. There was nothing for it, therefore, but to get a move on. With Captain Stephen and his command in tow, Washington and his small party left Great Crossing, marched over Laurel Hill, and, on May 24, located the main body of his troops, who, the road work being as hard as it was, had made little progress toward Redstone Creek.

They delivered to Washington a new message from the Half-King, translated—more or less—by the expedition's semiliterate interpreter, John Davison:

> To the forist, His Majesties Commander Offiverses to hom this meay concern: On acc't of a freench armey to meat Miger Georg Wassiontton therefore my Brotheres I deesir you to be awar of them for deisin'd to strik ye forist English they see ten days since they marchd I cannot tell what nomber the half-King and the rest of the Chiefs will be with you in five days to consel, no more at present but give my serves to my Brothers the English.

As far as he could determine, this meant that the French were advancing in unknown numbers ("I cannot tell what nomber") and the Half-King was on his way to counsel ("consel") with Washington. By intensively grilling an Indian messenger, Washington learned that about half the French garrison had left Fort Duquesne on a mission of some sort. A short time later, another Indian trader, this one fresh from Christopher Gist's settlement, reported having seen two Frenchmen at the settlement on May 23. He told Washington that this probably meant a strong French force was on the march.

With attack apparently imminent and the whereabouts of reinforcements unknown, Washington surveyed Great Meadows, the forest clearing on which he and his men happened to be standing at the moment. Spying a pair of gullies that ran parallel to one another, he envisioned them, somewhat wishfully, as trenches, positioned his wagons between them to form a defensive square, and ordered his men to climb down into them. Posting sentries, Washington bedded down with his men, passing the night of May 24 in the cold, wet ditches.

There was no attack. Still hopeful of capturing La Force, Washington, come morning, decided he could not afford to wait to be attacked. Even knowing he was outnumbered, he unhitched the wagons from the horses, put men on their bare backs, and sent them out to look for the French. In addition, he dispatched some foot patrols into the woods. Then, instead of digging the gullies deeper, to make them something more formidable than mere ditches, he put the rest of his men to work clearing brush. True, this exposed his position to any approaching enemy, but he wanted to see what was coming at *him* across what he described in a quick letter to Dinwiddie as a "charming field for an encounter."

Still, one after the other, Washington's scouts returned to report having seen no Frenchmen. Three more days passed before Christopher Gist rode into camp with a story to tell.

On May 26, Gist said, fifty French regulars had marched into his settlement while he was out. The two Indians who looked after things in his absence reported to him that Commissary La Force was their leader and, apparently upset by Gist's absence, threatened to kill a cow and destroy other property. The two Indians talked him out of it, and a sullen La Force rode off along with his troops. Gist told Washington that he saw, just five miles from Great Meadows, the tracks of many white men. Moreover, Gist said, he had been told that many French canoes were now beached at Redstone Creek, empty.

Gist's narrative transformed any fear of attack into the perception of opportunity. Washington reasoned that La Force with just fifty men was far from where they had landed, but very close to where he now was. This meant that the Frenchmen were cut off, isolated, and eminently vulnerable. In an instant, Washington ordered Captain Peter Hog to take seventy-five men and *find the French*. Next, he sat down to dash off a new letter to Dinwiddie, who was now at Winchester. After informing him that Captain Hog had been sent in pursuit of La Force and his detachment, he complained about a shortage of presents for the Indians— "I have been oblig'd to pay Shirts for what they [the Indians] have already done which I cannot continue to do"—and gave the letter to Gist to carry to Winchester.

About nine that evening, Silverheels, an Indian runner, arrived at Great Meadows with a message from the Half-King, who announced himself to be just six miles from Washington's camp. He noted that he had seen the footprints of two Frenchmen.

Laying the message aside, Washington picked forty of the eighty or so men remaining in camp and led them through a rainy, moonless night to the encampment of the Half-King. Feeling their way along, the going was painfully slow, and dawn was breaking by the time Washington sighted the sachem's shelter.

Although the Half-King was a supremely important figure in the Virginia–Pennsylvania–New York frontier, no description of him survives. Perhaps his years had dignified his appearance, or perhaps he was just prematurely aged, haggard with the signs of an illness that would kill him before winter. Whatever his appearance, Washington respected him, appreciated his importance, and was glad to see him. Surely, however, he must have been chagrined that, whereas Washington had been told to expect a fully equipped force of fifty, only Monacatoocha (the Oneida chief also known to the English as Scarouady), two warriors, and two boys carrying muskets accompanied him, along with six or seven other Indians, all unarmed. No matter. Washington omitted the usual flowery speeches and instead came directly to the point. He proposed that Half-King and his warriors join him and his men in immediately attacking La Force and his party. For his part, the Half-King instantly agreed and, without ceremony, led Washington and the others to the spot where he had seen the footprints. From here, he sent two Indians to follow the trail, locate the French camp, and report back.

The pair returned much sooner than expected. The Frenchmen were no more than a half mile off the trail, in a "bower" nestled among rocks.

Washington and the Half-King lowered themselves on their haunches and, with sticks, scratched a plan of attack into the soft Pennsylvania loam. The concept was simple. They would surround the French and attack them from all sides. The plan settled upon, Washington mustered his men, and the Half-King summoned his small entourage.

As they neared the bower, Washington saw that the approach of his left flank would be amply sheltered, but that the right would be exposed before the encirclement could be completed. He assigned Captain Stephen to command the left flank while he took the more dangerous right himself. The Half-King's warriors were positioned to Stephen's left, at the far left of the attack. Between seven and eight in the morning, the attackers were in position. At Washington's wordless signal, they crept to within one hundred yards of the bower. This was the maximum effective range of the "Brown Bess" muskets of the era. Washington had read enough drill manuals to know that, ideally, fire was to be withheld until troops had closed to fifty yards; he therefore looked to his right and then to his left, ensuring that all weapons were at the ready. Satisfied that they were, he rose to his full height, drew his sword, stepped into the clearing, and gave the command in a strong, steady voice. If he followed the European custom to which he would adhere years later, during the

Revolution, it was this: *The army will advance!* Then, at about fifty yards, it would be *Fire at will!*

The Frenchmen had posted no sentries. Those few soldiers loitering outside of the bower were not carrying their muskets, which, long and heavy, had been left in their place of concealment. At the sound of Washington's voice and the sight of the soldiers rising, they dashed into the bower to fetch their weapons.

After the battle, no one could remember who had actually fired first, but everyone agreed that men started falling right away, including, among the Virginians, Lieutenant Thomas Waggener, stricken right next to Washington. He was followed by another, who fell dead instantly. Two or three more were wounded. Everyone hit was a member of the exposed right wing, Washington's wing. The French, however, got the worst of it by far. A dozen fell, ten dying on the spot. Of the two wounded, one died soon after.

Death was the expected outcome of wounds inflicted by the musket balls of the period. About three-quarters of an inch across, made of lead, each ball weighed somewhat over an ounce. In theory, a ball fired from a properly loaded and charged weapon could inflict a wound at three hundred yards—though no competent commander would permit his soldiers to shoot their wildly inaccurate weapons from such a distance. At fifty yards, though, each ball would tear a very substantial hole through a man. *Through* a man. For at fifty yards, not only was the aim more accurate, but the force was most deadly. At this range, a ball usually bored both an entrance and an exit wound. Whereas the entrance trauma was little larger than the diameter of the ball, the exit injury was typically three or four inches across. Unlike a modern bullet, a lead ball does not expand on impact, but the tissue, shattered bone, and even the densely packed air the speeding ball pushes in front of it punch out a jagged exit wound that is very hard to bandage and is especially vulnerable to lethal infection. Not that Washington was thinking of flesh and blood when he wrote of the battle to his brother, John Augustine Washington, on May 31: "I can with truth assure you, I heard Bulletts whistle and believe me there was something charming in the sound."

Amid the flying lead, Washington and Stephen pressed their attack, and the French quickly gave ground. Some made a run for it. Summoned back by their commander, however, they meekly returned, hands raised. Washington understood why. The Frenchmen saw the Indians on the extreme left of the attack and, seeing them, knew in an instant that it was far better to surrender to the Virginians than to fall into the hands of the Half-King's warriors. The French wounded could neither raise their hands in surrender nor run, and so they fell, willy-nilly, under hatchets, clubs, and scalping knives of the warriors. Washington did nothing to stop the Indians. This, he understood, was how they fought, and he feared they would fight no other way. Besides, to be wounded in the woods pretty much always meant death sooner or later, and Washington certainly did not want to burden his command with care of the enemy's wounded; however, when the Half-King demanded the same bloody vengeance on the unhurt prisoners, all twenty-one of them, including Commissary La Force, Washington drew the line.

The fight had consumed no more than a quarter hour, cost few Virginia casualties, and inflicted total defeat on the French. The commander of the force, Joseph Coulon, sieur de Jumonville, was among the slain (the Half-King claimed credit), and La Force was a prisoner. To all appearances, George Washington's maiden battle was a signal triumph. One French soldier (his name was Mouceau) did get away, ran to Fort Duquesne, and there made a full report.

As Washington began marching his prisoners back to Great Meadows, one of their number protested that they were not common soldiers but diplomatic aides to M. Jumonville, who was—or *had* been—an ambassador of France, sent to the Ohio Country at the pleasure of Louis XV to serve notice on the English that they were trespassing on his royal domain. As members of an embassy, they must not be treated as prisoners of war—anymore than they should have been shot, killed, or scalped.

Washington did not record his reply to this protest, not in his diary nor in any letter to Dinwiddie. He may have responded with what he later told Dinwiddie and others—that ambassadors do not travel with large armed contingents, that they do not roam the wilderness in stealth, and that they do not hole up in secluded bowers. Had Jumonville traveled openly, he would have been granted safe passage. On May 29, Washington wrote to Dinwiddie, "In strict justice, they [the French prisoners] ought to be hanged as spies of the worst sort."

He was anxious that no stain dim his first battle and his first victory. For him, it was strictly personal, a point of honor. War? Act of war? He had no intention of starting a war. The French, he believed, had struck the first blow by taking the fort at the Forks of the Ohio. If anything, a war was already under way before the battle of the bower. That is not how historians have seen it. In 1822, the British diarist and letter writer Horace Walpole wrote in his *Memoirs of the Reign of King George II,* "The volley fired by a young Virginian in the backwoods of America set the world on fire." The French and Indian War had begun.

10

Fort Necessity

———❦———

WASHINGTON WAS HOLDING HIS prisoners at his Great
Meadows encampment when, on the morning of May 29, he was told
that they wanted to speak with him. When they asked "in what Manner I
looked upon them, whether as the Attendants of an Embassador, or as
Prisoners of War: I answered them it was in Quality of the Latter." Washington wrote to the lieutenant governor later that day to report the Half-
King's "Sense . . . that [the French] have bad Hearts, and that this [their
claim of being ambassadors] is a mere pretence, they never designed to
have come to us but in a hostile manner." Washington also explained to
Dinwiddie that, had he failed to attack, had "we [been] so foolish as to let
them go," the Half-King "never would assist us in taking another of
them." Thus Washington used the opinion of an Indian leader and the
importance of an Indian alliance to justify attacking a party of Frenchmen who claimed to be diplomats. When he went on to explain the importance of having captured Commissary La Force, he likewise framed
his justification in terms of relations with the Indians. To have let La
Force go "wd tend more to our disservice than [releasing] 50 other Men,
as he is a person whose active Spirit, leads him into all parlys [parleys—
diplomatic councils with Indians], and brought him acquainted with all

parts, add to this a perfect use of the Indian Tongue, and g[rea]t influence with the Indian." In effect, then, the French and Indian War was motivated by the business of territorial control but began as an English effort to hold Indian allies while preventing the French from acquiring them.

On May 30, Washington sent his prisoners, under a guard of two officers and twenty men, to Winchester, where Dinwiddie was waiting for them. He also sent along a letter to Dinwiddie, assuring him that the Half-King, emboldened by the battle, was now a firm ally and that he "has declar'd to send" the scalps of the Frenchmen just slain in battle, along with a hatchet, as a call to arms "to all the Nations of Indian's in union with" the Iroquois. He "promis'd me to send down the River for all the Mingo's & Shawnesse to our camp, where I expect him to Morrow with 30 or 40 Men."

In the meantime, however, Washington "expect[ed] every hour to be attackd and by unequal number's, which I must withstand if there is 5 to 1 or else I fear the Consequence will be we shall loose [lose] the Indians if we suffer ourselves to be drove Back." So he at last set his men to work improving his defenses at Great Meadows. No longer content to rely on the cover provided by a pair of gullies, he began construction on May 31 of what he described as "a Pallisado'd Fort." With remarkable frankness, he christened the resulting structure "Fort Necessity" when it was completed on June 3. The Half-King was singularly unimpressed, dismissing it later as "that little thing upon the Meadow." John B. W. Shaw, a member of the Virginia regiment at Great Meadows, left the most detailed description: "There was at this Place a Small Stocado Fort made in a Circular form round a Small House that Stood in the Middle of it to keep our Provisions and Ammunition in, And was cover'd with Bark and some Skins, and might be about fourteen feet Square, and the Walls of the Fort might be eight feet Distance from the said House all Round." In 1759, Colonel James Burd, who commanded two hundred men clearing a road from Chestnut Ridge to Redstone Creek, noted in his diary on September 10 that he "saw Col. Washington's fort, which was called Fort

Necessity. It is a small circular stockade, with a small house in the center; on the outside is a small ditch goes around it about 8 yards from the stockade. It is situate in a narrow part of the meadows commanded by three points of woods. There is a small run of water just by it."

Modern archaeologists have concluded that the stockade was indeed circular and quite small at 53 feet in diameter, with an overall perimeter circumference of 168 feet. The entrance, located on the southwest sector of the circle, was 3.5 feet wide. Archaeologists were able to locate what Burd called the "small ditch," which they determined was not a trench but two sets of mounded earthworks bracketing the fort—rather like angle brackets, with rounded points—on its east and west sides. These mounds were designed to provide cover for men shooting from a kneeling position.

Frontier stockades were usually triangular or diamond shaped, so the layout of Fort Necessity was unusual, if not unique. The conventional triangle or diamond floor plan was a simplification of the classic European pentagonal bastion and was designed to allow some opportunity for the members of the garrison to mount effective crossfire against attackers. In contrast, the strange circular plan Washington chose made it difficult for his men to concentrate their fire in any particular direction. On the other hand, it was probably easier to build for men in a hurry, requiring both less work and less material. Besides, the angle-bracket-shaped earthwork mounds did provide acute angles that allowed for good defensive crossfire, albeit from more exposed positions. Washington doubtless intended the fight to begin from these earthworks, outside of the fort itself, the stockade functioning to protect ammunition and to serve as a fallback position. That may be why it was so small. It was a last resort.

The more serious weakness of Fort Necessity was its situation (as Burd wrote) "in a narrow part of the meadows commanded by three points of woods." By "points of woods," Burd meant wooded points—hills with trees on them, one of which was no more than sixty yards from the stockade, easily within accurate and effective musket range. The tactical principle of defending from high ground is basic, yet Washington violated it by placing his fort below the level of any potential attack. It was a rookie mistake.

Late on June 2, the thirty-man escort Washington had sent with the Half-King to gather more warriors returned with some eighty Indians— not just fighters, however, but their families, including numerous women and children. Reporting to Dinwiddie, Washington tried to put this in the best light by relaying to him the Half-King's assurances that Big Kettle, a Seneca chief to whom he had spoken, pledged the "good Intentions" of most of the Indians in the Ohio Country to assist "the 6 Nations [the Iroquois League] and their Brother's the English agt [against] the French." According to the Half-King, Big Kettle was waiting "only . . . to see us begin."

The Half-King, Washington wrote, also sent Monactaoocha to Logstown "with 4 French Scalps two of which was to be sent to the Wyandotts &ca and the other two to the 6 Nations telling them that the French had trickd them out of their Lands for which with their Brother's the English [they] joyn'd hand in hand . . . for that they int[en]d with their Brothers to drive the French beyond the Lakes." According to Washington, this strong message—a message of lives taken in the battle he had just won—would "draw all the Indians from Ohio" into the English camp.

Say what he would about the developing Indian alliance, the fact was that, with all the women and children about, Washington now had many mouths to feed. Moreover, on June 9, the first of the promised reinforcements arrived at Great Meadows—three companies of the Virginia Regiment under the command of Major George Muse, 181 soldiers in all. They brought with them nine swivel guns—small cannon—but very little in the way of provisions. So the specter of hunger loomed that much larger. On the next day, June 10, Washington complained to Dinwiddie that "we have been extreamly ill used by Major Carlyle's Deputys." The trader and merchant John Carlyle was the expedition's commissary and had six "deputies" under contract to supply provisions.

For the acute shortages he was now experiencing, Washington blamed them rather than Carlyle himself because "he is a Gentleman," so must have been "deceiv'd, and we have suffer'd by those under him." As of June 10, Washington noted that Fort Necessity had "not Provision's of any sort in the Camp to serve us 2 Days."

The same day that he sent Dinwiddie the letter about the shortage of provisions, he welcomed into camp Christopher Gist. It must have been a relief to shake hands again with a reliable trader—but Gist brought the shocking news that Colonel Joshua Fry, Washington's commanding officer, was dead, killed by a fall from his horse. This put twenty-two-year-old Washington in command of the entire English field expedition to save the Ohio frontier for the Ohio Company and its investors—not to mention for the British Empire.

Major Muse brought more than reinforcements. His Indian interpreter, Andrew Montour, was famous throughout the English frontier. His father was the Oneida sachem Carondawana ("Big Tree"), and his mother the daughter of a Huron woman and a French trader (named Montour). Andrew Montour thus embodied the hybrid ethnic identity that characterized Franco-Indian civilization in North America but was apparently quite loyal to the English, a dedication he had imbibed from his mother, popularly called "Madame Montour." He lived among the Iroquois and was employed by the colonial government of Pennsylvania colony as an interpreter and commercial agent. A prosperous fur trader, Andrew Montour was fluent in French, English, and several Indian languages. To all appearances he was the very model of a blended Euro-American/Native American man, his face distinctly European but painted in the Iroquois manner. His attire combined elements of Euro-American and Native American garb, which the Moravian mission leader Count Nicholas Ludwig von Zinzendorf, founder of the Pennsylvania town of Bethlehem, described as consisting of "a brown broadcloth coat, a scarlet damaskin lapel waistcoat, breeches over which his shirt hung, a black cordovan neckerchief decked with silver bugles, shoes and stockings and a hat. His ears were hung with pendants of brass and other wires plaited together like the handle of a basket." Dinwiddie had commissioned Montour to recruit and command a force of two hundred Indians, and although Washington was grateful for another interpreter and adviser on dealing with Indians, he was also well aware that many on the frontier criticized Montour for consistently delivering less than he promised when it came to exercising influence on the Indians.

Also designed to help Washington in his dealings with the Indians was a medal Dinwiddie had sent, stamped with the lieutenant governor's likeness. Washington was to wear it around his neck as a token of Dinwiddie's confidence in him and as a sign to the Indians that he spoke for the highest authority in Virginia. Muse also presented Washington with a letter from Dinwiddie promoting him to full colonel and commander of the Virginia Regiment. The lieutenant governor had named his friend Colonel James Innes to overall command of all the forces. To this Washington had no objection, but he bridled at Dinwiddie's instructions concerning the officers of the independent companies, who, the governor explained, "having their Commos. [commissions] sign'd by His M[ajest]y imagine they claim a distinguish'd rank & being long trained in Arms expect suitable regards. You will therefore consult & agree with Yr Officers to shew them particular marks of Esteem, which will avoid such Causes of Uneasiness as otherwise might obstruct His Majesty's Service wherein All are alike engag'd." This confirmed Washington's fears that he, now a full colonial *colonel,* would be subordinate to James Mackay, who commanded an independent company as a mere *captain.* "Your Honour may depend," Washington replied to Dinwiddie on June 10, "I shall myself, and will endeavour to make my Officer's shew Captn McKay all the respect due to his Rank & merit." Then he added, "But should have been particularly oblig'd if your Honour had declar'd whether he was under my Command, or Independent of it."

Late on June 10, Washington's Indian scouts raised the alarm: *The French were coming.* It looked as if a night battle were imminent, and

Washington, along with his entire command, stayed wide awake. The attack failed to materialize, though, and at daybreak on June 11 he sent out another scouting party. Two of the scouts returned on the morning of the twelfth to report having seen some French troops in the woods— but only a few. Soon, however, came additional reports of about ninety Frenchmen nearby. Ordering Muse to man the swivel guns, he prepared to ride out at the head of 130 colonial troops and thirty Indians, intending to capture the French detachment. Before setting out, however, he learned that this latest intelligence had been mistranslated. There were not *ninety* French soldiers but *nine* French deserters, who had been seen straggling toward Great Meadows. Washington sent Montour to lead a detachment of Indians to bring them in. At the same time, he sent off a new "express" to Carlyle yet again demanding provisions and ammunition.

When the deserters were marched in, they reported that "more than One Hundred Soldiers were only waiting for a favourable Opportunity to come and join [battle with] us; that M. *de Contrecour* expected a Reinforcement of Four Hundred Men; that the Fort [Duquesne] was compleated; and its Artillery a shelter to its Front and Gates; that there was a double Pallisadoe next to the Water; that they have only eight small Pieces of Cannon; and know what Number of Men we are."

Five hundred men were ready to attack from a very well furnished fort. This was hardly welcome news to the commander of no more than four hundred men with little ammunition and less food, sheltered by nothing more than a small circular stockade. Yet more alarming than the five-to-four advantage of the French was the added intelligence that "the *Delaware* and *Shawanese* had taken up the Hatchet against us." In response to this, Washington instantly "resolved to invite those two Nations [the Delaware and the Shawnee] to come to a Council at Mr. *Gist's*. Sent for that Purpose Messengers and Wampum." He sincerely believed he could talk them out of turning against the English. Indeed, on June 13, Washington noted that he also "Perswaded the Deserters to write [a] Letter, to those of their Companions who had an Inclination to Desert." So not only did he intend to try to talk French-allied Indians into switching sides, he believed he could use a handful of French deserters to persuade their countrymen to give up the fight as well.

Probably on June 14, Captain Mackay arrived with the "independent company" of British regulars from South Carolina. Washington had been dreading this arrival even more than the French onslaught.

Born and raised in Scotland (he was the son of a military officer, Hugh Mackay, laird of Scoury), James Mackay immigrated to Georgia with no less a personage than the colony's founder, James Oglethorpe. For some fifteen years, he had fought Indians on the Georgia frontier and (as Washington had suspected) was in no mood to take orders from a provincial colonel. Although he responded to Washington's welcome most politely, he cleared a campsite entirely apart from that of Washington and his men. If this was meant as a provocation, Washington refused to take the bait. He did not presume to inspect either the camp or the independent company; however, he did send to Mackay the "parole and countersign," the secret password and acknowledgment used in Washington's command to prevent enemy infiltration. Mackay refused to receive either, however, explaining that he did not deem it proper to accept these from a provincial colonel because the independent company was a royal force. While Mackay did not demand that Washington be subordinate to him, he nevertheless asserted his separate and sovereign command over the king's forces. To Dinwiddie, Washington wrote on June 15 that "for want of proper Instructions from your Honour I am much at a loss to know how to act, or proceed in regard to [Mackay's] company," protesting that the independent company was bound to "impede the Service [rather] than forward it, for having Commissions from the King they look upon themselves as a distinct Body, and will not incorporate and do duty as our Men—but keep separate Guards, Incamp separate &ca." He assured Dinwiddie that he had "not offer'd to controul [Mackay] in anything, or shewd that I claimd a superior Command, but in giving the Parrole & Countersign which must be the same in an Army consisting of 10 Different Nation's, to distinguish Friends from Foes—He knows the necessity of this, yet does not think he is to receive it from me." He put the question to Dinwiddie: "Am I to Issue these order's to a

Company? or is an Independent Captn to prescribe Rules to the Virginia Regiment? . . . It must be known who is to Command before order's will be observ'd."

Perhaps it was the perceived necessity of asserting the primacy of his command authority that prompted Washington to lead his men out of Fort Necessity to resume clearing the road to Redstone Creek. What else can explain his decision to leave Fort Necessity virtually undefended when he knew that five hundred Frenchmen were nearby? If he hoped to put the men of the independent company to work alongside his soldiers, Washington was quickly disappointed. Captain Mackay refused to set his men to labor unless Washington agreed to authorize regular British army daily pay of one shilling (sterling) for this work. When Washington explained how the disparity between this pay and the mere eight pence his soldiers received would affect morale, Mackay did not disagree but protested that he had no authority to order his men to work for less. So on June 16, Washington left the independent company in camp as he led three hundred Virginians out of Fort Necessity to work on the Redstone Creek road.

Even as he labored toward Redstone on June 17, Washington sent an "express" to the "*Half-King,* in order to perswade him to send a Message to the *Loups* [the Delaware]; which he did." On June 18, he and his men reached Gist's settlement, where they were met by "eight *Mingoes,*" a small tribe associated with Iroquois and sometimes called the Ohio Seneca, who informed Washington that a "Council must be held" and proclaimed their desire to ally themselves with the English, even though the tribe was situated "amongst the *French*" and "complied with some of their Customs."

It was tempting to welcome this news, but to Washington it sounded too good to be true, and he suspected a French trick. He therefore delayed negotiating with the Mingoes "until the Arrival of the *Half-King.*" That worthy arrived later in the day, whereupon Washington convened a grand council that included "several of the *Six Nations* [Iroquois], *Loups and Shawanese,* to the Number of Forty."

Such councils were the chief vehicle of Anglo-Indian diplomacy. They were part hard-nosed negotiation and part elaborately tedious ritual. The one that began on June 18 dragged on until June 21 and, like all such occasions, consisted of a dreary procession of formal speeches and formal responses, long-winded in themselves, then subject to stammeringly imperfect translation. For Washington, the sum and substance was his declaration that he and the other English had come to fight alongside the Iroquois and the Delaware. He invited the Indian men to send their women and children to the English settlements, where they would be protected in the coming combat. In the end, the result seemed to be everything Washington could have hoped for. Not only did the Iroquois *and* the Delaware pledge to refrain from taking up the hatchet against the English, they also, more positively, renewed their standing pledge of allegiance. Next, turning to Gist, Washington was also able to obtain his promise that the desperately needed provisions would be forthcoming.

This left only the eight Mingoes to deal with. They "had told me there were Sixteen Hundred *French*, and Seven Hundred *Indians* on their March, to reinforce those at the Garrison" of Fort Duquesne. Washington believed this "News to be only Soldiers Discourse"—exaggerated rumor—or perhaps it was an outright Mingo lie. He accordingly "perswaded the *Half King* to send three of his Men to inquire into the Truth of it." They were "sent in a secret Manner, before the Council broke up, and had Orders to go to the Fort [Duquesne], and get what Information they could from all the *Indians* they should meet, and if there was any News worth while, one of them should return, and the other two continue their Rout[e] as far as [the French trading settlement of] *Venango* . . . in order to obtain a perfect Knowledge of every Thing."

Like the French, Washington had begun using Indians as spies. They were an obvious choice for this work, since they could travel more or less freely between French and English forts, camps, and settlements. Assuming that this was also how the French were using the Mingoes—whom Washington now referred to as "treacherous Devils"—the colonel sent them packing as soon as the council had broken up, "though not without some Tale ready prepared to amuse the *French*, which may be of Service to make our own Designs succeed." He filled their ears with what today would be called "disinformation," telling them that "we intended to keep on [advancing] across the Woods as far as the Fort [Duquesne], falling the Trees, &c. [but that] we were waiting here for the Reinforcement which was coming to us, our Artillery, and our Waggons to accompany us there." In this way, he gave them a spectacularly inflated picture of English strength. No sooner did the Mingoes leave than Washington continued work on the road.

Frontier diplomacy was almost always fluid. Both the Euro-Americans and Native Americans readily shifted allegiances and casually broke promises whenever it seemed advantageous to do so. Washington must have been pleased, therefore, that the alliance with the Half-King, founded on fur-trading relations that went back to the preceding century, had been so happily confirmed. Yet he did not have long to bask in the warmth of this comfortable conclusion. A Delaware chief, second in diplomatic influence on the frontier only to the Half-King himself, suddenly told Washington that the Delaware would not camp at Great Meadows, near Fort Necessity. He did allow that warriors *might* be persuaded to side with the Virginians if it came to a fight with the French, but he made no promises. As for the Shawnee, who had forthrightly declared their allegiance to the English at the council just concluded, they drifted wordlessly away.

Washington looked, then, to the Half-King, having assumed that he and his warriors would accompany the Virginia regiment as it hacked out the Redstone road. Instead, they withdrew to their camp at Great Meadows immediately after the council ended. One of the Iroquois party told Washington that the Half-King *might* join him on the progress toward Redstone Creek if Washington sent him wampum and a proper speech inviting him to join in greeting Monacatoocha, who was believed to be en route to Washington's position. On the evening of June 25, however, only three of the Half-King's warriors caught up with Washington. They handed him a message from Croghan "informing me what Pains he was at to perswade any *Indians* to come to us." Croghan mentioned that the Half-King really did want to join Washington but was now laid up nursing an injury.

The council, which had seemed a triumph, now looked to have been a complete failure. Washington's confidence in both Montour and Croghan melted away. What the critics said of Montour could be applied to Croghan as well. Both men talked much about the influence they wielded over the Indians, but that now seemed like just so much talk.

Washington pondered what seemed to him the imminent collapse of vital Indian alliances. He concluded that the root of the problem was entirely material. Loyalty, as he saw it, was a product of self-interest, and, for Indians and Euro-Americans alike, self-interest was essentially a matter of commerce. All military and political agreements between Euro-Americans and Native Americans were based on trade and, quite properly, were therefore solemnized by the earnest of gifts. These presents were symbolic tokens, but they were also eagerly sought-after merchandise, including rifles, ammunition, powder, and clothing. From the outset of his mission, Washington had been underfunded by the parsimonious House of Burgesses. Accordingly, his stock of presents was meager, and the new supply of gifts he had hoped to receive along with other provisions failed to arrive in time for the council. As Washington now saw it, the Indians had interpreted the poverty of his presents not as a mere failure of courtesy but as an indicator of the general poverty of the English—and who wants to do business with the poor?

If there was an upside to this precarious situation, it was that George Washington was learning the lessons of waging war on a shoestring. They would serve him well in the American Revolution—but, of course, that was more than twenty years in a future of which he knew nothing. For now, the situation was this: The Delaware and the Shawnee were gone, and the Iroquois of the Half-King, though camped at Great Meadows, showed hardly any inclination to join in a fight against the French.

Reducing his men's rations to carefully metered doles of parched corn supplemented by what little stringy meat could be cut from the expedition's few remaining emaciated cattle, he ordered his command to work faster in pushing the road to Redstone. He wanted to build there something more formidable than Fort Necessity, a fort that would give him a fighting chance to hold out until reinforcements could arrive. Then, properly reinforced, he intended to go on the offensive and retake Fort Duquesne.

The French had other ideas. Either on the night of June 27 or the next morning, Chief Monacatoocha sent a message to Washington, warning him that he had personally seen the arrival of reinforcements at Fort Duquesne and had overheard the French say they were going to attack Washington and his command with a mixed force of eight hundred white soldiers and four hundred Indians. Monacatoocha was an old ally, whose information jibed with what the French deserters had said earlier. Believing that he was about to be attacked, Washington convened his officers in a council of war. They decided to combine all available forces, including Mackay's independent company, for a stand at Gist's settlement, which is where the swivel guns had been deposited. Yet no sooner did Washington reach Gist's than he discovered that the Indians did not want to fight there. They warned the colonel that they would go their own way unless the force withdrew back to Fort Necessity on Great Meadows, where the Half-King and his warriors were still camped. Though loath to yield ground to the French, Washington decided to comply, not just to retain the warriors but because Fort Necessity was closer to promised supplies and because the two routes along which the French would have to advance from Fort Duquesne converged at Great Meadows, which meant that their approach would be detected no matter what route they used.

The only problem was that the troops had been hungry when Washington led them out of Fort Necessity and put them to work on the road to Redstone. Now, according to his own minutes of the council of war, they were in a "Starving Condition," having "wanted meat & Bread for Six days already." Yet he ordered them to march, and because he had already sent back the teams and wagons that had hauled the swivel guns and other baggage, those starving soldiers would have to pull the guns themselves and do so through thirteen wilderness miles. Subsisting on parched corn and being obliged to transform themselves into beasts of burden, the men found the way back a trail of agony. Perhaps Washington spurred them on with promises of the decent meal that surely would by now be waiting for them at Fort Necessity. Yet when they finally stumbled into the fort on July 1, the men discovered the storehouse as empty as ever.

Washington considered retreating closer to the English settlements, thereby yielding yet more of the Ohio Country to the French. Reasoning, however, that his men were too weak to haul the swivel guns any farther—which would therefore have to be abandoned to the French— and that, in fact, they might be too weak even to walk any farther, he decided to hold Fort Necessity and hope for the timely arrival of rein- forcements. Accordingly, he ordered soldiers to fell trees to strengthen the stockade and directed that the trenches outside the fort's wall be ex- tended past the small branch that ran nearby. This would ensure that, even under fire and siege, his men, protected by a mound of earthworks, would still be able to fetch water.

The Half-King was not impressed by these preparations. The fort was built on bottom land, which meant that it was surrounded by high ground, which gave any attacker a great advantage, especially since that high ground was wooded—so provided both cover and concealment— and was well within musket range.

By July 2, the Half-King and the warriors who had camped with him left. As the sachem later explained to Conrad Weiser, Washington, "a good-natured man but [without] experience," refused to "take Advice from the Indians." In particular, "he lay at [Great Meadows] from one full Moon to the other and made no Fortifications at all, but that little thing upon the Meadow"—that is, Fort Necessity. Moreover, the Half-King observed, Washington had placed the fort "where he thought the French would come up to him in open Field," whereas, had he followed the Half-King's advice concerning the placement of the fort, "he would certainly have beat the French off." (Just what that advice was, we do not know.)

Assessing the battle after it was over, the Half-King remarked that "the French had acted as great Cowards, and the English as Fools" at

Great Meadows. He had left before the fight, as "did other Indians . . . because Col. Washington would never listen to them, but was always driving them on to fight by his Directions."

Washington was more skilled in his dealings with Indians than many of his fellow Virginians were and was far more effective than most regular British military leaders; however, not only was he reluctant to follow their advice, he failed to appreciate the pragmatic sophistication of Indian diplomacy. Earlier, he had told the Half-King that the "only motive" the English had in fighting the French was "to put you again in possession of your lands, and to take care of your wives and children, to dispossess the French, to maintain your rights and to secure the whole country for you; for these very ends are the English arms now employed." Apparently, he sincerely believed that the sachem had swallowed this disingenuous speech whole, and now the Half-King's departure seemed to him a betrayal.

The fact was that the Half-King's first loyalty was to his people's self-interest, and he must have understood that Washington's promises, presented as selfless, were actually motivated by English self-interest. To put his life and the lives of his people in the hands of a young Virginian who was counting on a puny, poorly sited fort to withstand an attack by superior numbers, the Half-King knew, was a bad bargain. So he left.

Washington's lapse of frontier diplomacy was both typical of and the product of a more universal failure of Anglo-Indian diplomacy. He had inherited the general English refusal to deal with the Indians as politically, socially, and economically sophisticated individuals. In the long term, this would greatly weaken the British position in the French and Indian War. In the short term, it left George Washington without the reconnaissance assets he had come to rely on. During the night of July 2–3, therefore, he had to send out a reconnoitering party. In addition, he detached men to serve as outlying pickets to provide advance warning of the approach of the French. His ranks, already thinned by hunger, exhaustion, privation, and sickness, were rendered even thinner by the absence of those out reconnoitering. When the sun set on July 2, he counted just 284 men fit for duty.

. . .

First light, July 3: a single musket shot, followed by a call for help from one of Washington's sentinels. He had been shot in the heel. The colonel ordered his men to arms.

Instead of an onslaught of Frenchmen, however, came a torrent of rain. Since Fort Necessity occupied the lowest point in a surrounding marsh, it rapidly became a basin, the defensive trenches filling with water in which the men had no choice but to crouch, waiting for the assault. At nine in the morning, some five soaked hours after Washington had issued his order to arms, the sentinels began sending reports. One breathless Virginian said the French and Indians were on the march, just four miles off—and all of them naked! A second, rather less hysterical report estimated nine hundred French regulars approaching from the Monongahela.

Writing about the events a year or two after they happened, George Washington noted that the Battle of Fort Necessity began when a sentinel fired his musket at about ten; however, in his report of July 19 to Dinwiddie, Washington put the shot at eleven o'clock. Whatever the hour, it was the first of several shots that (Washington reported to Dinwiddie) cut down three Frenchmen in quick succession. The opening volleys, according to Washington, brought down a "fire upon us, at about 600 Yards Distance." Fire from so far away—at least six times the effective range of eighteenth-century muskets—Washington believed was "only an Artifice to intimidate, or draw our Fire from us." Resolving not to take the bait, he ordered his men to refrain from returning the French "Salute" until the enemy was nearer.

Washington reported to Dinwiddie that the French advanced "in a very irregular Manner," an assessment corroborated by the French commander himself, Captain Louis Coulon de Villiers, who admitted in a report to his own superiors that he had ordered his men to fire too soon. The older brother of Jumonville, the "ambassador" killed in the Battle of the Bower, Coulon de Villiers was probably overeager for vengeance. Yet the more serious mistake was Washington's failure to capitalize on Coulon de Villiers's tactical blunder. We know that he had deployed a number of his men in the open field in advance of his trenches. They should have fired on the exposed French flank as soon as Coulon de Villiers had paused to commence firing. Instead, the French were permitted to advance to "another Point of Woods, about 60 Yards off, and from thence [make] a second Discharge." In other words, Washington made little effort to hold the French at a distance, and he instead ordered his men to retreat to the trenches.

Once they were entrenched, Washington (according to his report to Dinwiddie) "gave Orders to fire, which was done with great Alacrity and Undauntedness."

The "Undauntedness" Washington reported was flatly contradicted by the diary of one Landon Carter, a well-to-do planter who served in the Virginia Regiment. He noted that Washington's second in command, Lieutenant Colonel George Muse, "instead of bringing up the 2d division to make the Attack with the first, . . . marched them or rather frightened them back to the trenches, so that the Colo. [that is, Captain Mackay] at the head of the Carolina Independent Company was greatly exposed to the French Fire and were forced to retire to the same trenches, where they were galled on All sides by 1,100 French and Indians who never came to an Open ground but fired from behind trees." It was this "galling fire"—Washington's adjective echoes Carter's verb—from "every little rising, tree, stump, stone and bush" that wore down the defenders of Fort Necessity.

"We continued this unequal Fight, with an Enemy sheltered behind the Trees, ourselves without Shelter, in Trenches full of Water, in a settled Rain, and the Enemy galling us on all Sides incessantly from the Woods," Washington reported to Dinwiddie, in effect describing how he and his men were caught in a trap of his own making.

Built in a swamp, Fort Necessity provided only wet misery, no real shelter. Perhaps *this* is what the Half-King had tried to talk him out of. The Half-King had also called the French cowards—presumably because they failed to storm the fort. Yet with his quarry trapped in a diminutive stockade surrounded by woods and now practically underwater, what reason did Coulon de Villiers have to risk his men in a charge across an open field? After all, Washington and his command weren't going anywhere.

"The Enemy," Washington wrote, "deprived us of all our Creatures; by killing, in the Beginning of the Engagement, our Horses, Cattle, and every living Thing they could, even to the very Dogs." The last of the meat shot away, together with the remaining means of transportation, the jaws of the trap clamped down harder. Nevertheless, Washington kept his men in the fight all day. Then, at about eight in the evening, came a call from the woods: *"Voulez-vous parler?"*

No, Washington replied.

The answer was motivated by more than unthinking defiance. Why, he asked himself, would the commander of so vastly superior a force be the first to call for a parley? There was only one reason. The Frenchman wanted to get a look behind the stockade. He wanted to count heads before coming in for the kill. Washington was not about to let that happen, but a short time later, when Coulon de Villiers asked Washington to send an officer to *him* under a guarantee of safe conduct, Washington reconsidered. As the din of musketry had died down, he could now clearly hear the cries and moans of the wounded, and he could see that more than a third of the men who had been fit for fighting now lay dead or wounded. The rain, ceaseless, had soaked powder and cartridges. Cattle? Dead. Horses? Dead. Provisions remaining? Two bags of flour and a bit of bacon. Rum, he noted, was to be had in plenty, the most recent supply train having brought a large supply of it to be used as presents for the Indians. With a lull in the shooting, the soldiers occupied themselves drowning their sorrows in it. It occurred to the colonel that most of them would not be fit to fight again anytime soon. He called up his two French-speaking troops, Jacob Van Braam and a scout named William La Péronie, and sent them into the woods, into the rain, into the ranks of the French.

La Péronie and Van Braam spent little time in conference with the enemy before returning to Fort Necessity. The French, they said, were willing to allow the English to withdraw from Fort Necessity and return to Virginia. Washington was defeated, but at least he and his men would not be made prisoners. Though not one to look a gift horse in the mouth, he sent La Péronie and Van Braam back to the French to obtain more particulars. On this second foray, La Péronie was somehow seriously wounded, leaving Van Braam, whose first language was Dutch, second language French, and third English, to conduct the parley on his own. Coulon de Villiers recorded in his journal what he said to the Dutchman:

> I sent M. *le Mercier* to receive [Van Braam], and I went to the Meadow, where I told him, that as we were not at War, we were very willing to save them from the Cruelties to which they exposed themselves, on Account of the *Indians*; but if they were stubborn, we would take away from them all Hopes of escaping; that we consented to be favourable to them at present, *as we were come only to revenge my Brother's Assassination,* and to oblige them to quit the Lands of the King our Master; . . . We considered that . . . it was not proper to make Prisoners in a Time of Peace.

Around midnight, Van Braam returned to Washington with the *"Capitulation,"* the surrender document. The text, scrawled in a barely legible hand, was runny and blurred with the incessant rain. Van Braam translated it for Washington, who signed it. In modern translation, the document begins:

> As our Intentions have never been to trouble the Peace and good Harmony subsisting between the two Princes in Amity, but only to revenge the Assassination [*seulement de venger L'assasin*] committed on one of our Officers, bearer of a Summons, as also on his Escorte, and to hinder any Establishment on the Lands of the Dominions of the King my Master: Upon these Considerations, we are willing to shew Favour to all the English who are in the said Fort.

Although it goes on to make a second mention of the "Assassination of M. *de Jumonville* [l'assasinat du Sr. de Jumonville]," only later, after the document had been signed and Washington and the surviving members of his command were on the march back to Virginia, did some officer, a man who possessed at least a rudimentary reading knowledge of French, review the *Capitulation* and point out to Washington the words *l'assassin* and *l'assassinat*.

George Washington had confessed himself an assassin. The self-accusation—Washington blamed Van Braam for having translated the words as "loss" or "death"—would haunt the young colonel for some time, although mostly in his own mind rather than in the opinion of others. For when he reached Williamsburg, on July 17, he was generally greeted as a hero. His fame even reached London, where the *Gentleman's Magazine* for July 1754 reproduced the letter to his brother, wherein he wrote of "something charming in the sound" of bullets as he fought the Battle of the Bower. King George II reportedly read the article and remarked that Washington would not have found the sound of bullets quite so charming "if he had been used to hear many."

Before long, there would be many, very many. Few battles, no matter how great or small, have been of more consequence than that at Great Meadows. Here began in earnest the French and Indian War, which was in turn the commencement and North American theater of the cataclysmic Seven Years' War, truly the first "world" war, engulfing Europe, India, the Caribbean, and vast portions of the Atlantic Ocean, killing some 900,000 combatants, savagely recarving the political contours of the planet, and setting the colonial stage for a war of independence.

11

Mercenary War

—◆—

THE FRENCH AND INDIAN War started with George Washington, in a Pennsylvania swamp, but it was the culmination of nearly two centuries of conflicting *imperial* aspirations driven most immediately by conflicting *commercial* ambitions plus commercial and military relations between the competing French and English and their Indian clients, trading partners, allies, rivals, and enemies. On Washington's return from Great Meadows, Lieutenant Governor Dinwiddie was eager to put the young officer in command of a new expedition but, on further consideration, decided to wait for help from the crown in the form of some regiments of British regulars. He reported Washington's two battles to the authority he deemed could be most helpful in getting him the soldiers he wanted. It was not a member of the royal cabinet or an influential member of Parliament but the Lords Commissioners of Trade and Foreign Plantations—more familiarly called the Board of Trade—a body of eight paid commissioners in London that had been formed in 1696 by King William III not to create empire but to promote trade in the American plantations and elsewhere. To these men of commerce, Dinwiddie collectively characterized the battles as a "small Engagement, conducted with Judgment by the Officers, and great Bravery by our few Forces," but went on to appeal for assistance in mounting a major offensive to evict the French. The Board of Trade made its recommendation to King George II, who tasked his son the Duke of Cumberland, as captain general of the army, to draw up plans for ousting the French from North America once and for all.

Cumberland drafted a four-pronged assault against everything France claimed on the continent. The main prong would consist of two regular British infantry regiments (plus provincials and whatever Indian allies could be recruited along the way) to follow Washington's route to the Forks of the Ohio. This task force was to capture and garrison Fort Duquesne. The other three units would strike Nova Scotia, the Niagara forts on Lake Ontario, and the forts on Lake Champlain. Cumberland was confident that if all of these forts were taken, the French would no longer have any hold on the Ohio Valley.

Major General Edward Braddock was tapped to sail to America in command of the Fort Duquesne expedition. At sixty, he was old, but not unusually so for a regular British general officer. Although he had seen battle for some four decades, he had never fought outside of Europe and therefore was ignorant of the nature of wilderness warfare. This led him to dismiss his enemy as a rabble of Frenchmen, backwoods Canadians, and savage Indians, none of whom, he believed, could possibly stand up to well-drilled regular British soldiers. He thought of the Virginia militia and other "provincials," as well as their Indian "auxiliaries," in much the same way. He expected them to be more of a hindrance than a help. These attitudes were typical of the regular British military of the time but may well have been even more pronounced in Braddock. There is no question that he was a courageous field officer, but, as Monacatoocha characterized him, he was intolerant of any judgment that differed from his. He was full of "pride and ignorance," Monacatoocha testified to the Pennsylvania Council after Braddock's single cataclysmic engagement in the French and Indian War, "a bad man when he was alive; he looked upon us as dogs, and would never hear anything what was said to him. . . . He never appeared pleased with us and that was the reason that a great many of our Warriors left him and would not be under his Command."

In sending Braddock to America, the Duke of Cumberland offered neither his best nor his worst officer, but the two units he gave Braddock to command, the 44th and the 48th Regiments of Foot, were decidedly second string. They were pulled from garrison duty in Ireland. That unruly island was, apart from North America, the wildest province of the British Empire, so perhaps Cumberland believed he was sending his most suitable soldiers; however, no army puts its best troops in garrison posts. Braddock may have sought to compensate for the weakness of his infantry by transporting with him a remarkably large array of artillery: four 12-pounder cannon, six 6-pounders, four 8-inch howitzers, and fifteen Coehorn mortars. If such compensation was his motive, it showed a certain tactical savvy; however, the inclusion of the weighty, cumbersome Coehorns at the same time showed how little he knew of the field into which he was being sent. Firing a heavy projectile in a high trajectory, the Coehorn was intended to be used against fortifications in siege operations. Because Braddock was told that he was to take a fort, he brought along the kind of siege artillery that would be used against the forts he knew in Europe, weapons intended to batter down stone walls or fly above such walls to the structures and personnel within them. Both the Coehorns and the heavy howitzers—also high-trajectory weapons—were ridiculous overkill for the taking of a frontier stockade and would require a Herculean labor to transport through a nearly trackless wilderness. Indeed, Braddock's artillery train necessitated construction of a major road.

Braddock, his regiments, and his hardware set sail in January 1755 and arrived in Virginia on February 20. Six weeks of stormy sea passage in close quarters with his army did not mellow the irascible commander. He was stunned, when he disembarked, to find the Virginians going about their business as usual, propelled by no sense of urgency, let alone zeal for the empire. It was his first lesson in North American colonial politics. The Tidewater was disconnected from the Piedmont, the coastal establishment out of touch with the frontier. Impatient by nature, Braddock fumed. The colonies were at war! Where was the stockpiling of arms? The recruiting of regiments? The drilling of companies? He peremptorily demanded an audience with Dinwiddie.

The lieutenant governor presented Braddock with a remarkably detailed map and plan of his assigned objective. When Washington, in defeat, marched out of Fort Necessity, he left with Coulon de Villiers one Captain Robert Stobo, who was to serve as hostage against the promised return of the prisoners Washington had taken at the Battle of the Bower and sent to Dinwiddie at Winchester. Having been told by Washington that the prisoners were really spies who, if anything, deserved shooting, and having been apprised (also by Washington) of the great importance of one prisoner in particular, Commissary La Force, Dinwiddie was loath to release them. Stobo, therefore, remained a hostage. He used his time in captivity most productively, however, drawing a detailed plan of Fort Duquesene, which he managed to smuggle to Williamsburg in a packet of letters. Dinwiddie was able to show Braddock that the fort was now garrisoned by just four hundred men, not the eleven hundred or so reported earlier.

Braddock brought with him two thousand British regulars, who were to be supplemented by nine hundred provincials, which gave him a spectacular numerical advantage. Dinwiddie or someone else in the conference pointed out, however, that capturing Fort Duquesne was less of a problem than getting to Fort Duquesne. That is when the subject of George Washington came up. The young officer, Dinwiddie said, knew the Alleghenies firsthand and had already fought the French—twice. In fact, Braddock had already heard of Washington because Washington himself had wasted no time in dashing off a letter congratulating Braddock on his safe arrival in Virginia. Obviously, he wanted the general to know who he was—and yet, when it came down to it, he was ambivalent about serving with him. More than likely, his experience with Captain Mackay and the independent company had left him with a bad taste. He understood that his provincial rank would make him inferior to one of the king's majors, and while a colonial colonel was theoretically accepted as equal to a regular captain, those captains would, in practice, look down upon him as well.

Before accepting an appointment with Braddock, Washington shared his concerns with Dinwiddie, who assured him that he had a solution.

Dinwiddie spoke to Braddock about Washington's misgivings. The lieutenant governor said that he understood the general had no authority to
give Washington a *royal* commission as captain of regulars, but he did have
absolute discretion when it came to appointing his personal staff, did he
not? Braddock answered that he did. Dinwiddie therefore proposed that
he appoint Washington as his personal aide-de-camp. This would remove
him from the ordinary chain of command because Washington would report directly to Braddock. Although Braddock did regard provincials with
contempt, he agreed that a man with Washington's experience would be
valuable in his service, and he issued the appointment. As Dinwiddie knew
it would, all ambivalence melted away, and Washington eagerly accepted.

For a young man who had confessed himself charmed by the sound of
flying lead, the opportunity to again risk life and limb was thrilling. Even
more appealing, however, was the opportunity for an apprenticeship
with an experienced, high-ranking British officer. Washington was ready
to learn the application of Old World military muscle to New World
military objectives.

Braddock sent his forces marching ahead of him at the start of April
1755, from their landing place in Alexandria to the forward British outpost
at Wills Creek, Virginia, while he remained behind to hold a grand council
of war with Dinwiddie and the governors of Maryland, Pennsylvania, New
York, and Massachusetts. He caught up with his troops later in the month,
finding that they had made numbingly little progress, having been idled by
local promises of supplies that, day after day, failed to materialize.

Washington watched, listened, and learned. He learned that the more
Braddock threw his royally commissioned weight around, the less willing the locals were to comply with his demands. No one knew better
than George Washington how much Virginia and the other English colonies needed a real European army to save the empire in North America.
Yet he was also learning that such an army needed the cooperation and
goodwill of local traders and merchants. The locals did not see the big
picture—or they simply did not think in terms of empire. All they saw

was a stout, blustering man in a scarlet uniform making demands and offering little by way of compensation.

By the third week in April, Braddock's regiments were well enough supplied to begin their inland trek in earnest. If Lesson #1 concerned the importance of securing local cooperation, Lesson #2 went something like this: *The bigger the army, the harder it is to move.* To what must have been Washington's mounting chagrin, Lesson #3 was *Braddock had learned neither Lesson #1 nor Lesson #2.*

Loaded down with baggage, pack animals, cumbersome wagons, and all that heavy artillery, Braddock's British army seemed absurdly out of place in the North American backwoods. "Our march must be regulated by the slow movements of the [artillery] Train," Washington wrote to Virginia's William Fairfax on April 23. This difficulty, he continued, was "answerable to the expectation I have long conceived, tho' few believ'd." To Fairfax, the young man could say what he could not to his commanding officer: *I told you so.*

It was May 10 by the time the army reached Fort Cumberland, the British forward outpost at Wills Creek, Maryland. They arrived without the Indian auxiliaries who were supposed to have met them at Winchester, Virginia; however, a large number of potential Indian allies had come directly to Fort Cumberland, apparently willing to be persuaded to serve. Firsthand, Washington had learned that Indian alliances could not be taken for granted. The Indians' presence at Fort Cumberland meant nothing more or less than that they were weighing the value of joining the expedition. Washington was dismayed, though not surprised, by Braddock's high-handed refusal to concede to the gathered chiefs any rights whatsoever within the territory of the Ohio Valley. Braddock knew the crown's position: the Indians occupying the Ohio Country, which was part of the British Empire, were subject to British government and law. Monacatoocha put it another way: "He looked upon us as dogs."

So, on May 29, 1755, Braddock and his command lumbered out of Fort Cumberland with no more than a handful of Indian auxiliaries. Nearly three thousand men, dragging the ball and chain of Old World artillery, clawed their way over trails that had been "improved" by soldiers' hard labor. Braddock ordered some baggage to be sent back to Fort Cumberland, but, even relieved in this way, he despaired of reaching Fort Duquesne in anything under a matter of months. Seeing an opportunity, his aide-de-camp, Washington, made bold to suggest detaching from the supply and artillery train what he called a "flying column" to make the initial assault against Fort Duquesne. Stobo's inside intelligence reported a garrison of four hundred. It made sense to attack as soon as possible, before this number was reinforced. Braddock agreed. He handpicked eight hundred of his best regulars, added to this some six hundred provincials, took along just eight cannon, and consolidated his supplies into thirty wagons. The rest of his army was to keep advancing and catch up when it could.

The pace picked up—until it was retarded by Braddock himself, who insisted on slowing down so that a wider, leveler road could be built ahead of the flying column. Washington believed that this activity defeated the very purpose of the flying column, for which the existing trail seemed to him perfectly adequate. The European commanding officer did not see it this way. In any case, the issue never came to a dispute because Washington suddenly fell ill with fever, becoming so sick that he could no longer ride. On June 23, he asked Braddock to leave him behind near the Youghiogheny River, promising that he would catch up as soon as he recovered. The general left him with a packet of "Dr. James's Fever Powder" and tried to make him feel better with a promise that he would not start the fight without sending for him first.

On June 24, the flying column, minus Washington, ran across dead campfires, beached canoes, and even taunting messages painted on the trees. Clearly, the French and the Indians were nearby. The troops bivouacked for the night, and when they awoke the next morning, they found a new message. Three of His Majesty's soldiers had been killed—and scalped. The work had been done with such stealth that no one, not even the sentries, had heard so much as a whimper.

Washington caught up with the flying column within scant miles of Fort Duquesne on July 8. He was emaciated, exhausted, and apparently so plagued by hemorrhoids that his orderly had had to tie cushions to his saddle. Nevertheless, on the ninth, he rode out ahead with Braddock and five hundred regulars to rendezvous with a three-hundred-man vanguard under Lieutenant Colonel Thomas Gage of the 44th Regiment of Foot. Nineteen years from this time, in May 1774, Gage would serve as royal governor and military commander in chief of Massachusetts, commissioned by George III to nip an incipient rebellion in the bud.

Just behind Gage's vanguard were the hundred soldiers of a New York independent company, co-captained by Robert Cholmley and Horatio Gates—the latter destined to serve as a troublesome Continental Army general in the American Revolution. The independent company functioned as a guard to a 250-man working party. Braddock, Washington, and the five hundred regulars were behind the working party. They, in turn, were backed up by a rear guard of a hundred Virginia provincials commanded by former captain—now Major—Adam Stephen.

It was after two in the afternoon by the time the main body of five hundred completed crossing the Monongahela. Everything was so quiet that Braddock came to believe that the French, overawed by the approach of English artillery, had withdrawn from the fort. Just as his men were setting up camp some ten miles from the fort, however, a distant rattle of musketry made it clear that they had by no means withdrawn. They were attacking Gage and his vanguard.

Both Braddock and Washington had taken comfort in Captain Stobo's on-the-scene intelligence reporting no more than four hundred men garrisoning Fort Duquesne. That was months earlier, though, and the fort had since been reinforced. Still, Commandant Claude-Pierre Pécaudy de Contrecoeur knew that he was facing superior numbers, and he seriously contemplated surrender. Contrecoeur's youthful second in command, Captain Daniel Liénard de Beaujeu, pointed out reports from Indian scouts that Braddock's force was large but also slow and strung out over a great distance, dragging behind it eight pieces of artillery and thirty wagons. It would make a formidable siege force, to be sure, but, unwieldy as it was, it was also highly vulnerable to a preemptive attack. Beaujeu pleaded for bold action. Contrecoeur agreed, assigning him to march out at the head of 72 regulars of the marine and 146 Canadian militiamen, link up with 637 Indians just outside of the fort, and make a surprise attack on Braddock's column.

After taking holy communion before dawn on July 9, Beaujeu marched southeast and attacked Gage ten miles out. Braddock sent half his men on a double-quick march to the sound of the muskets. The remainder he ordered to take a stand with the wagons and baggage. He then sent an aide to ride ahead to see what was happening but, with the volume of musket fire increasing, did not wait for him to return with his report. Instead, mounting up, he galloped off himself—Washington and the other staff officers close behind.

Pounding full tilt, they soon collided with red-coated regulars, stumbling over themselves, running the other way. We have no eyewitness account of the collision but can only imagine Braddock wheeling his horse about in an effort to put the spine back into his men. The few breathless officers he was able to corral reported that Frenchmen, Canadians, and Indians—a great many Indians—fell upon the work party and Gage's advance party. They reported that, at first, the soldiers responded quite well and even managed to kill the commanding officer, Beaujeu, early in the fight. That had thrown the French and Canadians into disarray, but it seemed only to make way for the Indians, who fought like—what else?—savages. At the sight of this, Beaujeu's second in command, Jean-Daniel Dumas, contained the rout among the white warriors, who rallied and opened fire again. The Indians stirred terror and created chaos, causing some of the redcoats to fire wildly, often hitting one another, and the others either to run or—most terrible of all—to just throw down their Brown Besses, huddle together like sheep, and, like sheep, meekly accept the slaughter, either at the hands of the Indians or under fire from the whites.

Doubtless these tales of terror were scarcely gasped out before the retreating advance party and work party ran headlong into the main body of reinforcements. On the narrow trail, hemmed in by old-growth forest, maneuver was impossible, and once a military formation loses the option of maneuver, the battle is lost. The French, Canadians, and Indians pressed in upon the mingled British and Virginians as a ramrod drives a ball against gunpowder. There was no place to go and nothing to do except fall under bullet, sword, and hatchet—or do as Braddock did. The portly sixty-year-old blusterer waded into the storm of lead and steel. He rode among his troops in a vain attempt to tie knots of them into something like effective fighting order. Form up enough men, and he might even be able to mount a counterattack.

It was no use. What had been an army was now a terrified mob. Washington was in the thick of it with Braddock and the rest of Braddock's staff officers. On July 18 he would write to his mother of how he "had four Bullets through my Coat, and two Horses shot under me." Yet he remained unhurt, even as everyone else attending the general fell wounded or dead. At the time, he was almost certainly unaware that Adam Stephen and his Virginians were performing far more effectively than the regulars. They were returning fire and taking lives. Washington did bear witness to Edward Braddock's remarkable stubborn valor. For all his failings as a commander, he was a hero toe to toe with death. Four horses were shot from beneath his sturdy frame before he himself was toppled from the saddle, a ball having penetrated (according to Washington) his shoulder and lodged in his chest.

What happened next is not certain. According to some sources, the dying Braddock asked nothing more than to be left behind. Others report that he asked for a pistol, so that he could make a clean end of it. Still others say that he uttered a bewildered "Who would have thought it?" then lingered three days before speaking his final, oddly hopeful, words, "We shall do better next time."

It is generally agreed that Washington personally saw to it that he was put on a wagon and sent toward the rear shortly before the surviving members of his command followed him, abandoning to the French and Indians the tightly packed baggage train they had hauled so very far and with so much labor. Braddock died less than a mile from Fort Necessity, at Great Meadows, on July 13. He was one of 456 killed, 520 wounded, and a dozen or so given up as prisoners. A total of 1,373 men had been engaged.

. . .

It was not of Braddock's courage that Washington wrote in his letter to his mother from Fort Cumberland on July 18, 1755, but of the craven timidity of the British regulars, who "were struck with such panick, that they behavd with more cowardice than it is possible to conceive." To this he contrasted the behavior of the Virginians, who "shewd a good deal of Bravery, & were near all killd." Every scrap of writing George Washington committed to paper is of great interest to historians, but virtually nothing he wrote appeals to students of American literature. Typically, he expressed himself awkwardly as well as abstractly. He does not make us *see* the world through his eyes. Yet the "dastardly" (his adjective) conduct of the regulars before Fort Duquesne moved him to uncharacteristically concrete vividness. He painted for his mother a picture of the redcoats fleeing "as Sheep pursued by dogs; and it was impossible to rally them." To Dinwiddie, he reported their "inconceivable Panick," so severe "that nothing but confusion and disobedience of order's prevailed amongst them." In contrast, the troops of the "Virginian Companies . . . behavd like Men, and died like Soldier's." He embellished for Dinwiddie what he had already written to his mother, describing how the British "broke & run as Sheep before Hounds" and explaining that attempting to rally them met with "as little success as if we had attempted to have stopd the wild Bears of the Mountains."

Washington had embarked on a mission to evict the French from land on which his family's future wealth depended. Viewed this way, the issue was straightforward; however, he soon found himself entangled in Anglo-Indian/ Franco-Indian relations, which were complicated by relations among the British North American colonies and between soldiers who had received commissions from the British crown and those, like himself, whose authority came from colonial governments. He had earlier confessed great zeal to serve his "country," by which, when he said it, he meant the British Empire and Virginia as part of that empire. He came to understand that the commanders of that empire's army regarded him and his fellow Virginians with contempt, however, and he came to see that the soldiers of that empire's army were capable of incompetence and cowardice.

Much of the rest that occurred in the French and Indian War created similar impressions in many citizens of the British colonies. Yet neither the threat posed by the French nor the unreliability of the British regulars to defend colonial interests succeeded in promoting intercolonial unity. A panicky "congress," convened at Albany from June 19 to July 10, 1754, failed to produce an acceptable plan for collaborative colonial action and concluded a poorly thought-out treaty with the Iroquois that succeeded only in sending the Delaware and other tribes into the arms of the French.

Throughout the war, the alliances between the Euro-Americans and the Native Americans played out this way. Most Indian leaders understood that the Euro-Americans, whether French or English, looked out for their own interests, which included taking as much Indian land as possible. In their diplomatic strategy, the Indians sought ways to suffer the least at the hands of the Euro-Americans while gaining some advantage against rival tribes. As the war developed, the Iroquois, whose hunger for English trade had made enemies of the French and the tribes allied with the French, especially in fur country, now struggled to remain neutral. They saw that the French push to the west—where beaver peltries still abounded—had outpaced that of the English. Moreover, they found it easier to deal with unlicensed, independent French-Canadian traders than with the English, who were rigidly committed to the Hudson's Bay factory model. On the other hand, they had long experience with the power of the British crown and the stubbornness of the English colonists. The very centralization that often made trade with the English a hard bargain also gave the English trader a better selection of merchandise and suggested to many Iroquois leaders that, in the long run, the English, not the French, would prevail in North America. Thus, except for the staunchly pro-English Mohawks, the Iroquois tried to bide their time, to ride out the war between the French and the English, and to do business with the victor.

In contrast to the Iroquois, most of the other tribes sided in varying degrees with the French. The Delaware and other eastern tribes, having good reason to fear dispossession from their lands at the hands of the English, were fairly reliable French allies. Later in the war, however, when the English finally deigned to negotiate with them, they did show a willingness to stop raiding on behalf of the French. In the Northeast, the Abenaki continued to prove extremely loyal to the French. Here, the enmity with the English colonists transcended issues of trade and had become crystallized as a matter of tribal tradition and heritage.

To the west, in the hotly disputed Ohio Country, the Shawnee were not so much pro-French as they were allied to the Delaware, their eastern neighbors, and thus posed a danger to the English on the frontier fringe. More enthusiastic toward the French in the West were the Ohio Country tribes who called themselves the Three Fires: the Ojibwa, Ottawas, and Potawatomis. Like the Hurons in the East, they were linked to French fur traders through generations of trade as well as intermarriage. As mentioned earlier, cultural intimacy went a long way toward creating a kind of Franco-Indian microcivilization that stood as a formidable barrier against the English, whose approach to Indian relations was typically a mixture of arrogance and parsimony. In more strictly business terms, though, the English had an edge. While French fur traders reached out into the Indian communities whereas the English compelled the Indians to come to their settlements, the French usually had on offer goods of less variety, less desirability, and greater cost than those of the English traders. Moreover, the administration of New France was not above coldly manipulating Indian affairs in much the same way that the English did. If English colonial governors had wielded the Mohawks against other tribes, so the French sometimes employed their western allies to menace recalcitrant eastern tribes and bring them into line.

The governors of New France had ventured into the Ohio Country to exploit the still-rich beaver peltries after those in the East had been trapped and hunted to virtual extinction. They understood what Louis XIV did not understand: that beaver pelts were currency and represented the liquidity necessary to drive even the kind of agricultural empire the king wanted to create. Let the English gain control of the western realm, and the flow of cash would be stanched. Throughout the seventeenth century and during the first half of the eighteenth, the struggle to control the western peltries had driven Indian relations and fueled wars. Now, in this biggest of wars, in this French and Indian War, the Ohio Country served a new purpose for New France. It was a vast staging area for raids into the East. The new French strategy was to confine the British colonies to the seaboard south of Canada. Maybe—someday—the English could be pushed into the sea itself, but for now containment was a goal sufficient.

The instruments of this containment were the Shawnee, Delaware, and even some French-allied Iroquois. The headquarters of operations from the West was Fort Duquesne, which controlled the confluence of two rivers, the Monongahela and the Allegheny, into the great Ohio, and thereby commanded the gateway to the Ohio Country frontier. Fort Duquesne was the rallying point for the raiders, who, sustained and supplied there, would be launched into Pennsylvania, Maryland, and Virginia. Often, one or two French regulars would lead the raiding party, though sometimes raids were motivated solely by Indian concerns and were, therefore, led by the Indians themselves.

In the aftermath of Braddock's defeat, the Pennsylvania, Maryland, and Virginia frontiers were convulsed by Indian raids. Braddock, however, had laid out a three-pronged war plan, only one prong of which had thus far failed. William Johnson, the wily Irish trader we met in chapter 6, was encamped at the southern tip of Lake George, at the southeastern base of the Adirondacks, preparing to move against Fort St. Frédéric at Crown Point on Lake Champlain per Braddock's plan. Pierre François de Rigaud, marquis de Vaudreuil-Cavagnal, governor of New France, had sent his Saxon-born commander in chief of French regulars, Baron Ludwig August Dieskau, with a mixed force of three thousand men to reinforce the fort. Seven hundred of these were regulars, sixteen hundred Canadians, and seven hundred Indians, three hundred of whom were so-called mission, or "domiciliated," Iroquois. Theoretically, these mission Iroquois should have been among the more reliable of Dieskau's Native American military assets, but, as the baron wrote to Count d'Argenson after the battle, he doubted "the fidelity of the domiciliated Iroquois." He complained that, "for more than [the] 15 days that I was encamped [at Fort St. Frédéric], I encountered nothing but difficulties from the Indians." He explained that "those who were good, were spoiled by the Iroquois," meaning those Iroquois who did not live in a mission village. The result was that "never was

I able to obtain from them a faithful scout; at one time they refused to make any [scouting reconnaissance at all]; at another time, seeming to obey me, they set forth, but when a few leagues from the camp, they sent back the Frenchmen I had associated with them, and used to return within a few days without bringing me any intelligence."

For his part, Johnson also labored under poor intelligence, which inflated the French numbers to as high as eight thousand. (In fact, Johnson's forces were about equal to Dieskau's—which, combined with the garrison already in place at Fort St. Frédéric, came to some three thousand.) Accordingly, Johnson grimly prepared to make a desperate defensive stand instead of mounting the offensive assault Braddock's plan called for. Dieskau, in the meantime, perplexed by his inability to obtain solid battlefield intelligence, decided to act contrary to Vaudreuil's instructions. The governor had wanted him to do no more than hold the vital fort. Instead, unwilling to await the blow he anticipated from Johnson, Dieskau detached about fourteen hundred of his regular and Indian troops, moved out of the fort, and launched a preemptive strike on Johnson's camp. News of his approach reached Johnson late on the night of September 7, 1755. Instead of consolidating his forces in camp, Johnson ordered a thousand militiamen and two hundred Mohawks to reconnoiter the approach. Theyanoguin, whom the English called Hendrick, chief of Johnson's Mohawk allies, instantly grasped this as a tactical error. "If they are to be killed, they are too many," he observed. "If they are to fight, they are too few." Johnson overrode his objections, however; the detachment, including Hendrick, left camp at sunrise while the rest of Johnson's troops remained behind, felling trees and working feverishly to fortify the camp as best they could.

The column was ambushed; its militia commander, Colonel Ephraim Williams, and Hendrick were both shot dead. Under intense fire, the survivors fell back on the camp. Johnson, however, had ordered a relief party to march to the sound of the firing, and the combined forces were able to check Dieskau's pursuit. Dieskau retreated to regroup for a fresh assault on the camp itself—but, suddenly gunshy, refrained from launching an all-out, go-for-broke attack. Instead, he arrayed his troops in a stationary line of fire, which, against Johnson's dug-in command, had little effect. For his part, Johnson was able to return a devastating fire, in particular training his two cannon against Dieskau's ill-conceived firing line, sending ball after ball crashing fiercely through the thick forest. After four hours of this terrifying pounding, Dieskau's line wavered, then broke. Johnson took this as his cue to charge. He overwhelmed the French and took a wounded Dieskau captive.

Braddock's plan had been boldly offensive, calling for Johnson to advance to Fort St. Frédéric on Lake Champlain. Instead, still believing that there was a large French force garrisoning the fort, Johnson built a fort of his own, William Henry, on the south end of Lake George. Indeed, George Washington, having returned from Braddock's defeat, persuaded authorities to build even more forts between the Potomac and James and Roanoke rivers, down into South Carolina. Between them, Johnson and Washington transformed the British strategy of offense—which had begun with Washington's own mission to throw the French out of the Ohio Country—into a broadly defensive strategy, by which they hoped to prevent the French and the French-allied Indians from pushing them any farther east. The English were now playing the game the French had begun late in the previous century. Instead of controlling territory by winning the trade of Indians, they were claiming turf with forts.

Even as the English were starting to play by French rules, Governor Vaudreuil was changing them. Rejecting Dieskau's criticism of his Indian allies, he was persuaded by the Battle of Lake George to prosecute the war guerrilla fashion, making extensive use of Indians and directing them specifically against civilian targets.

Through the balance of 1755 and well into 1756, the new strategy proved devastatingly effective. An abstract of French military dispatches from Canada for the winter of 1755–56 reported that "the French and Indians have, since Admiral [sic] Braddock's defeat, disposed of more than 700 people in the Provinces of Pennsylvania, Virginia and Carolina, including those killed and those taken prisoner." New York was similarly ravaged, while New England, perhaps more accustomed to Indian warfare, seems to have suffered less. Meanwhile, early in 1756, having failed to take Forts Frontenac and Niagara as prescribed in the third prong of Braddock's battle plan, Massachusetts governor William Shirley retreated to Albany to regroup and, on March 17, 1756, dispatched Lieutenant Colonel John Bradstreet to reinforce Fort Oswego, on the southeast shore of Lake Ontario, which was one of the most important English bases. The adjutant general of Massachusetts, Bradstreet was yet another example of hybrid North American civilization. He had been born in Nova Scotia, the son of a British army lieutenant and an Acadian mother.

By the time Bradstreet approached Fort Oswego, the French were already well on their way to cutting the supply line to the fort. On March 27, 1756, 360 Indians, Canadians, and French regulars under the command of Lieutenant Gaspard-Joseph Chaussegros de Léry attacked Fort Bull at the west end of the portage between the Mohawk River and Wood Creek, which feeds into Lake Oneida. Here they destroyed great quantities of munitions and stores, all intended for Fort Oswego, and the French-allied Indians massacred the Fort Bull garrison. Bradstreet responded to this disaster with a swiftness and resolve that astounded the French. Withdrawing to Albany, he built a hundred new bateaux (riverboats), added them to the 250 he managed to commandeer, and pressed into service "bateaumen" to handle them all. By definition, these were rough-and-ready traders and fur trappers, to all appearances wild men, who nevertheless were eager to save their country. Using these forces, Bradstreet managed to deliver food and other supplies over 160 miles from Albany to Oswego by the end of May, thereby averting collapse of the fort due to starvation. On July 3, as Bradstreet and his men were returning from one of their supply runs to the fort, a combined force of about seven hundred Canadian militiamen and Indians ambushed his advance group of about three hundred.

If the French and Indians expected a reprise of Braddock's defeat, they were stunningly surprised. Bradstreet rallied his outnumbered troops and charged the attackers, wresting hatchets from the Indians and using them in the counterattack as well as their muskets. Dumbfounded by the ferocity of the counterattack, the larger force turned in retreat to the banks of the Oswego River. Panic had dictated a poor choice of refuge. Backed against the river, they could either fight or swim. There was no third alternative. Spooked, they chose to swim, and thereby transformed themselves into easy targets for Bradstreet's men.

Such British triumphs were rare during the entire first three years of the war. By June 1756, British settlers in Virginia had withdrawn 150 miles from the prewar frontier, and George Washington moaned to Governor Dinwiddie that "the Bleu-Ridge is now our Frontier."

On May 11, 1756, Louis-Joseph, marquis de Montcalm, at forty-four a distinguished veteran of the War of the Polish Succession and the War of the Austrian Succession, arrived in Canada to take charge of French and provincial forces. Less than a week later, on May 17, England formally declared war on France in the start of the Seven Years' War. After successfully supplying Fort Oswego and defeating the ambush, Bradstreet, on July 12, warned his commanders that the vital fort was nevertheless in grave danger, but by this time Governor Shirley, who had great respect for Bradstreet, had been relieved of command of provincial forces by a newly arrived British regular, Major General James Abercromby. Not only did he turn a deaf ear to the warning of a mere provincial officer, Abercromby excluded Bradstreet from the council of war he convened on July 16. Abercromby was particularly put off by the bateaumen, whom he dismissed as so many uncouth fur trappers. He summarily dismissed four hundred of these remarkable riverborne fighters.

Having disposed of the colonial riffraff, Abercromby ordered another British regular, Major General Daniel Webb, to prepare his regiment for departure to Oswego. Yet, having issued the order, he conveyed—and apparently felt—no sense of great urgency. When John Campbell, fourth Earl of Loudoun, arrived in the colonies on July 23 to take overall charge of all British forces, regular and provincial, he immediately set off for Albany, summoned Webb, and tried to light a fire under him. Webb and his regiment marched out on July 29 and got as far as Schenectady, just fifteen miles away, where Webb spent more than two weeks dickering over provision contracts. It was August 14 by the time his regiment had reached German Flatts (modern Herkimer, New York), still a hundred miles from Oswego. On that date, Fort Oswego fell to Montcalm and three thousand French and Indian troops.

The loss of the fort meant that the British had yielded all of Lake Ontario to the French, giving eastern New France unhindered communication with Fort Duquesne and the West. Not only was attacking Fort Niagara now out of the question, but the Iroquois—save the Mohawks—though still professing neutrality, clearly inclined toward the French victors. Strategically, it was a blow even more severe than the defeat of Braddock.

The fall of Fort Oswego should have taught the British commanders the value of Indian allies and provincial troops, but Loudoun nevertheless continued to alienate both groups. He made official what had only been vaguely understood before, that the most senior provincial commanders were outranked by any captain of regulars. When General Edward Winslow, a commander of provincials, pointed out that this effectively enlisted his men into the British regular army, thereby violating the resolutions of the colonial assemblies, which specified that local forces must remain under local command, Loudon remained unmovable. Weary of wasting time in further argument, Winslow acted on his own, marching his colonial troops to Lake George to attack Fort Ticonderoga. Before he could launch the attack, however, he received a dispatch from Loudoun urgently recalling his forces to "protect" Albany. Winslow knew the town was in no immediate danger, but even he dared not disregard a lawful and direct order. Arriving in the capital, Winslow reported to Loudoun, who accused him of mutiny and relieved this highly capable general of command.

In the meantime, on August 20, having received word of Fort Oswego's fall, General Webb advanced to the portage known as the "Great Carrying Place" (present-day Rome, New York). There a colonial major was directing the rebuilding of forts, but Webb, appalled by the absence of conventional military discipline among the provincials and noting that the forts were far from completed, panicked. He ordered them burned, lest they fall into enemy hands, and withdrew all forces east to German Flatts without having even sighted the enemy.

. . .

In this way, 1756 went very badly for the British. Fort Oswego fell, and Webb ran from any possibility of retaking it; Winslow was forced by his own commander to relinquish Lake George; Loudoun spent more time and energy arguing with colonial governors and officers than he did fighting the French; and the Iroquois, long associated with the English by profitable trade, turned increasingly to the French.

In December 1756, William Pitt became British secretary of state for the Southern Department, which put him in charge of American colonial affairs. Despite halfhearted support from the king and outright opposition from the powerful Duke of Cumberland, within three weeks of taking office Pitt ordered two thousand additional troops to Halifax, Nova Scotia, intending to take the war into the very heart of French Canada, through the St. Lawrence Valley, and against Quebec. The first objective was the always troublesome French naval base at Louisbourg. With its defeat, Acadia would fall, cutting off New France from communication with Europe. While this plan was sound, its execution suffered from massive logistical bottlenecks, which delayed its contemplated execution until August 1757, when the British commanders concluded that the season was too late and the enemy now too strong to attempt an assault on Louisbourg. They withdrew to New York.

In the meantime, back in New York, Webb was camped with four thousand troops near Fort William Henry on the southern tip of Lake George. Since April he had been receiving intelligence of a massing of French troops at Fort Ticonderoga but had done nothing about it. July brought further information, making it clear that Montcalm was preparing for an assault on Fort William Henry itself. Webb sat tight.

By capturing Fort William Henry, Montcalm intended to seize control of what was generally known as the Warpath of Nations, the chain from the Atlantic to the Hudson River, to Lake George, Lake Champlain, and to the Richelieu River, and thence into the St. Lawrence. The most critical link in this chain was that between Lake George and Lake Champlain. The French Forts Ticonderoga and St. Frédéric, and the British Fort William Henry (at the south end of Lake George) and, south of that, Fort Edward (on the headwaters of the Hudson) had all been built to contest this region. In fact, for much of the French and Indian War, armies fighting in the eastern theater faced one another between these sets of forts. No tract of North American real estate was of greater strategic consequence, and yet Webb ended weeks of inaction with nothing more useful than panic. He decided to withdraw from the forward fort, William Henry, and by cover of night began a retreat to Fort Edward. His stunned subordinates persuaded him to wait until morning, but he marched off as early on August 3 as possible, taking with him much of the available artillery and nearly half the men, leaving Fort William Henry to be defended by Lieutenant Colonel George Monro and a provincial colonel, together commanding a garrison of 2,372. His parting advice to Monro was "to make the best [surrender] terms left in your power."

Things were not only bad. They were worse than they appeared. Of Monro's complement of 2,372, only 1,100 were listed as fit for duty. The rest were down with disease or injury. Opposing him, Montcalm commanded 7,626 men, including 1,600 Indian allies. Yet Monro could not find it in himself to follow Webb's surrender advice. Outnumbered seven to one, he managed to hold out for nearly a week before finally capitulating on August 9, 1757. Montcalm promised the defeated commandant and his gallant men safe conduct out of the fort.

What happened next has been subject to much bitter debate. According to English accounts of the period, once the garrison emerged from an entrenched encampment just outside the fort, they were set upon by Montcalm's Indians. About fifteen thousand soldiers, women, and children were massacred or taken prisoner. Montcalm decried the outcome, claiming that the Indians had acted on their own, but the English knew otherwise.

Tales of the "Fort William Henry Massacre" circulated quickly, convincing many English colonists that the French were treacherous and the Indians inherently bloodthirsty or, at any rate, knew only one brutal way of making war. In fact, the "massacre" suggests more about the nature of Franco-Indian relations at this point in the war than it does about the nature of Indian warfare. It was not that the Indians were ruthless so much as that they were restless, eager—as mercenary troops always are—for the spoils of victory. Clothing, arms, ammunition, provisions, rum: These were the prizes of conquest, and they were the only payment the Indians accompanying Montcalm had been promised. When the booty was not forthcoming, tensions mounted. Indeed, sensing trouble, Montcalm suggested that Monro delay his march out of the entrenched camp until morning. Indians were already pestering the garrison soldiers, wanting to appropriate their baggage, and Montcalm decided to post French guards, not to control the English but to protect the now unarmed men against the Indians.

Come the morning of August 10, Monro, mounted, ordered his command to march out of the entrenched camp. A two-hundred-man French escort was standing by. The British marched out by regiment, and after the last regiment had departed, the Indians descended upon seventeen wounded men who had been left behind in huts. They were scalped. This done, Indians attacked Monro's rear guard, which consisted of a Massachusetts regiment and some New Hampshire militiamen, plus an assortment of camp followers. The account of this attack reads almost generically: "The savages fell upon the rear killing and scalping . . . tearing the Children from their Mothers Bosoms and their mothers from their Husbands, then Singling out the men and Carrying them in the woods and killing a great many whom we saw lying on the road side."

Fifteen hundred was the number of slain most frequently reported by panic-stricken stragglers arriving at Fort Edward. They spoke of a three-hour slaughter against the unarmed garrison. Monro, however, reported 129 of his regulars killed and wounded, which included casualties from the siege, not just the "massacre" that followed. He did not have a casualty count for the militia but estimated that "their Numbers Kill'd Could not be Less than Four Officers & about 40 Men. And very near as many Men Wounded."

Massacre? It was more like armed robbery. The Indians took the baggage, supplies, and clothing they believed was their due. If anyone resisted, he was knocked down, and, to be sure, some were killed; however, the Indians knew that live soldiers were worth more than dead ones. The French wanted prisoners to ransom; therefore, most of Monro's soldiers who broke and ran from them were pursued and captured—alive. The numbers tell the tale. Of the 2,372 soldiers who left Fort William Henry on August 9, 1,783 reported to Fort Edward by August 31. Before the end of the year, another 217 were accounted for. Interestingly, just 500, among them "wives, servants, & sutlers," arrived at Fort Edward *with* Monro, which means that many had fled into the woods at least temporarily, whereas others, taken captive, were soon paroled. Officially, by the end of the year, the number of missing and presumed dead was nowhere near 1,500 but just 308—and who knows how many of these simply deserted?

While the fall of Fort William Henry represented the nadir of British fortunes in the French and Indian War, Montcalm's inability to control his Indian allies, to be able to claim them as anything more than mercenaries—and discontented mercenaries at that—did not bode well for the French, either. As William Pitt's military reforms began to take effect, the tide of the war slowly turned. Pitt reversed crown policy by ordering his officers to cooperate with provincial forces and colonial governments rather than simply dictate to them. He also ensured that colonial assemblies would have a voice in managing funds used to prosecute the war. In response to the new policy, Massachusetts, which Loudoun had accused of mutiny, quickly raised a large and effective army, and on December 30, 1757, Pitt recalled Loudoun and appointed James Abercromby as commander in chief of American operations.

As we have already seen, Abercromby was hardly one of history's great captains, but he was a considerable improvement on Loudoun, and, besides, Pitt reduced the scope of his office so that abler commanders, nominally serving under him—including provincials—were given more freedom of movement and power of decision. Perhaps most important of all, Pitt sought, rather than shunned, Indian allies, promising them that after the war Great Britain would enforce a boundary line to restrict white encroachment into their lands. *That* was the promise that meant the most to the Indians, and it would prove of profound consequence to the colonists as well.

12

"All North America in the Hands of a Single Power"

———◆◆◆———

PITT PERSONALLY SELECTED BRIGADIER General John Forbes, one of his best commanders, to assault Fort Duquesne. In contrast to the stiff-necked Braddock, Forbes willingly worked with the Pennsylvania governor and colonial assembly to obtain the supplies and recruit the men he needed for the campaign. Initially, he was also more successful in recruiting Indian allies; however, problems with supply and disputes among commanders delayed Forbes's expedition and made his new Indian allies restless, many of whom abandoned the enterprise before it got under way. In September, an army of five thousand provincials, fourteen hundred elite Scottish Highlanders, and dwindling numbers of Indians at last slowly advanced toward Fort Duquesne only to bog down in the rain-soaked quagmire of Loyalhanna (present-day Ligonier, Pennsylvania). As a result of this setback, even more Indians deserted the expedition.

The Indians were not the only impatient warriors. One of Forbes's subordinate commanders, Colonel Henry Bouquet, could stand the waiting at Loyalhanna no longer. On September 11, he ordered eight hundred Highlanders under Major James Grant to reconnoiter the environs of Fort Duquesne. The troops arrived near the fort on the night of September 14. Come dawn, Grant ordered the drums to beat, thinking to inspire and inspirit his men. Whatever effect the martial noisemaking had on the Highlanders, it definitely alerted the enemy. Suddenly, a sortie of French and Indians poured from the fort and overran the Highlanders, killing a third of them, including Grant.

To Forbes, literally stuck in the mud, his Indian allies deserting him, his provincial forces soon to leave as well when their enlistments expired, Grant's defeat came as a terrible blow. Yet this disaster was not an unalloyed triumph for the French. Losses among their Indian auxiliaries were heavy, prompting many to reconsider the alliance. Seizing their plunder, most deserted the fort. When the so-called Far Indians (Potawatomis, Ojibwa, and Ottawas) left the French fold, only the Ohio allies were left. Unknown to the French, these were about to be neutralized by a pact concluded at Easton, Pennsylvania. In October 1758, the Treaty of Easton returned to the Iroquois western lands the Six Nations had earlier ceded to Pennsylvania. It further stipulated that the Iroquois would freely grant the Delaware—hitherto, for the most part, French allies—the right to hunt and live on these lands. The Iroquois thus became landlords to the Delaware, a position of power that pleased them while providing the Delaware with land west of the Appalachians and Alleghenies. Insofar as the Iroquois were allies of the English, the new relationship also meant peace between the English and the Delaware. This was enforced by a provision that European settlement would not encroach on the returned territory. The Treaty of Easton was the single most important diplomatic move of the war.

While French-Indian alliances were crumbling, General Abercromby assembled sixteen thousand troops at Lake George for a march against Fort Ticonderoga, which the French had renamed Fort Carillon. Abercromby sent ahead Lieutenant Colonel John Bradstreet, whose provincials quickly overcame the fort's outer defenses. Bradstreet asked Abercromby for permission to attack the fort itself, before Montcalm had time to call up reinforcements, but the conventional British regular insisted that Bradstreet await the arrival of the main body of troops.

It was a decision both cautious and fatal. It gave Montcalm time not only to bring up reinforcements from Fort St. Frédéric but also to erect highly effective entrenchments and fascines, using fallen trees and branches much as later armies would employ barbed wire. Even reinforced, Montcalm had only three thousand men to defend Fort Ticonderoga, but he had transformed it into a formidable objective. Of course, the British also occupied a good position. They held a place called Mount Defiance, which was ideal high ground for artillery—had Abercromby chosen to put artillery there; instead, he planted William Johnson with four hundred Mohawks atop Mount Defiance, a position from which they, as infantry, could never even be committed to battle.

Johnson's lofty perch did give him a fine view of the debacle that unfolded when Abercromby attacked on July 8. Previously, he had fatally delayed to allow his full forces to assemble; now he blundered into action prematurely. Instead of waiting for the main body of his artillery to arrive—for, even poorly placed, cannon could have blasted away at the French lines—he sent his regulars against Montcalm's defenses in a series of bayonet charges. Montcalm, who had been fully resigned to beating a retreat, now found that his greatly outnumbered forces could simply mow down the charging Highlanders. In a series of bayonet charges, 464 British regulars fell dead and 1,117 were wounded; provincial losses were 87 dead and 239 wounded. The French, who were outnumbered more than five to one, lost 112 officers and men, with 273 wounded. A stunned Abercromby retreated to Albany.

Ticonderoga was the last major French triumph of the war. The British promise of a definite line separating English and Indian lands, a pledge echoed by William Johnson, who spoke in 1758 of creating "clear and fixed Boundaries between our Settlements and [Indian] Hunting Grounds," was already eroding Franco-Indian alliances. The Treaty of Easton began a process of negotiation between the English and the Indians, and, gradually, three important Delaware sachems—Tamaqua, Pisquetomen, and Shingas—began actively advocating peace. In the summer of 1758, Frederick Post, a German Moravian who had twice married Delaware women and who favored the English far over the French, acted as interpreter in negotiations between colonial officials and the Delaware tribe. The traders George Croghan and Andrew Montour joined the negotiations as well.

The Delaware took a different tack from the Iroquois and the Hurons. Instead of accepting the French and English proposition, which was an exclusive alliance with one or the other, the tribal representatives proposed an alliance with the British based on the withdrawal of the French *as well as the British* from the Ohio Country. "We have great reason to believe you intend to drive us away and settle the country," a Delaware negotiator declared, "or else why do you come to fight in the Land that God gave us . . . ? Why don't you and the French fight in the old Country, and on the Sea? Why do you come to fight on our Land? This makes every Body believe you want to take the Land from us, by force and settle it." Surprisingly, Henry Bouquet, who represented General Forbes in the negotiations, allowed that this was a possibility. Unlike Washington and the other Virginians, he had no particular stake in the Ohio Country—except to ensure that the French did not control it. Besides, what the Indians held could always be negotiated for purchase later, provided that the French had no stake in the territory. The great thing, as Forbes saw it, was not to grab the Ohio Country but to evict the French from it, and if that meant agreeing to let the Indians have it, so be it—for now, at least. In any event, this would not bar the English from trading in the West—the Indians would not have wanted such an exclusion in any case—but merely from settling there.

While Anglo-Indian negotiations undermined the long-standing Franco-Indian alliances that had been built on a combination of missionary and fur-trading relationships, Major General James Wolfe and Brigadier General Jeffrey Amherst succeeded in taking Louisbourg, Nova Scotia, on July 26, 1758. At the end of the very next month, Bradstreet assembled a provincial task force—1,112 men from New York, 675 from Massachusetts, 412 from New Jersey, and 318 from Rhode Island, supplemented by 300 bateaumen, 135 British regulars, and 70 Iroquois—to seize Fort Frontenac, near present-day Kingston, Ontario. The objective seemed so formidable that when they learned of it, the Iroquois contingent, small as it was, promptly deserted. Actually, as it turned out, Fort Frontenac was practically defenseless. Governor Vaudreuil and General Montcalm had withdrawn most of the garrison to Fort Ticonderoga in anticipation of a renewed assault there. Although he did not know it, Bradstreet and his three thousand men surrounded a mere 110 inmates of the fort, men, women, and children included. Fort Frontenac fell on August 27, after a token resistance of two days. Bradstreet captured sixty precious cannon and 800,000 livres' worth of provisions. The loss of Fort Frontenac severed the lifeline to Forts Niagara and Duquesne. The French were forced to relinquish control of Lake Ontario to the English, and Bradstreet took possession of a nine-vessel French fleet, loading two ships to carry off booty and burning the rest.

Fort Duquesne was now cut off from ammunition and other supplies. Aware that he would soon be forced to release his militiamen from Illinois and Louisiana, along with his dwindling Indian auxiliaries, François-Marie Le Marchand de Lignery, the fort's commandant, launched what can only be described as a desperation raid on Forbes's position at Loyalhanna on October 12, 1758. Forbes repulsed the attack, forcing Lignery to withdraw into the fort, leaving his few remaining Indian allies badly shaken. A month later, he launched another raid. While chasing this force off, Forbes's men captured three prisoners, who revealed just how weakly Fort Duquesne was held.

Forbes resolved to close in for the kill. His men were hardly in the best shape to mount a major assault. Inadequately fed and subject to abysmal sanitation on the march as well as in the camp, hundreds of soldiers fell ill with pneumonia and intestinal infections. No one was sicker than Forbes himself, and no one knew this better than he, since, as a youth, he had studied medicine at the University of Edinburgh. He self-diagnosed his disorder as the "bloody flux," presumably dysentery, which was endemic to army life. In fact, he suffered from far more. He was plagued by migraines that blinded him throughout their excruciating duration. Chronically dehydrated by the "flux," he would then be seized by epic sieges of constipation so severe that he was sometimes unable to walk. Unwilling to slow progress toward Fort Duquesne, he ordered a litter slung between two horses and settled his beleaguered frame into it.

At last, on November 24, within striking distance of the fort, there came the rolling thunder of a distant explosion. Forbes sent out his advance guard on the double-quick. By the time they reached Fort Duquesne, they found it gutted and deserted. Lignery had blown it up, leaving in front of the partially ruined stockade a line of stakes on which the heads of Highlanders captured earlier were skewered, their kilts tied below. Lignery had retired to Fort Machault (present-day Franklin, Pennsylvania) to plan a counterattack.

Even in ruins, Fort Duquesne was a great prize. The power that controlled the Forks of the Ohio controlled the gateway to the West. Forbes renamed Duquesne Fort Pitt, but, having taken it, he had now to garrison and hold it. Victorious though his forces were, Forbes had suffered massive troop desertion and was left with just two hundred men. This number was far too small to withstand a determined counterattack, especially with so much of the fort's structure burned down or blown apart. Forbes also knew that his Indian auxiliaries traditionally disliked the static warfare a fort represented and so were certain to melt away, unless he could ply them with presents. Israel Pemberton, a Philadelphia merchant and Quaker pacifist, sent Forbes £1,400 worth of gifts, soon followed by an additional £3,000. Pemberton's understanding was that these would buy peace. In fact, they set the French up for 1759, destined to be chronicled as their "year of disaster."

Seeking to capitalize on what had been gained so far, Pitt proposed a new three-pronged campaign against the French, which included, first, the capture of Fort Niagara and the reinforcement of Fort Oswego to sever the West from the St. Lawrence River. Second would be a strike via Lake Champlain into the St. Lawrence Valley; third, an amphibious assault on Quebec itself.

Early in 1759, the Fort Pitt garrison was expanded to 350 as Brigadier General John Stanwix arrived and prepared to use the fort as a base for a 3,500-man force that was to operate throughout the Ohio Country. In

February, William Johnson proposed an expedition against Fort Niagara through the country of the Six Nations. Indian auxiliaries, he argued, could be acquired along the way. In April, the Seneca, the Iroquois tribe still most inclined toward the French, at last became discouraged by the failure of the French to provide satisfactory trade goods. Accordingly, in April, they proposed to assist the English in the attack on Fort Niagara. That same month, the Oneida chief Conochquieson told William Johnson that all the Six Nations were "ready to join and revenge both Your Blood and ours upon the French."

As Johnson assembled Indian auxiliaries for the assault on Fort Niagara, Wolfe prepared to take Quebec. On May 28, 1759, Rear Admiral Philip Durell landed a detachment on the Île-aux-Coudres, in the St. Lawrence River, northeast of Quebec. His troops advanced downriver to Île d'Orléans, nearer to Quebec, to await the main amphibious force under Wolfe and Vice Admiral Charles Saunders, which landed on June 27. By July, Wolfe's nine-thousand-man army was in possession of the north shore of the St. Lawrence above Quebec. Montcalm attempted to burn the British fleet at anchor by chaining rafts together, setting them ablaze, and sending them downriver, but British seamen in small boats managed to repel these assaults.

For the next two and a half months, Wolfe probed Quebec's defenses without success. Failing to penetrate, the British commander turned to terrorism against the civilian population, bombarding the city day and night with his artillery, purposely concentrating his fire on residential rather than military targets. For his part, Montcalm was no less ruthless. When, after weeks of siege and bombardment, the citizens of Quebec expressed their desire to surrender, the general threatened to turn his Indians loose upon them. We do not know if Montcalm consulted the sachems about this. It would have been risky to do so. Contrary to what many colonists had been told, the Indians had no racial hatred of whites and did not seize on any and all opportunities to commit mayhem. However, had Montcalm turned them loose against Quebec, giving them leave to appropriate whatever booty they could carry off, the situation might well have rapidly escalated out of control. On the other hand, the mere suggestion that

Montcalm was willing to kill his own people might have prompted his Indian auxiliaries to leave him or even to embrace the English.

While the siege of Quebec ground on, General Amherst decided to put the Niagara expedition under the command of a regular army officer, Brigadier General John Prideaux, with William Johnson as his second in command. On July 8, Prideaux presented Fort Niagara's commandant, Captain Pierre Pouchot, with a demand for surrender. Pouchot responded by pretending not to understand English. To his protests of incomprehension, Prideaux responded with a siege.

Pouchot appealed to Lignery, now at Fort Machault, for reinforcements. Lignery had been putting together a force of a thousand men to counterattack Fort Pitt but abandoned this to relieve Fort Niagara. As the British forces prepared for the assault on the fort, about one in the afternoon of July 19, General Prideaux stepped in front of an active mortar. The blast carried off his head and put William Johnson in command of the assault—at least as Johnson saw the situation. Lieutenant Colonel Eyre Massey, a regular British army officer, objected, Johnson acknowledged the protest but assumed command just the same. At this very moment, a scout reported the approach of Lignery leading the French reinforcements. Cutting short his dispute with Johnson, Lieutenant Colonel Massey immediately rode out to a position held by New York captain James De Lancey, who had erected barricades against Lignery's approach. It is not clear whether Massey did this in obedience to an order from Johnson or on his own initiative. Simultaneously, some six hundred Mohawks, under the command of nineteen-year-old Joseph Brant and apparently operating independently of both Johnson and Massey, attacked from the sides of the road. Seeing this, De Lancey led a bayonet charge against Lignery and Massey and, either acting according to plan or in response to what he saw, ordered a volley of fire.

"We killed 200 and took 100 prisoners," De Lancey later reported concisely. Among the prisoners were five senior officers. Pouchot capitulated, and Niagara fell to the British on July 25. On the very next day, the French garrison, facing superior numbers led by Jeffrey Amherst, unceremoniously abandoned and blew up Fort Ticonderoga. Amherst moved against Fort St. Frédéric next, taking it on July 31. The French retreated down the Richelieu River.

Despite the year of unfolding French disaster, Quebec remained an objective apparently unattainable. Throughout the summer of 1759, Wolfe had made several costly attempts to storm the town, but it wasn't until September 12 that he managed a stealthy approach to the Plains of Abraham, the adjacent high ground. Failing to anticipate an attack from this unlikely direction, Montcalm had fortified another position, at Beaumont. At daybreak on September 14, he, his soldiers, and the people of Quebec were stupefied by the sight of an army forming battle lines on the Plains. The French commander could have attacked while Wolfe's forces were still gathering, which would have given him a fair chance to defeat the British in detail. Instead, he waited until he had brought up all of his own forces from their positions at Beaumont. Having done this, however, he inexplicably decided not to await the arrival of additional reinforcements from Cap-Rouge. Thus he ended up ordering a charge against the advancing British that was simultaneously too late and yet premature.

Montcalm committed 4,500 troops, mostly Canadians, to the battle. James Wolfe was a temperamental commander, considered high-strung. He reportedly summoned his officers to him the night before the Battle of the Plains of Abraham, recited to them Thomas Gray's "Elegy Written in a Country Churchyard"—with its celebrated line "The paths of glory lead but to the grave"—in its entirety, then proclaimed, "Gentlemen, I would rather have written that poem than take Quebec tomorrow." When it came to combat, however, he was a man of preternatural courage. So careless was he of his own life and limb that some considered him downright suicidal. With steely nerves, he ordered his commanders to restrain their men's fire until the very last possible moment. When they finally opened up on the poorly organized French ranks, it was with devastating effect.

After months of failed assaults, the climactic battle was over in no more than a quarter of an hour. Two hundred French troops fell dead, and another twelve hundred were wounded. British losses were sixty killed and six hundred wounded. Among the fatalities on either side were the two commanders, Montcalm and Wolfe.

By the time the comte de Bougainville arrived with reinforcements, the British forces were securely ensconced on the high ground, and the fresh French troops could do nothing but withdraw. Quebec formally surrendered on September 18, 1759, effectively spelling the end to French power in North America.

The fall of Quebec had decided the war, but the fighting did not end. The French still held Montreal and the Richelieu River as far as Île-aux-Noix, at the bottom of Lake Champlain. Britain's commander in chief, Jeffrey Amherst, could have pushed his advantages, but, always cautious, he chose instead to consolidate his positions, and the winter passed without further event.

In the meantime, all was not well in Quebec. While fewer than 250 English soldiers died during the siege of the city, a thousand succumbed to disease while garrisoning it, and twice that number became so ill as to be unfit for service. After the long siege and the effects of Wolfe's policy of laying waste the countryside, there was little left in Quebec to sustain an occupying force. What is more, Wolfe's victory had not severed all of the ties between the French and the Indians. Local warriors frequently attacked British hauling parties, sent to gather precious firewood. General James Murray, commanding the garrison, made attempts to foil the mounting French effort to retake the capital and in May 1760 was badly beaten in a battle before the city. One thousand of his men—a third of his troops fit for service—were killed before he finally retreated back into Quebec, where he and the surviving members of his command now endured a French siege until the arrival of the British fleet relieved them.

Nevertheless, from the fall of Quebec on, the British steadily gained ground, as William Haviland, marching from Crown Point (the former French Fort St. Frédéric), captured Chambly on September 1, 1760, and Amherst and Murray joined forces in an assault on Montreal. At last, on September 8, 1760, Governor Vaudreuil surrendered the province of Canada.

Yet this did not stop the remaining French forces, with attendant Indians, bonds forged mainly by generations of trade, from fighting on in hopes of salvaging something they could bring to the peace table. Soon, however, the French dropped out, and most of the action throughout the remainder of the war was between the English and various groups of Indians.

There was good reason for this. General Thomas Gage put the British understanding precisely, when he wrote to a friend in 1762, "All North America in the hands of a single power robs them [the Indians] of their Consequence, presents & pay." Experienced traders, heirs to the Euro-American/Native American civilization of trade founded on the currency called beaver fur, warned General Amherst that it was a grave mistake to view relations with the Indians exclusively through a military prism. Pressured to reduce costs by Parliament, which was appalled by the accumulated price of the French and Indian War (a conflict that had to be financed in the shadow of the much larger Seven Years' War with which it was linked), Amherst protested that traders such as George Croghan and William Johnson were wrong to persist in seeing the Indians to be of greater "consequence than they really are." Croghan countered that the British military had defeated the French military but had "nothing to boast from the War with the natives." He believed the Indians had to be conciliated, not fought, and he was eager to reestablish the hybrid civilization, based on mutually profitable trade, that had existed before the war.

As a means of pleasing Parliament by sharply and quickly cutting expenses in North America, Amherst was intent on immediately ending the custom of furnishing presents to the Indians. He justified this with the claim that presents encouraged the natural shiftlessness of "savages," whereas compelling the Indians to make their own way would promote their evolution toward (a European style of) civilization. Croghan and others explained that the "middle ground," the hybrid cultural territory in which Euro-American and Native American cultures and economies met and mingled, was defined in large measure by the symbolism of the presents. To deprive the Indians of these would be to destroy what had become a uniquely American civilization. The resulting sense of bewilderment and betrayal would fuel nothing but further war.

Amherst would not yield. In fact, his dismissal of the Indians went well beyond the elimination of presents. During 1760, having promised the Delaware and Shawnee that the English had no intention of occupying their lands, Amherst nevertheless built new forts in the West. The Seneca, westernmost of the Iroquois tribes, had come over to the English side in order to rid themselves of the French. Now Amherst began granting land—Seneca land—to his officers as payment for faithful service. The Ottawas, Potawatomis, and Ojibwa also had reason for alarm, first over the ever-growing presence of the English at Fort Pitt and then at Detroit. On September 12, 1760, Amherst ordered Major Robert Rogers, celebrated as the heroic guerrilla leader of his famous rangers, to take *actual* possession of Detroit, Fort Michilimackinac (on Michigan's Upper Peninsula), and other western outposts *formally* ceded to the English after the fall of Montreal.

As the British took over Detroit, most of the local Indians ostensibly renounced their loyalty to the French. The Seneca, however, were wary and resentful of the continued and increasing British presence at Niagara. At last, they consulted with other Iroquois League chiefs at Onondaga to plan a coordinated uprising. On July 3, 1761, encouraged by unreconstructed French traders, two Seneca chiefs bore a war belt to Indians in the vicinity of Detroit, inviting the western tribes to join them in resisting the English. The Detroit Indians rejected the belt and disclosed the planned rebellion to the British commandant of Fort Detroit. This was enough to drive even William Johnson, long a supporter of the Iroquois Six Nations, to adopt a new approach. He found himself agreeing with Amherst that, with the French defeated, the Iroquois had become a threat rather than an asset. Accordingly, he set about stirring up intertribal discord, which he hoped would break up the Iroquois League.

On February 10, 1763, the kingdoms of Great Britain, France, and Spain signed the Treaty of Paris, which concluded both the Seven Years' War and the French and Indian War. This event in a far-off European capital was quite unknown to Obwandiyag, the Ottawa tribal leader the English

233

called Pontiac, who, a few days after it, led members of his tribe, along with Delaware, Seneca, and Shawnee warriors, in the first of a series of extremely violent attacks on the western outposts the French had just formally relinquished to the English.

"Pontiac's Rebellion"—the label was bestowed by the nineteenth-century American historian Francis Parkman, and it has stuck ever since—was the result of what the Ohio Country tribes perceived as the sudden collapse of the "middle ground" that had defined their relations with the Euro-Americans. Beginning with Washington at the very outbreak of the French and Indian War and continuing through Amherst at the war's end, the English had promised to behave as brothers or as fathers to the Indians who sided with them, but they consistently failed to behave as either.

In contrast to the English, the French had, since the seventeenth century, developed a genuine middle-ground civilization. True, the French missionaries were often overbearing and even brought disease, but they also offered a certain caring attitude and secured from the government of New France the protective treatment a father or a brother is bound to deliver. Moreover, the French model of trade, in which traders lived among the Indians instead of demanding (as the English did) that the Indians live separately and come to them only at trading settlements and then only to trade, promoted intermarriage and other aspects of cultural blending. This, among other things, the French and Indian War had ended. During the 1640s, tribes in New France addressed Governor Charles Jacques Huault de Montmagny as "Onontio." It was a Mohawk word meaning "great mountain" and, as such, a literal translation of "Montmagny." The form of address survived the particular governor and became the name the French-allied Indians applied to all successive governors. As such, the term took on symbolic significance. The "Great Mountain" became a "Father." In this rich word and the concept it represented was contained much of the emotional and cultural currency the Indians invested in the French. It expressed an understanding of the middle-ground civilization that existed in New France, especially where the fur trade abounded and joined Euro-American to Native American. Now, with French defeat, Onontio, the Great Mountain, the Father, was vanished altogether and at once.

What was left to the western tribes that had bound themselves to New France? They could follow the example of the Iroquois and create a confederacy to resist the British usurpation of their land. To a degree, this was precisely Pontiac's aim.

How deeply Pontiac and the leaders of the Delaware, Seneca, and Shawnee felt the English betrayal and the French defeat as the end of the civilization they had come to know, we can only speculate. Perhaps, in fact, they were conscious of no such thing. In any case, they did not need a theoretical analysis to formulate a reason for war. Jeffrey Amherst provided reason enough when, upon the fall of Detroit to the British on November 29, 1760, he announced his decision to abolish the custom of giving presents to the Indians. What was especially galling was his assertion that the unlimited supply of gifts made the Indians lazy and overly dependent on British largesse, discouraging them from hunting, the means by which they obtained their own sustenance as well as merchandise for trade. Even as Amherst made this assertion, he was most particular about cutting off the Indians' supply of ammunition—the very thing they most needed for the hunt.

In the wake of Amherst's edict ending the flow of gifts, a prophet arose among the Delaware, counseling the Indians to reject all the ways of the white man and return to a pure Indian life, the way of the ancestors. Although Neolin—whom the English called alternately "the Delaware Prophet" and "the Impostor"—charged his listeners to keep the peace, English traders in and around Detroit were worried. They regarded the Delaware Prophet as an agent of a "conspiracy" (they did not use the word "confederacy") among local tribes. What they did not understand was that Neolin filled the vacuum left by the bad faith of the English and the defeat of the French. In any case, his call to peace was heeded. Indians gathered, and many became disciples of the Delaware Prophet.

Yet there was no armed uprising—at least not until Pontiac entered the picture.

The Treaty of Paris, including the cession of all French territory in North America, was concluded without the participation of France's Indian allies, of course, and news that the English were suddenly in uncontested possession of the Ohio Country prompted Pontiac to call a grand council on April 27, 1763. Here he urged the Potowatomis and Hurons to join his Ottawas in an attack upon Detroit. Four days later, Chief Pontiac visited the fort with a group of his warriors, ostensibly to entertain the garrison with a ceremonial dance. His real purpose was to size up the outpost's defenses. On May 5, Pontiac outlined his plan of assault: The warriors would conceal muskets, tomahawks, and knives under their blankets. Once they were inside the fort, the attack would begin. The operation was scheduled for May 7 but was thwarted by an informant whose identity has never been discovered. Fort Detroit's garrison of 120 Royal Americans and Queen's Rangers was prepared for Pontiac's entrance on the appointed day. The chief came with three hundred warriors, each with a blanket thrown over his shoulder, but Pontiac quickly realized that he had lost the element of surprise. Though his warriors outnumbered the garrison two to one, he withdrew from the fort without firing a shot.

Yielding to pressure from some of the warriors, who accused him of cowardice, Pontiac tried to enter the fort again on May 8, but garrison commander Henry Gladwin told him that he would admit only the chiefs, no warriors. In a bid to demonstrate innocence of intention, Pontiac organized an intertribal game of lacrosse just outside the fort. At the game's conclusion, he told Gladwin that he and his warriors would be back the next day for council, whereupon the commandant reiterated that he would admit only the chiefs.

Again frustrated, but pressured by his warriors, Pontiac led a quick series of raids against the settlements in the vicinity of the fort. Next, his Ottawa warriors, joined by Wyandots, Potawatomis, and Ojibwa, began firing into the fort. After some six hours, the attackers withdrew, exhausted. Five of Gladwin's men had been wounded in the firing. On May 10, following this exchange, Pontiac conferred with other Indian leaders and local French traders. The French counseled a truce, and Pontiac allowed that he, too, desired peace. Accordingly, he sent a few of the traders, along with four Indian chiefs, to the fort with a request that Captain Donald Campbell, Gladwin's second in command, be sent out to negotiate. Gladwin, who did not trust Pontiac, refused to order Campbell to go; the captain, however, volunteered, reassured by the French that he would be treated as an ambassador.

No sooner had the stockade gate closed behind him than Campbell was set upon and taken off as a hostage. On the next day, May 11, Pontiac ordered Gladwin and his garrison out of Fort Detroit, telling him that he, with fifteen hundred warriors, would storm it within an hour. Gladwin refused, whereupon some six hundred warriors opened fire on the fort, maintaining the assault until after seven in the evening. Again Pontiac demanded surrender; again Gladwin refused, declaring that he would discuss no terms of settlement until Campbell was released. In the meantime, small raiding parties ambushed travelers and struck at nearby settlements, and Pontiac distributed war belts to the Miami Indians as well as to French traders and farmers in Illinois Country, inviting their support. While Miami warriors showed interest, the French, no longer confident of Pontiac's ability to control his warriors, demurred. They had been hearing tales of harassment at the hands of Indians allied to Pontiac. Seeking to put an end to the settlers' misgivings, Pontiac met with a delegation and delivered a memorable speech of apology for the actions of some of his followers. He then pledged his undying loyalty to France. This was largely interpreted as a moot point, since the war was over, but the chief nevertheless managed to win sufficient support from local Frenchmen to make battle in full earnest.

Early in June, after the Indians had attacked Michilimackinac and a number of other forts, they advanced east, laying siege to Forts Pitt, Ligonier, and Bedford in Pennsylvania. Those large outposts held out, but, about June 16, 1763, Seneca killed all fifteen or sixteen men of the garrison at Fort Venango (Franklin, Pennsylvania), except for the commandant, Lieutenant Francis Gordon, to whom they dictated a list of grievances addressed to the king of England. Having written the list as he was directed, Gordon endured three days of torture before he died. From Venango, the Seneca moved on to Fort LeBoeuf (present-day Waterford, Pennsylvania) on June 18. They put it to the torch, killing six or seven of its thirteen-man garrison. Joined by Ottawa, Huron, and Ojibwa warriors, the Seneca attacked Fort Presque Isle (Erie, Pennsylvania) on June 20, razing the fort to the ground. Thirty English soldiers surrendered in return for a pledge of safe conduct to Fort Pitt. The pledge notwithstanding, the Indians divided up the defeated men among the four tribes as prisoners. Some were killed; some went missing; a handful returned to the white settlements.

In at least one case, the attacks on the forts brought an extraordinary response. When a party of Delaware warriors demanded the surrender of Fort Pitt on June 24, Simon Ecuyer, commanding in the absence of Colonel Henry Bouquet, refused. He informed Bouquet, who sent off a dispatch to General Amherst on July 13, reporting on the situation and including the following postscript: "I will try to inocculate the Indians by means of [smallpox-contaminated] Blankets that may fall in their hands, taking care however not to get the disease myself." He added, "As it is pity to oppose good men against them, I wish we could make use of the Spaniard's Method, and hunt them with English Dogs, supported by Rangers, and some Light Horse, who would I think effectively extirpate or remove that Vermine." Amherst replied on July 16, 1763, "You will Do well to try to Innoculate the Indians by means of Blankets, as well as to try Every other method that can serve to Extirpate this Execrable Race. I should be very glad your Scheme for Hunting them Down by Dogs could take Effect, but England is at too great a Distance to think of that at present." Bouquet ordered Ecuyer to summon the Delaware chiefs to the fort for a conference. There Ecuyer presented them with a handkerchief and two blankets from the fort's smallpox-ridden hospital. Not only did the attackers soon retreat, but a rescued white captive of the Delaware later reported that the disease had become epidemic in the tribe.

Other forts fell under attack. Fort Niagara endured a Seneca siege and was never taken. Detroit likewise survived a siege—this one of five months' duration, from May to September, at the hands of the Ottawas, Ojibwa, Potawatomis, Hurons, Shawnee, Delaware, and Eries. In the meantime, Bouquet led a column to the relief of Fort Pitt, about 460 men, including Highlanders of the famous Black Watch regiment. On August 5, when they were within thirty miles of the fort, at a spot called Edge Hill, a party of Delaware, Shawnee, Mingoes, and Hurons ambushed the column's advance guard. Bouquet's forces held the high ground throughout the long afternoon of battle, but they were nevertheless surrounded. Bouquet responded by planting a thin line of men along the crest of Edge Hill, so that, when the sun came up on August 6, the Indians would be lured by the sight of a weakly held position. The gambit worked. Seeing the soldiers, the warriors made a radical departure from their accustomed fighting style. Abandoning the stealthy tactics of forest warfare, they rushed into the open to charge the English position. Breaching the line without difficulty, they suddenly found themselves set upon by two full companies, which had been held in reserve. In number, losses were probably about equal on both sides. For Bouquet it was fifty killed and sixty wounded, but the Delaware counted two chiefs among their casualties and, having failed to stop the relief column from reaching Fort Pitt, gave up a battle decisive enough to earn a name, the Battle of Bushy Run, named for the stream beside which Bouquet was camped.

Unlike most so-called Indian uprisings, Pontiac's Rebellion ended decisively and with profound consequences. The chief lifted the siege of Detroit in September, and on October 31, 1763, he agreed to peace in return for a pledge that English settlement would stop at the Allegheny Mountains. The promise came directly from King George III in the form of a royal proclamation that was binding not on the Indians, but on his own colonial subjects:

> And whereas it is just and reasonable, and essential to our Interest, and the Security of our Colonies, that the several Nations or Tribes of Indians with whom We are connected, and who live under our Protection, should not be molested or disturbed in the Possession of such Parts of Our Dominions and Territories as, not having been ceded to or purchased by Us, are reserved to them or any of them, as their Hunting Grounds—We do therefore, with the Advice of our Privy Council, declare it to be our Royal Will and Pleasure that no Governor or Commander in Chief in any of our

Colonies of Quebec, East Florida or West Florida, do presume, upon any Pretence whatever, to grant Warrants of Survey, or pass any Patents for Lands beyond the Bounds of their respective Governments as described in their Commissions: as also that no Governor or Commander in Chief in any of our other Colonies or Plantations in America do presume for the present, and until our further Pleasure be known, to grant Warrants of Survey, or pass Patents for any Lands beyond the Heads or Sources of any of the Rivers which fall into the Atlantic Ocean from the West and North West, or upon any Lands whatever, which, not having been ceded to or purchased by Us as aforesaid, are reserved to the said Indians, or any of them.

. . . And whereas great Frauds and Abuses have been committed in purchasing Lands of the Indians, to the great Prejudice of our Interests. and to the great Dissatisfaction of the said Indians: In order, therefore, to prevent such Irregularities for the future, and to the end that the Indians may be convinced of our Justice and determined Resolution to remove all reasonable Cause of Discontent, We do with the Advice of our Privy Council strictly enjoin and require that no private Person do presume to make any purchase from the said Indians of any Lands reserved to the said Indians, within those parts of our Colonies where We have thought proper to allow Settlement.

For the first time in American history—perhaps even in all history—an emperor had proclaimed a limit to his own empire. The action was intended to buy the goodwill of the Indians not in the interest of promoting a middle-ground civilization in the French manner but because defending the North American frontier had proven to be a ruinous drain on the British exchequer. What neither king nor Parliament foresaw, however, was that the effect of the proclamation, while temporarily salutary for relations with the western tribes, would permanently erode those that existed between the colonies and their mother country.

13

White Savages

—=≻◆≺=—

VICTORY! STARTING IN THE Pennsylvania backwoods with
something at the very least resembling an assassination followed by the
desperate defense of a miserable little stockade imprudently raised in a
swampy meadow, then nearly reducing British settlement in North America to a narrow coastal strip, the French and Indian War ended far better
than crown, Parliament, and the English colonists had any reason to expect. The French were utterly defeated, their American empire extin-
guished. True, a brief but very bloody Indian uprising followed the Treaty
of Paris in 1763, but King George III's royal proclamation of that year, by
voluntarily contracting the frontier of English settlement (at least for the
time being), brought the promise of resolution and peace.

France's King Louis XIV had wanted an empire in North America.
England's King George III ended up with one instead.

Or did he?

Thomas Gage was born in 1719 or 1720 at Firle Place, East Sussex, where
his family had lived since the 1400s. His father, the first Viscount Gage,
sent the boy to Westminster School in 1728, at which his classmates

included John Burgoyne and Richard Howe, with whom he would, years later, unsuccessfully attempt to extinguish a great American rebellion. Sometime after he graduated from Westminster in 1736, Gage joined the army. In January 1741, he purchased (as was the custom of the day) a lieutenant's commission in the 1st Northampton Regiment, which was the start of his rise through the military. He fought in the ongoing War of the Austrian Succession (1740–48), serving as the Earl of Albemarle's aide-de-camp in the harrowing 1745 Battle of Fontenoy, then fought at the brutal Battle of Culloden, April 16, 1746, which brought the Second Jacobite Uprising to a sudden, bloody end.

Gage purchased a major's commission in the 55th Foot Regiment (later renumbered as the 44th) in 1748 and was promoted to lieutenant colonel in 1751. This veteran of battles particularly fierce became a mildly effete clubman prominent in British high society. He made gentlemanly connections with such figures of power and influence as Jeffrey Amherst, who would become his benefactor in the French and Indian War, which Gage joined in 1755, when his regiment was sent to North America as part of Braddock's expeditionary force.

Gage and his regiment, as we saw in chapter 12, were the first to be hit in the catastrophic Battle of the Monongahela, in which Braddock as well as Sir Peter Halkett, colonel of the 44th, were killed. When Halkett fell, Gage assumed command of the beleaguered regiment and thereby absorbed much of the blame for its defeat. Although this resulted in his failure to rise to permanent command of the 44th, his friendship with Amherst led to his appointment as military governor of occupied Montreal late in the war, followed by his promotion to major general in 1761 and his assignment to command of the 22nd Regiment. Gage disliked the thoroughly thankless task of governing Montreal, and as soon as the Treaty of Paris was announced in 1763, he sought a new post. It came quickly, in October, when Amherst, about to begin an extended leave of absence in England, named him acting commander in chief of North America. This meant a welcome removal from Montreal to New York City on November 17, 1763. It also meant that he had the responsibility of dealing with the intense violence of Pontiac's Rebellion.

Doubtless in the course of his education at Westminster, which, like all English public schools, was strongly grounded in classical history, Gage had read Plutarch and likely encountered the story of King Pyrrhus of Epirus, who defeated the Roman Legion at Heraclea in 280 BC and Asculum in 279 BC during the Pyrrhic War, incurring in these battles severe casualties. Retailing a report by Dionysius, Plutarch wrote of how "it is said, Pyrrhus replied to one that gave him joy of his victory that one more such victory would utterly undo him." Pyrrhus of Epirus had won a "Pyrrhic victory." Now Gage was about to understand just what that phrase meant.

War weary and well aware that Parliament was adamant against appropriating any more funds for fighting colonial wars, Gage sent Colonel John Bradstreet and Colonel Henry Bouquet to deal with Pontiac by force of arms even as he also put Sir William Johnson on the case. His brief from Gage was to negotiate an end to the war—and to do so with as small an investment of treasure and blood as possible.

In choosing Johnson for the assignment, Gage knew his man. As we have already noted, he had rapport and credibility with the Iroquois (who had long-standing trade relations with the English), as well as with the traditionally anti-English Algonquian tribes, which was virtually unique among the English. Born in Ireland in 1715, Johnson began the settlement of his uncle's lands at the eastern end of the Mohawk Valley near present-day Amsterdam, New York, about 1738. He entered the fur trade, in which he prospered, investing most of his profits in the purchase of land directly from the Indians. In this way, he became a powerful force in colonial New York as well as among the tribes of the Iroquois League and their dependent peoples. Like the French, he operated comfortably between the Euro-American and Native American cultures, and in 1759 his Mohawk common-law wife, Molly Brant, gave birth to the first of their eight children. Molly's brother, Joseph Brant, became a warrior of renown and a man of great influence among the Mohawks, thanks largely to Johnson's sponsorship. It is a measure of Johnson's thoroughly hybrid identity that even as he frequently donned Iroquois ceremonial dress and was unashamed to perform the ritual dances and other ceremonies he knew so well, he also enthusiastically supported the work of English missionaries who were attempting to Christianize the Indians.

Johnson's standing with the Iroquois was instrumental in discouraging the western tribes' support of the French during King George's War of 1744–48. Recognizing this, New York governor George Clinton appointed Johnson provincial superintendent of Indian affairs in 1746. Some years later, during the Albany Congress, convened in 1754 on the eve of the French and Indian War, Johnson was again instrumental in keeping the Iroquois out of the French camp—though, except for the Mohawks, they remained mostly neutral, and the Seneca, westernmost of the tribes, sometimes inclined actively toward the French. In 1755, Johnson led British, provincial, and Mohawk forces (under Chief Hendrick) in an assault against the French and their Indian allies at Crown Point on Lake Champlain and also defended British positions on Lake George. The next year, he was named superintendent of Indian affairs for the Northern Department and colonel of the Six Nations.

Johnson proved himself a capable commander of mixed Anglo-Indian forces throughout the war, and after the French surrender of Detroit in 1761, he was appointed the crown's principal emissary to the Indians of the Ohio Country. Gage recommended his appointment as Indian administrator after the 1763 Treaty of Paris delivered tribes formerly allied with France to British control.

Of course, that "control" was nominal, and Johnson knew it. He believed that the most effective means of actually enforcing influence over the western tribes was to find a way to regulate relations between Euro-Americans and Native Americans on the frontier. As he saw it, this meant regulating the fur trade in the western Ohio Country, which, under the unlicensed trading of the French, had been mostly unregulated. His concern was to assert authority—the rule of law—not merely over the Indians but also over the white traders with whom they came into contact. He well understood that the Indians would respond to abuse at the hands of traders with acts of vengeance, which could very quickly rise to the level of outright war. The fur trade was something whites and Indians had in common, a cultural and commercial nexus. It therefore seemed to Johnson the great rein by which he could guide relationships on the frontier among the English, the French, and the Indians.

It was one thing, of course, to promulgate regulation of the fur trade and quite another to enforce it. Johnson appointed enforcement deputies, supervised by his nephew Guy Johnson, his son John Johnson, and the fur traders George Croghan and Daniel Claus, both of whom were fluent in Iroquoian and Algonquian languages and were well regarded among a variety of tribes. He also built trading forts, thereby merging the military and the commercial functions.

In the meantime, Johnson was hearing the rumblings of what would soon erupt as Pontiac's Rebellion. He warned Jeffrey Amherst about it and protested the announcement of Amherst's new policy discontinuing the custom of giving presents to the Indians, predicting that it would provoke a war. As we saw in chapter 12, Amherst, yielding to parliamentary parsimony, failed to heed Johnson's warning.

William Johnson was unable to prevent Pontiac's Rebellion, but he did succeed in keeping most of the Iroquois neutral during it, except for some Seneca bands. He welcomed King George III's Proclamation of 1763, which he considered a necessary precondition to imposing law on a frontier that was so uncomfortably occupied by English, Indians, and dispossessed (but still present) Frenchmen. The proclamation would bar English settlers from encroaching on Indian land, but it would still permit Anglo-Indian interaction through the fur trade, which, if regulated, would represent a form of law that all parties could subscribe to. Johnson knew that the "Proclamation Line" was not intended as a permanent limit on English settlement; however, he hoped that it would buy time for order to develop on the frontier. In part, this would require all parties to accept English laws that applied equally to English, French, and Indians; but Johnson also wanted to go beyond this basic step. His chief goal for shaping Anglo-Indian relations now that New France was out of the picture was to train the English to emulate, in their relations with the Indians, the very people they had defeated: the French.

If the British victory in the French and Indian War had taken away the Indians' Onontio—their "Great Mountain," their French "father"—Johnson reasoned that the English themselves would have to assume the role and become the new "father." The most visible tokens of this were gift giving and the regulation of trade, so that Indians would feel that they enjoyed the protection of the same English laws they were required to obey. First and foremost, Johnson intended his policy to elicit good behavior from the Indians; however, this was predicated on his ability to secure good behavior from the white residents of the frontier, which, in turn, depended on the commitment of the British government to provide presents and to enforce law and regulation. Johnson would get nothing of the kind.

Settlers largely ignored the 1763 Proclamation Line, and Parliament failed to fund measures to enforce compliance. Johnson himself explained the result in a 1772 letter to the Earl of Dartmouth, British secretary of state for the colonies. What he wrote applied equally to conditions in the mid-1760s: The "back inhabitants [frontier people] particularly those who daily go over the Mountains of Virginia employ much of their time in hunting, interfere with them [the Indians] therein, have a hatred for, ill treat, Rob and murder the Indians, that they are in generall a lawless sett of People, as fond of independency as themselves, and more regardless of Governmt owning to ignorance, prejudice, democratical principles, & their remote situation."

It was a most incisive analysis of life (and death) on the Ohio Country frontier in the years after the French and Indian War. Consider it closely. Clearly, the Proclamation Line was porous, with colonists crossing it "daily." Once ensconced in the royally proscribed country, they spent their time hunting. In the Indian view, land was not so much *owned* as it was *used*. Its exclusivity as "property" lay in its resources, especially the physical and cultural sustenance embodied in hunting. Traders (who did not use the land) were not considered trespassers, but hunters (who did use it) were.

Had the "back inhabitants" who crossed the Proclamation Line "interfered" with the Indians only by hunting, this would have been provocation enough to create combat conditions on the frontier, but, Johnson wrote, they did more and they did worse. In his letter to Dartmouth, he accused them of hatred, which motivated their ill treatment, robbery, and murder of the Indians. Having broken the law by crossing the Proclamation Line, they were an entirely "lawless sett of People," who would be bound by no law whatsoever but instead considered themselves independent and "democratical." Johnson had a plan for governing the *Indians*, but he found the illegal *white settlers* literally ungovernable, combining as they did a philosophy of independence with ignorance and prejudice.

Thomas Gage, in 1770, described the frontier people as "almost out of the Reach of Law and Government. Neither the Endeavors of Government, or Fear of Indians has kept them properly within Bounds." The English missionary David McClure referred to them as "white Savages," who "subsist by hunting, and live like the Indians." The worst aspect of living like an Indian, as far as missionaries and government officials were concerned, was indulging in a wildness that transgressed all social restraint. The white people of the frontier went "naked," meaning that they wore Indian clothing. They engaged in sex with Indians—not intermarriage, as in Franco-Indian culture (which most of the English nevertheless found unacceptable), but fornication (which was a sin) and rape (which was crime). They got drunk—rum having become as valid a form of frontier currency as fur. They committed murder.

The Ohio Country was becoming a casual killing ground. Murder had devolved into a form of social exchange between whites and Indians. Fired up by rum, a settler might resolve any dispute or perceived insult by murder, for which the murdered man's Indian relatives and friends would exact vengeance in kind. William Johnson sought in vain to bring killers to justice under English law. In the case of accused white men, however, juries would almost never hand up a conviction; indeed, law enforcement officials—if any could be found or recruited—rarely consented to make an arrest, and if transgressors were hauled east to Philadelphia to stand trial, white mobs would often free them. In the case of accused Indians, the tribes objected to being subject to laws the whites did not obey. Like other Englishmen, Johnson understood that English law was supposed to apply equally to all subjects of the empire, which included the Indians of the territory ceded by the French. On the other hand, he also accepted the reality of his inability to apply the law to anyone, white or Indian, on the lawless frontier, writing to Gage, who had himself complained that local colonial officials protected rather than punished white criminals, that "from the present disposition of our People we can expect little Justice for the Indians."

In the spring of 1766, Johnson sent his lieutenant, the trader George Croghan, to explain to a council of Ohio Indians the necessity of submitting to English justice. Croghan recorded in his journal the gist of what the Indians said by way of response: "Before when accidents [apparently their euphemism for murders] happened . . . we made up by Condoling with each other, which is the antient Custom of all Our Nations in this Country"—that is, on the frontier, where Euro-Americans and Native Americans interacted. Croghan's journal entry continued: "But you have broke tho. [through?] our old Customs and made New Ones which we are not well acquainted with; And you Can't Expect, let us be ever so desirous of living in Peace, that we will Sit Still and See our People murdered by yours without having the Same Satisfaction from you that you Demand of Us."

In June, Croghan advised Johnson to return to the "antient Custom" of "condoling" the relatives of murdered Indians by covering the slain person's grave with presents of both symbolic and practical value. A Shawnee with whom Croghan spoke told him that, in the past, this practice "had made their young men's & women's hearts perfectly easy," extinguishing any desire they had for revenge. From about the summer of 1766 on, Johnson, with Gage's agreement, tried to embrace this policy. Publicly, both men continued to assert the authority of English law. In practice, however, Gage ordered the military to refrain from reprisals against Indians who took revenge against white murderers, and Johnson approved of condolence through the presentation of gifts. The problem was that neither colonial nor royal governments were willing to fund gift giving on any effective scale. In an effort to prevent the culture of murder (and rape and robbery) from escalating up the vengeance ladder to full-scale war, Johnson was willing to compromise the absolute sovereignty of English law by resorting to "antient Custom," but he lacked the government appropriations necessary to do so.

Condolence through gift giving might have gone a long way toward mollifying the Indians of the frontier, but in the end it was at best a partial solution, a gesture. When the French had controlled the western Ohio Country, they lived in relative harmony with the Indians of the trading villages they shared, Detroit, Kaskaskia, Michilimackinac, Vincennes, and others. These villages became worlds unto themselves and were largely autonomous, but not defiantly or militantly independence seeking. The self-regulation they practiced was not intended to undermine the central authority of New France or the French Empire. It was practiced because it worked, period.

William Johnson might nevertheless have denounced the French attitude as "democratical" and exhibiting "independency," yet the product of this attitude was very different on the Franco-Indian frontier than on the Anglo-Indian frontier. George Croghan understood this when he wrote to Johnson in 1765 that the French and Indians had been "bred up together like Children in their Country, & the French have always adopted the Indians Customs & manners, Treated them Civily & supplied their wants generously," becoming (now in Gage's words) "almost one People with them." The French model of fur trade, in which the traders went to the Indians, lived among them, and even married with them, was both creator and product of this attitude, whereas the English model, which demanded that the Indians come to a Hudson's Bay Company "factory" to trade their pelts, both flowed from and reinforced an attitude of cultural segregation, misunderstanding, prejudice, and even racial hatred.

There were exceptions to the customary English model, including men like Johnson, married to a Mohawk, and Croghan, a trader universally respected by his Indian partners, but these exceptions were notable precisely because they were rare. By and large, English colonial society condemned the kind of hybrid cultural relationships common in French frontier life. Stories of English frontiersmen "going native"—becoming "white Savages"—were a kind of Ohio Country pornography, exciting, titillating, sensational, but unacceptable. For instance, a trader known to history only as Bruce was raided, robbed, and financially ruined by an Ojibwa raid against Michilimackinac in 1763. His response was not to appeal to English authorities (if he could even have found any to hear his appeal) but to seek refuge among the Fox, whom he knew as enemies of the Ojibwa. In the course of time, Bruce was adopted by the tribe and rose to become a war leader among them. In 1770, seven years after his business had been destroyed, Bruce led a Fox war party against the Ojibwa leader, known as the Grand Saulteur, who had led the 1763 Michilimackinac raid. Bruce's warriors killed the Grand Saulteur, which was both a triumph for the Fox and a sweet helping of personal vengeance for Bruce. Because the Grand Saulteur happened to be a relative and ally of Pontiac, the English authorities also approved of what Bruce had accomplished, even though his choice of life among an Indian tribe remained socially unacceptable.

A military victory against a hated enemy somewhat redeemed the otherwise aberrant Bruce in English eyes, but in reading most accounts of English frontier people who allowed themselves to become "white Savages," one soon gets the impression that the ultimate taboo—the final frontier—was sexual intimacy. Rape and prostitution were conventionally objectionable, whereas intimacy of the kind the French and Indians routinely embraced was taboo. The English trader James Kenny, eager to gain an edge in doing business with Indians, employed as an interpreter and adviser an ex-captive of the Indians, who, in the course of his captivity, had learned much about tribal customs. Kenny followed his employee's advice up to the point at which Indian women demanded to sleep with him as a condition of trade. When Kenny responded to the demand by locking the women out of his trading house, they showered his shutters with stones. Despite whatever his knowledgeable employee might have tried to explain to him about tribal customs, Kenny could not overcome his own cultural prejudices to accept sex as a necessary component of trade.

Kenny was trading in the 1760s, immediately after the conclusion of Pontiac's Rebellion. Within a few years, many English traders, it seems, would learn to accept sexual exchange as part of the business they did. It *was* business, not an expression of cultural intimacy. Among Delaware women, for example, trading sex for rum became routine, acceptable to traders, but obnoxious to tribal leaders, who, seeking ways to curb this prostitution, gave women increasing control over trading other commodities, especially furs. By the 1770s, among the Delaware, this reduced prostitution, but it increased the consumption of rum—not among the women who traded furs for it but among Delaware men, to whom the women retailed the rum they had bought. The consumption of liquor was generally deleterious to the Delaware and, throughout the frontier, it served to increase violence within tribes as well as between whites and Indians. To be sure, Franco-Indian relations had never been pure bliss, but they were far more generally peaceful and mutually profitable than relations between the English and the Indians. As the Franco-Indian frontier became the Anglo-Indian frontier, its people, both white and Indian, suffered a notable degradation.

As the 1760s wore on, the Anglo-Indian frontier did become united—albeit united in the cultural degradation and general lawlessness shared among Euro-American and Native American inhabitants alike. This dysfunctional commonality was the de facto essence of local Anglo-Indian relations, and it eroded the attempts of English authorities and Indian leaders to create relations that were both official and more productive. The Franco-Indian frontier had been largely independent of central authority. Although Louis XIV had not approved, this independence by no means constituted a deliberate act of defiance. For all its violence and the mutual enmity of its inhabitants, the Anglo-Indian frontier also became increasingly independent of both the seaboard colonial establishment and the mother country beyond. Unlike the frontier under French hegemony, however, this independence was lawless, violent, destructive, and, ultimately, defiant.

Acutely frustrated, William Johnson made in 1768 a grand effort to push back. He convened a council at Fort Stanwix (modern Rome, New York), attracting more than three thousand representatives of the Iroquois League to meet with him for the purpose of adjusting and rendering permanent the boundary line established by the Proclamation of 1763. The result of the meeting, signed on November 5, was the Treaty of Fort Stanwix, which pushed the original Proclamation Line far to the west, back from the Alleghenies to the Ohio River as far as the Tennessee River, thereby securing for white settlement Kentucky and most of present-day West Virginia. Unable to control violation of the 1763 Proclamation Line, Johnson rendered the lawless settlements lawful simply by pushing the line back. Yet in negotiating only with the Iroquois, Johnson left out of the agreement the tribes most affected by it, the Algonquians, many of whom were traditional enemies of the Iroquois and, in the seventeenth century, had even been on the receiving end of a genocidal campaign of conquest during the Beaver Wars.

The Treaty of Fort Stanwix was, in part, an attempt to cement an alliance between the English and the Iroquois, but it achieved this by dealing in real estate neither the British nor the Iroquois owned. It was therefore less a bold assertion of authority than a bald abdication of authority. In the very same spirit of lawlessness that characterized violators of the Proclamation Line, it threw open vast tracts of the West to settlement, ensuring conflict between the Algonquian tribes and the new settlers and demonstrating to those tribes an imperial willingness to betray them. In the aftermath of British victory in the French and Indian War, William Johnson had seen his task as persuading the Indians of the Ohio Country that the English were their new Onontio, their new "father." By the Treaty of Fort Stanwix, the new father summarily disowned all those he had claimed as his children.

In 1763, the British Empire had triumphed over the French Empire in North America only, five years later, to surrender to the criminals of the Ohio Country all that it had won below Canada. The Treaty of Fort

Stanwix proclaimed the expansion of British imperial sovereignty, but did so with neither legal basis nor the intention of enforcing by military or other practical means the sovereignty it claimed. Thus this new assertion of an empire had the paradoxical effect of diminishing that empire, creating a vacuum of authority and power in the West that the Shawnee rushed in to fill with an effort to lead the western tribes in a united war against the expansion of English settlement.

It is the nature of a vacuum to draw in everything and everyone indiscriminately, and so the Shawnee were not alone in acting on the far frontier. Early in the 1770s, Lord Dunmore, the royal governor of Virginia, announced his intention to issue patents for land on both sides of the Ohio River in the vast western territory his colony had long claimed. Early in the spring of 1774, Michael Cresap, a Virginia militia captain who operated a trading post at Redstone Old Fort (modern Brownsville, Pennsylvania) on the Monongahela River, acted on Dunmore's authority to survey and claim a large expanse of land in what is today West Virginia, in the vicinity of Middle Island Creek (the modern town of Sistersville). Dunmore also sent Ebenezer Zane—who would earn fame after the American Revolution as the builder of Zane's Trace into the Northwest Territory—to survey and settle lands near the mouth of Sandy Creek. Finally, another party, under George Rogers Clark—an able frontiersman and notorious "Indian hater" (such was the contemporary term) who would become an important general during the American Revolution—gathered at the mouth of the Little Kanawha River (today Parkersburg, West Virginia) to await the arrival of an additional Virginia contingent. Once fully assembled, Clark's force would begin the settlement of territory in Kentucky.

While waiting, Clark received word that the Shawnee and Indians associated with them—some called the grouping the "Ohio Confederacy"—were on the march down the Ohio, clearly intent on war. Clark's first thought was to strike preemptively at an Indian village called Horsehead Bottom, near the mouth of the Scioto River. He sent for Cresap, whose party was some fifteen miles upriver, because he knew that the militia captain was the only one among all the officers who had some experience fighting Indians. On his arrival at the Little Kanawha camp, however, Cresap talked Clark out of making the attack. He advised Clark that war was not inevitable, unless the Shawnee were provoked by the very attack Clark contemplated. Instead, Cresap proposed withdrawing to Wheeling, Virginia (today West Virginia), where they should watch and wait. Once the frontier settled down, they could all—together—resume their westward march.

On reaching Wheeling, the group found not the calm safety they had sought but panic. Survivors of Shawnee attacks had been trickling in, and their stories were harrowing. Cresap suddenly found himself overwhelmed by volunteers, eager to wipe out the Shawnee menace. Shortly before Cresap was about to lead his force out of Wheeling, Captain John Connolly, commanding officer of Fort Pitt, sent an express asking him to remain in Wheeling until he, Connolly, had received replies to messages he had sent to local tribes. Connolly wanted to assess their intentions before risking the ignition of a major regional war. Cresap was willing to comply and sent off a message to that effect. It crossed paths with a second message from Connolly: The Shawnee-led Ohio Confederacy was bent on war.

Convening a council of war on April 26, Cresap dramatically read Connolly's message to all those assembled. Everyone agreed to war.

The first engagement came the very next day, with shots exchanged between a few Indians and some local settlers, who chased the Indians a full fifteen miles to Pipe Creek. There the warriors took a stand. The resulting skirmish was brief and cost both sides relatively little blood. On April 28, however, Clark, anticipating retaliation for the skirmish, joined his forces to those of Cresap at Redstone Old Fort and braced for the onslaught.

In the meantime, a hunting party led by a prominent local Mingo known as Logan was camped on the west bank of the Ohio at Yellow Creek, some thirty miles upstream from Wheeling. Logan was a rare and influential voice of conciliation along the turbulent frontier. On April 30, his younger brother, known to the whites as John Petty, and two female relatives, one of whom was pregnant and also accompanied by an infant girl, left Logan to cross the river to Baker's Bottom, home of

Joshua Baker, a rum trader. No sooner did they enter the cabin than they were set upon by thirty settlers, led by an "Indian hater" named Daniel Greathouse. The mob killed all the Indians, except for the infant. Soon hearing of the massacre, Logan jumped to the conclusion that it had been the work of Cresap and resolved to go on the warpath.

The panic that had been concentrated at Wheeling now swept the frontier. Settlers, fearing a major war to be waged by what they believed was a vast "Ohio Confederacy," either holed up in rude forts and block-houses or hightailed it back east, clambering across the Alleghenies, some never to return. Alarmed by the influx of frontier refugees, Lord Dunmore preemptively declared war on June 10, 1774, and raised a militia. It was September 8 by the time he personally led fifteen hundred men toward Fort Pitt, from which he intended to descend the Ohio River to its juncture with the Kanawha. There he planned to rendezvous with Colonel Andrew Lewis, whom he had tasked with recruiting an additional fifteen hundred militiamen. The combined forces of Dunmore and Lewis were then to cross the Ohio and destroy the Shawnee villages there.

On September 30, Dunmore reached Fort Fincastle (later called Fort Henry), which he had recently ordered built at Wheeling. In the meantime, Lewis, with eleven hundred men, marched out of his rallying point, Camp Union (now Lewisburg, West Virginia), and reached the Kanawha's mouth on October 6. Seeing that Dunmore had not yet arrived, he sent messengers up the Ohio to find him. Dunmore met them on October 9 and gave them a dispatch to carry back to Lewis, announcing his intention to proceed to the Shawnee towns on the Scioto River and ordering Lewis to cross the Ohio and meet him at the towns.

Lewis received the dispatch and was about to commence his crossing when, on October 10, he and his militia force were attacked by warriors under the Shawnee chief Cornstalk at Point Pleasant.

Most battles between whites and Indians were brief if bloody skirmishes, but the fight at Point Pleasant lasted throughout the day and concluded with desperate hand-to-hand combat. At the cost of some two hundred casualties, Lewis forced Cornstalk to retreat back across the Ohio. Lewis then rendezvoused with Dunmore on Sippo Creek, about eight miles from a major Shawnee town on the Scioto. Cornstalk came to this place—the two commanders called it Camp Charlotte—to talk peace. He told Dunmore that Logan had agreed to stop fighting but refused to participate in the peace talks. This had the effect of stalling the talks, whereupon Major William Crawford led a force of 240 militiamen against the Shawnee village of Seekunk, destroying it. That was enough to prompt Cornstalk and his Mingo allies to surrender unconditionally on October 26, 1774.

Lord Dunmore had reason to conclude that he had scored a signal triumph, for he believed that he had defeated a great regional Indian uprising. In fact, Cornstalk had fallen far short of raising the "Ohio Confederacy" the settlers so feared. All Lord Dunmore's War had done was to alert all the Indians of the formerly French-controlled Ohio Country that the English, regardless of what they might say, definitely meant to usurp their lands. When the American Revolution erupted in earnest in 1776 (from the Indians' perspective, it was a fight between one set of Englishmen and another), the Shawnee united with the renegade Cherokee chief Dragging Canoe in making war on Virginia, fighting not the British Empire but the frontier people—long filled with notions of "independency" and "democratical" ideas—who sought to break free from the empire once and for all. At the same time, the Iroquois (especially the Mohawks), with whom William Johnson had pretended to divide the vast Ohio Country, sought to protect what they regarded as their stake in the British Empire. William Johnson had died in 1774, but his nephew Guy Johnson, succeeding him as the empire's Indian superintendent, commissioned the Mohawk Joseph Brant to lead Iroquois forces against the rebellious frontier. The American Revolution, with its threat to Britain's North American empire, would accomplish what Britain's destruction of France's North American empire had failed to achieve. It made, at long last, common cause between Indians and Englishmen.

14

Big Knives and Red People

———◆———

AFTER TWO AND A quarter centuries of schoolteachers and schoolbooks, we all know the drill. There was the Stamp Act and all those other parliamentary instances of taxation without representation that, perceived as tyranny, stirred to action the urban radicals who were concentrated in Boston. Some, disguising themselves as Mohawks, held the Boston Tea Party in 1773, which brought reprisals from Parliament and crown that escalated into armed confrontation at Lexington and Concord in 1775 and motivated a Declaration of Independence a year after that. Lexington and Concord kicked off a very long war, even longer than the French and Indian War, spanning eight years from 1775 to 1783. Most of us recognize the names of at least some of the major battles of that war. After Lexington and Concord came Bunker Hill, Ticonderoga, the Boston Siege, Valcour Island, Brandywine, Germantown, Long Island, Trenton, Princeton, Oriskany, Saratoga (Freeman's Farm and Bemis Heights), Monmouth Court House, King's Mountain, Cowpens, Yorktown. These historical mile markers leave a lot of territory unaccounted for. Was it empty? A time of idleness and peace?

Of course not. Most of the American Revolution was not fought in the battles we know best, those seaboard contests between formally organized armies or parts of armies, but was a continuation of the violence on a frontier whose inhabitants had years earlier either declared their independence by their lawless and ungovernable behavior or found themselves cut loose from those they had considered "Onontio," their collective father. Most of the American Revolution was a frontier war. This statement will surprise some, but it will hardly come as a revelation to those who have read one or two modern books on the subject. Yet, typically, even these books don't get the nature of the frontier war quite right. In an effort to understand the American Revolution, they attempt to integrate the frontier theater into the same narrative that contains the seaboard theater, emphasizing that both sides employed Indian allies and auxiliaries in their effort to prevail and that the Indians endeavored to exploit the conflict between the two sets of Englishmen to stem the ongoing invasion of their lands. This interpretation is certainly not false, but it is hardly complete. Although both British and Patriot politicians and military leaders tried to enlist Indian allies, they often discovered—as British general Frederick Haldimand complained in 1781—that "there is no dependence [depending] upon even those Indians who are declared in our favor." What is more, the backcountry *white* settlers were equally unreliable. General Haldimand again spoke for the British side, but his complaint can readily be extrapolated to the Patriot cause as well. The settlers retired to the far frontier (Haldimand observed) "upon Pretense of separating themselves from Rebellion," but their actual motive was self-interest: to encroach "upon the most valuable Hunting grounds of the Indians and [secure] themselves rich settlements." This not only caused conflict with the Indians, undercutting their loyalty to the English, but the rogue settlers often attacked British soldiers, only to "profess their loyalty" if they happened to be taken prisoner by the British.

General Haldimand got it right, at least partly. Neither the Indians nor the whites of the backcountry were reliable allies of the British Empire. In his complaint about the white settlers, he also correctly identified self-interest as a leading motive. The settlers' objective was wholly self-interest, namely the usurpation of Indian land, and so they had need for unsettled conflict rather than placid alliance. Had he followed his analysis a step further, Haldimand might have taken some comfort in the realization that self-interest disqualified the settlers not only as reliably loyal British subjects but also as reliable Patriot rebels.

Haldimand was also correct in identifying self-interest as the motivation of the Algonquian Indians who professed themselves allies of the British: "There has not been a single Instance where the Indians have fulfilled their engagements but influenced by Caprice, a dream or a desire of protracting the war, to obtain presents, have dispersed and deserted the Troops." What he got wrong, however, was that the Indians' idea of self-interest was very different from that of the backcountry whites. Haldimand believed that the Indians wanted to prolong the war in order "to obtain presents," much as the whites wanted to exploit the war in order to obtain "rich settlements." Yet what he seems not to have appreciated is that, whereas land was an end in itself, presents were both desirable in themselves *and* symbolic of a beneficial relationship between the Euro-Americans and the Native Americans. A father gives presents to his children. In their desire for presents, the Algonquians expressed their desire for a new "father," not the self-centered independence the backcountry whites wanted, lawless freedom from *both* the British Empire and whatever government might emerge as a result of the revolution.

This was the great irony of the American Revolution in the West. The Indians resident there were more eager for a protective and profitable connection with a white governing authority than were their white neighbors, for whom "loyalty" meant loyalty to their own immediate self-interest, and "independence" meant freedom from both sides in the conflict.

The frontier of the American Revolution was really two theaters, the fringe of the seaboard establishment and the West—the far frontier, including the Ohio Country and Kentucky. What General Haldimand called the unreliability of Indian allies as well as white settlers was far more pronounced in the West than in the seaboard fringe. As a result, the fighting on the nearer frontier was often more intense, more "terrible"—in that the Euro-American combatants employed their Indian allies explicitly as instruments of terror.

For instance, William Tryon, the Loyalist governor of New York, urged British military commanders to "loose the savages against the miserable Rebels in order to impose a reign of terror on the frontiers." In London, Whig leader and former prime minister William Pitt the Elder recoiled from such statements, condemning the recommended tactics as "unconstitutional, inhuman, and unchristian," but attempted no steps beyond mild protest to curb the routine practice of terror.

On the near frontier, relations between the Iroquois—especially the Mohawks—and the British were of very long standing and, while founded on the fur trade, had evolved far beyond it, to the point at which British military leaders felt they could employ the Mohawks essentially as mercenaries, dealing with the chiefs in much the same way as the ministers in the mother country dealt with the German princes who retailed to the British the services of the so-called Hessians. Nevertheless, determined to take a lesson from the French and Indian War, in which the French had so many more Indian allies than the British did, the crown also created an Indian Department, charging it with improving Anglo-Indian relations. In 1775, almost immediately after Lexington and Concord, the Continental Congress emulated this example by creating an Indian Department of its own. The fact was, however, that many Indian leaders had decided to try to remain neutral in the war between the Englishmen, and others perceived a stake for themselves in a British victory. While it was true that King George III's Proclamation of 1763 had been ineffective, at least the king had tried to keep his people from invading Indian land. Many Indian leaders were all too familiar with the difficulty of bending their people to their will. If King George had been unable to control all of his people, so Indian elders often found themselves powerless to rein in the passions of young warriors. In any event, agents of the crown's Indian Department made it clear to as many tribal leaders who would listen that once they were independent of the king, the Americans would do nothing even to try to control their people. A Patriot victory would mean the loss of "Onontio George," and there would be no protection from the rapacity of white settlers.

By far the single most important Anglo-Indian alliance had been forged well before the outbreak of the American Revolution, between

William Johnson and Joseph Brant, whose Mohawk name was Thayen-danegea. Johnson was the common-law husband of Brant's sister, Degonwadonti—whose English name was Molly Brant—the daughter of his friend Nichus Brant and Nichus's Indian wife, Owandah. The union was a boon to Johnson's already thriving fur-trading business, which he enhanced further by informally adopting Joseph Brant, thereby giving him the benefit of education, money, and social station, while more firmly binding his business to Mohawk affairs.

Brant acquitted himself courageously fighting for the British in the French and Indian War, and, after Johnson died in 1774, he continued a close relationship with Johnson's nephew Guy. This relationship was the nucleus of the British alliance with the Mohawks during the American Revolution. Of all the eastern tribes, they were the prize allies, with their reputation as fierce warriors and their leading role at the "head" of the Iroquois Confederacy. Brant and other Mohawk leaders managed to per-suade three other Iroquois tribes, the Seneca, Cayuga, and Onondaga, to side with the British and against the Patriots—though this had the effect of splitting the Iroquois Confederacy, since the Oneida and the Tuscaro-ras did fight on the side of the Patriots. Significantly, the Oneida-Patriot alliance, like that between the British and the Mohawks, grew out of a personal relationship. Samuel Kirkland, a teacher and Presbyterian min-ister, had, before the outbreak of the war, worked among the Oneida and earned the friendship of tribal leaders. The Oneida, in turn, brought into the alliance members of the Mahican tribe (also called the Stock-bridge Indians), who had once been numerous and powerful but were now greatly diminished by ruinous warfare with the Mohawks. Another man, James Dean, an agent for the Continental Congress's Indian De-partment, was able to rally the Tuscaroras to the American cause. Valu-able though these alliances were, they could not offset the more powerful alliance the British made with the Mohawks and associated tribes.

Brant and other British-allied warriors, sometimes acting in concert with British regulars and Loyalists, sometimes acting on their own, raided the frontiers of Virginia, Pennsylvania, and New York. The raids became so common that in New York's Mohawk Valley, many Loyalists who had been forced out of their homes and lands by Patriots disguised themselves as Indians in order to terrify the usurping settlers. As 1777 drew to a close, the New York and Pennsylvania frontier, especially the Cherry, Mohawk, and Wyoming valleys, descended into a sickeningly predictable pattern of raid and reprisal. In April 1778, a combined force of Loyalists and Indians mounted a massive raid along the upper Susquehanna River, hoping to break the raid-and-reprisal cycle with a decisive action. At the Indian town of Tioga, Pennsylvania, the Loyalist colonel John Butler gathered four hundred Tory Rangers and Loyalist militiamen along with nine hundred Seneca and Cayuga, aiming to strike out against the Wyoming Valley of northern Pennsylvania. Butler and some of his Indian allies started building canoes for the trip down the Susquehanna while the Seneca chief Gu-cinge led four hundred warriors to make initial assaults on settlements along the river's west branch. While this was going on, Joseph Brant mustered 450 Indians and Loyalist militiamen for an attack on New York's Cherry Valley, at the headwaters of the Susquehanna.

Cherry Valley had been a target of raids since 1776, but the settlers there did remarkably little to defend themselves. Colonel Samuel Campbell took the desperate action of padding his small militia by dressing twenty-six boys in pointy paper hats and giving them wooden muskets to brandish as they marched back and forth. This crude deception was enough to deceive Brant (though not for long), sending him to attack nearby Cobleskill instead of Cherry Valley. Cobleskill was a knot of twenty houses, defended by twenty militiamen under Captain Christian Brown, whose command was reinforced by thirty-seven Continental Army soldiers from Colonel Ichabod Alden's 7th Massachusetts Regiment. Against Brant's 450 men they didn't stand a chance. Thirty-one (some sources say twenty-two) Patriots were killed and six wounded. Brant's raiders put Cobleskill to the torch.

In the meantime, the Wyoming Valley seemed a more formidable target. It was defended by a number of so-called forts, which were really nothing more than partly fortified houses, including Wintermoot's (or Wintermot's) Fort, Forty Fort, Jenkins' Fort, Wilkes-Barre Fort, and Pittston Fort. Most of these fell quickly to the raiders. The little garrison at Wintermoot's Fort professed itself to be Loyalist and gave up without firing a shot. Jenkins'

Fort fell on July 2, 1778, but Forty Fort, garrisoned by 450 Continental troops and militiamen under Continental colonel Zebulon Butler (no relation to John Butler) and militia colonel Nathan Denison, refused to surrender. John Butler withdrew, then burned down the captured Wintermoot's Fort on July 3 to make the defenders of Forty Fort believe that his Loyalist and Indian forces had given up. This, combined with wishful thinking, prompted Denison to propose a sortie out of Forty Fort to pursue John Butler's retreating forces. Zebulon Butler, far more experienced than the militia officer, warned him that he sensed a trap, but Denison and most of the others were tired of being cooped up. Denison's point of view carried the day, and he led the entire 450-man garrison out of Forty Fort. They had traveled no more than a matter of yards before they were enveloped in an ambush, which killed or wounded three hundred of their number.

The loss of Forty Fort and its garrison, by far the most substantial Patriot military force in the area, left the Wyoming Valley defenseless. John Butler burned every building to the ground even as Joseph Brant finally resolved to return to Cherry Valley. He raided Andrustown, seven miles west of Cherry Valley, on July 18, capturing fourteen settlers, killing eleven, then burning the town. After staging more raids in the area, he attacked the Mohawk River settlement of German Flatts (present-day Herkimer, New York) on September 17. By this time, however, Cherry Valley had largely emptied out, the residents having fled to the nearest forts. Brant burned the vacant buildings.

Devastating though these raids were, they did not have the decisive effect Butler and Brant had hoped for. Rather, they galvanized local Patriot militias to retaliate against Indian villages mercilessly. The retaliation spared not old men, women, or children. Learning of the cruel vengeance visited on his people, Brant returned to Cherry Valley in November 1778. By this time 250 soldiers of Alden's 7th Massachusetts had been sent to defend the valley. They were overwhelmed early in the morning of November 11 by eight hundred Tories and Indians, who not only killed the defenders but scalped, mutilated, and even cannibalized them. By two o'clock in the afternoon, Cherry Valley had been razed to the ground and wiped from the earth.

. . .

General George Washington, in command of the Continental Army and in charge of coordinating its operations with state forces and local militia, typically let frontier commanders take care of their own problems, but the "Cherry Valley Massacre" could not be ignored. Washington decided to launch a campaign of outright extermination against the Iroquois. He authorized the operation to begin early in 1779, but it was June 18 of that year before General John Sullivan, a New Hampshire schoolmaster's son, competent but cautious to a fault, marched his twenty-five hundred Continentals from Easton, Pennsylvania, to the Susquehanna River. The plan was for Sullivan to burn a swath through the Susquehanna Valley, moving up to the southern border of New York, while General James Clinton, who had been a colonel in the French and Indian War and whose brother was governor of New York, led fifteen hundred soldiers through the Mohawk Valley to Lake Otsego, then down the Susquehanna. While these two forces set about raking the countryside, Colonel Daniel Brodhead was assigned to lead six hundred men from Fort Pitt up the Allegheny. Unlike either Sullivan or Clinton, Brodhead had been raised on the turbulent frontier. Born in Marbletown, New York, in 1736, he grew up in what is now East Stroudsburg, Pennsylvania, where the Brodhead farm fell under Indian assault many times. By the time he reached adulthood, Daniel Brodhead was both an avid antitax advocate and an Indian hater. He both understood and embraced the common mission of all three forces: to destroy every Iroquois village and every Iroquois Indian they encountered as they converged.

Sullivan and Clinton planned to rendezvous at Tioga and march north to Niagara, to meet Brodhead at Genesee. Thus united, they would continue their sweep of total devastation. Such was the plan. In actuality, Sullivan took so much time to get under way that Clinton, impatient, took it upon himself to launch a six-day raid from his base of operations at Canajoharie on the Mohawk River beginning on April 21. Twelve Onondaga were killed, thirty-four captured, and fifty Indian houses were destroyed, but far from demoralizing the Iroquois, the attack served only to incite Brant to strike against the Mohawk Valley town of Minisink, which he destroyed, killing in the process 170 militiamen.

At last, on August 9, Sullivan had advanced as far as Newtychanning, formerly an important Seneca village, but now deserted. This notwithstanding, he burned its twenty-eight vacant structures before marching on to Tioga, where he made his rendezvous with Clinton. With a show of ceremony, he posted general orders calling for the total destruction of the Indians. Then, throughout August and September 1779, his men and those of General Clinton laid waste the Iroquois settlements throughout the region. Like Newtychanning, almost all had been abandoned before the arrival of the soldiers, so that, while Sullivan and Clinton occupied themselves in the destruction of empty buildings, the Iroquois remained at large, raiding the frontier. "I flatter myself that the orders with which I was entrusted are fully executed, as we have not left a single settlement or field of corn in the country of the [Iroquois], nor is there even the appearance of an Indian on this side of the Niagara," Sullivan wrote to the Continental Congress in September 1779. Even so, as Continental Army major Jeremiah Fogg observed in his journal on September 30, "The question will naturally arise, what have you to show for your exploits? Where are your prisoners? To which I reply that the rags and emaciated bodies of our soldiers must speak for our fatigue; and when the querist will point out a mode to tame a partridge, or the expedience of hunting wild turkey with light horse, I will show them our prisoners. The nests are destroyed, but the birds are still on the wing."

Such was the American Revolution on the near frontier. Simultaneously, farther west, the Ohio Country was also at war. As early as July 2, 1775, the leaders of the five Shawnee septs (bands) met at Chillicothe on the Little Miami River, in what is today the state of Ohio, to talk about how they should respond to the white invasion of Kentucky. One of the main Shawnee leaders, Chief Cornstalk, advocated neutrality in the ongoing fight among the whites. Despite his counsel, Shawnee warriors raided the new Kentucky settlements during the fall of 1775. This did nothing to stem the white tide, and in June 1776 George Rogers Clark traveled to Williamsburg to ask Virginia authorities (Virginia had jurisdiction over frontier Kentucky) to send troops to help resist the Indian raids.

Clark was a young man, having been born in 1752 in Charlottesville, Virginia, then growing up on a two-thousand-acre plantation in Caroline County. At nineteen, like fellow Virginian George Washington, Clark left the planter's life to become a surveyor, thereby casting his lot with frontiersmen and land speculators. In 1772, aged twenty, he made his first trip to Kentucky, which had recently been opened to settlement by the Treaty of Fort Stanwix. As we saw in the previous chapter, in 1774, while Clark was preparing to lead an expedition of settlers into Kentucky, Lord Dunmore's War erupted, in which Clark served as a Virginia militia captain. As the violence associated with Lord Dunmore's War melted into the American Revolution, the Kentuckians found themselves not only menaced by Shawnee but locked in a dispute over the sovereignty of their territory. Judge Richard Henderson of North Carolina, a hyperambitious land speculator, had recently "purchased" much of Kentucky from the Cherokee by means of an exuberantly illegal treaty. His aim was to become proprietor—as William Penn had been of Pennsylvania—of a colony he planned to call Transylvania, but most of the new settlers far preferred to remain under the jurisdiction of Virginia, and in June 1776 they sent Clark and the settler John Gabriel Jones to present a petition to the Virginia Assembly, asking for the formal extension of Virginia's boundaries to take in Kentucky. Clark and Jones succeeded in talking Governor Patrick Henry into creating Kentucky County, and Clark, summarily commissioned major of the Kentucky County militia, was given five hundred pounds of gunpowder to use in the defense of the new settlements.

While Clark was off on this errand, Pluck-kemeh-notee, a Shawnee subchief known to the whites as Pluggy, staged a series of fierce raids throughout the Kentucky settlements. En route to attack Harrodsburg, Pluggy was killed by settlers. The Shawnee chief Black Fish used this as a cause around which he rallied two hundred warriors in what he intended to be the ultimate raid; he meant to kill every last Kentucky settler.

On or about July 4, 1776, in council with Shawnee, Iroquois, Delaware, Ottawa, Cherokee, Wyandot, and Mingo war chiefs, Cornstalk caught the war fever and renounced his earlier inclination toward conciliation. Reasoning that it would be easier to kill the settlers if the Indians joined the British fight against the rebels, he abandoned his neutrality, declaring that it was "better for the red men to die like warriors than to diminish away by inches. Now is the time to begin. If we fight like men, we may hope to enlarge our bounds."

By this time, Black Fish had begun his campaign, and by the end of January 1777 he had driven most whites out of Kentucky. On April 24, Black Fish attacked the diehards at Boonesboro, laying it under a four-day siege in which one settler was killed and seven wounded, including Daniel Boone, who had founded the settlement. Boonesboro held out, and Black Fish withdrew, returning periodically to jab at other settlements.

Clark by now was raising his Kentucky militia; however, he was not planning to use it in the obvious way, the local defense of Kentucky. Although he was wholly untutored in the military art, Clark was a natural strategist. He immediately grasped that the way to stop the raids was to destroy the outposts from which the raids were launched and the raiders supplied. The main British forts were at Kaskaskia, Cahokia, and Vincennes. All were in modern Illinois and Indiana, not Kentucky, but destroy them, Clark reasoned, and the raiders would be without support. Moreover, destroy them, and the most important prize would be laid bare to attack: Detroit, the major British outpost in the Northwest and headquarters of Henry Hamilton, the crown's chief liaison with the Indians, who called him "Hair Buyer" because of the generous bounties he reputedly paid for Patriot scalps.

Before Clark could get his expedition under way, however, Shawnee warriors, together with Wyandots, Mingoes, and Cherokee, raided the area of Wheeling (in present-day West Virginia) during midsummer 1777. This prompted the Continental Congress to send General Edward Hand to recruit Pennsylvanians, Virginians, and Kentuckians for an assault on a Cuyahoga River outpost (near present-day Cleveland) from which the British supplied their western Indian allies. Learning of Hand's plan, Cornstalk, bearing a flag of truce, ventured into Fort Randolph on Point Pleasant at the confluence of the Ohio and the Kanawha rivers to deliver a dire warning: Attack, and all the Shawnee and allied nations would retaliate.

Captain Matthew Arbuckle, veteran of the Battle of Point Pleasant in Lord Dunmore's War and now commanding Fort Randolph, was contemptuous of both the message and the messenger. The white flag notwithstanding, he ordered Cornstalk, his son Silverheels, and another warrior taken prisoner. His idea was to hold them all to extort the good behavior of the Shawnee. Indian haters, however, were beyond the reach of military discipline and authority. On November 10, 1777, a party of locals broke into Fort Randolph, brushed by the light guard that hovered near the prisoners, and killed all the Indians. In a gesture of utmost contempt—learned, perhaps, from Indian warriors—they mutilated the remains.

The Shawnee, naturally, retaliated. During this campaign, on February 8, 1778, Chief Blue Jacket, with 102 warriors, captured a twenty-seven-man salt-making party at Blue Licks, Kentucky. Among the captives was Daniel Boone, founder of Boonesboro and, even at this early date, the most famous of the Kentucky settlers, a man who stayed in that hard country even now that newcomers were leaving in droves. He did not resist his captivity but instead pretended to turn traitor, accepted adoption into the Shawnee tribe, and offered to cooperate with none other than the Hair Buyer, Henry Hamilton. Boone supplied enough disinformation to the British leader, greatly exaggerating the size of Patriot forces in the region, to delay his decision to attack American-held Fort Pitt. At the same time, Boone also quietly acquired intelligence concerning the ongoing assault on Boonesboro. Once he determined for himself that he had heard enough, Boone made his escape, arriving at Boonesboro in time to lead the resistance there and to alert Fort Pitt to the imminent attack.

Major Clark, in the meantime, struggled to recruit an army, and by the end of May 1778, he had mustered no more than 175 men to march against Kaskaskia and Cahokia. He embarked with this diminutive force on June 26, 1778, in flatboats, reaching the mouth of the Tennessee River in four days. He made a stealthy attack on Kaskaskia, which he took without firing a shot. Clark was an Indian hater, who doubted that Euro-American and Native Americans could peacefully coexist, but he noted in a later memoir that "my situation and weekness convinced me that more depended on my own Behaviour and Conduct, than all the Troops that I had far removed from the Body of my Country." He was, he recognized, "Situated among French, Spanyards and numerous Bands of Savages on every Quarter." The requisite "Behaviour and Conduct" in this situation, he perceived, was not to give expression to his Indian-hating impulses but, rather, to win over the cooperation of local French traders (France had signed a Treaty of Alliance with the United States on February 6, 1778) and the Algonquian Indians friendly to them. (Local Spanish traders were somewhat less critically important, since Spain would not enter the American Revolution as a French ally until June of the following year.) Clark understood what some English commanders had understood in the French and Indian War, that the French were "more beloved by [the Indians] than any other Europeans," and he wanted to take advantage of this in addition to their extensive fur-trading connections with the tribes of the Illinois country and the upper Mississippi River to extend Patriot influence into these regions by identifying the Americans with the French at the expense of the British. True, the British also had trading relations with the Indians, but Clark understood that the intimate "French and Spanish mode [was] preferable" to British officiousness and was therefore to be emulated—even though the American tendency (and his own!) was to treat Indians as the British traditionally had, with contempt and loathing.

At Kaskaskia, where he established his forward base of operations, Clark met with representatives of various Algonquian tribes who visited him in the course of the year. For each he had the same message, as he paraphrased in a memoir: "The Big Knife"—that was the fiercely rapacious term by which the Algonquians called the Virginians—"are very much like the Red people they don't know well how to make Blanket powder and cloath &c they buy from the English (whom they formerly descended from) and live chiefly by making corn Hunting and Trade as you and the French your Neighbours do." Clark amplified this definition of common cause between the Algonquians and the Americans by explaining that the current war, the revolution, had started because the Americans wanted to begin making their own cloth and gunpowder and the British didn't want to let them. Clark's point was that the Americans, despite differences of race and language, had more in common with the Algonquians and the French than with the British, from whom they were "formerly descended" and whose language they spoke. Clark added to this a number of speeches in which he scorned the British ally and common enemy of the Algonquians and the Americans, the Iroquois. In this way, he sought to make an alliance with the Patriots appear to be a highly attractive option.

In his effort to win Algonquian hearts and minds, Clark had significant, though hardly complete, success. His British counterpart, Henry Hamilton, the Hair Buyer, was a formidable diplomatic opponent. Clark repeatedly explained that Americans traded with the British for goods they could not "know well how to make," but he went on to explain that their desire to make them had brought war. In this way, Clark offered the Algonquians the prospect of Americans as trading partners, even as he unfavorably compared with the British their ability to make the desired trade goods. Unconsciously, perhaps, this was Clark's acknowledgment that Hamilton held the ace. He could offer the Indians superior and more plentiful merchandise. Throughout the seventeenth century, this had been the problem in Franco-Indian relations. The Indians liked the French far more than they did the English—and for good reason—yet the English, obnoxious though they were, always had more and better goods to trade for Indian furs.

In addition, Hamilton, unlike his English predecessors during the French and Indian War, did not depend entirely on his superior trade inventory to cement favorable relations with the Indians. He did his best to reach out, to listen attentively at councils, and to participate decorously in Indian ceremonials—though he could never quite pull this off. For example, in preparing to lead a group of Indians to defend Vincennes against Clark's attack, Hamilton participated in a war dance, presented the requisite wampum belts, and even sang his war song, yet he declined to pour rum on the grindstone the warriors used to sharpen their axes. This was an important symbolic gesture, but he feared that distributing rum to the Indians would be detrimental to military discipline. Doubtless, it would have been—but his failure to observe this portion of the prebattle ritual stirred argument, eroded morale, created delay, and generally compromised the effectiveness of the alliance. Most of all, it revealed the brittle nature of the material out of which Hamilton's relations with his Indian allies was fashioned. He believed in the necessity of humoring the Indians—"to find some method to quiet their superstition, rather than mock or insult them"—but, like William Johnson in the French and Indian War, he was profoundly frustrated by his inability to persuade the Indians that their interests coincided with those of the British. How could they? Like Clark, Hamilton had to work with Algonquian Indians and the French at Vincennes. As he wrote of the local Wabash Indians, however, they were "in the dark with respect to the power of the British Nation" because "few but contemptible Renegadoes from the English" had "been among them, & the French traders from interest as well as a mortified pride, decrying as much as possible every thing that was not French."

Henry Hamilton was discovering, to his dismay, the truth of the old expression: When all you have is a hammer, everything looks like a nail. He tried to fake interest in the concerns of the Indians and the French, but he could not, in the end, accept their interests as genuinely valuable, and thus he continually beat his head against the stone wall of *their* inability to look at *their* situation from the *British* point of view.

This was all a very good thing for Clark.

Advancing from Kaskaskia, he easily took Cahokia, then set his sights on the fort at Vincennes. He believed this would be no easy objective. Hair Buyer was waiting for him there, and he commanded forces far larger than the small band Clark had been able to muster. What Clark did not know was that Hamilton himself had little confidence in his forces, especially his Indian allies, whom the French, he believed, had generally poisoned against the English through "poltronnerie and treachery." All Clark knew was that Hamilton had more men than he, and he therefore decided that his only chance against these superior numbers was speed. Thus, on February 5, 1779, he began a 150-mile march from Cahokia to Vincennes through a hostile wilderness, in the depths of winter, at as quick a pace as he could extract from his men. They reached Vincennes on February 23 and quietly took a few prisoners, who readily revealed that Hamilton's nearby stronghold, Fort Sackville, was defended by only a few hundred men. Things were looking up, but Clark nevertheless assumed that a "few hundred" was still more than 150. If he laid siege to Fort Sackville, all Hair Buyer had to do was hold out for British reinforcements—but Clark had not come so far to turn back. He resorted to pure bluff.

Summoning one of his prisoners, Clark wrote out a letter, handed it to him, and told him that he was being sent back to Vincennes, where he was to convey the contents of the letter to the village leaders and to Henry Hamilton. The text proclaimed Clark's intention of capturing Vincennes, then issued a stern warning to all those loyal to King George III: Withdraw into Fort Sackville, because they would get no quarter, not from Clark, not from his soldiers, and certainly not from the Indians at his command. Clark signed the letter with the names of many officers, all of whom were quite real, of course, but by no means present in his command. While waiting for Hamilton and the good people of Vincennes to contemplate the contents of the letter, Clark cherry-picked a number of his men, issued to each of them a stick on which he had tied a cloth painted to resemble a regimental banner, then directed them to march to and fro, holding their makeshift standards aloft. When he was satisfied that this had given Hamilton the impression that he was facing a large, well-organized, and highly disciplined force, Clark launched his attack.

Almost instantly, Hamilton's Indians deserted him. Worse—for the Hair Buyer—a group of Kickapoo and Piankashaw Indians, formerly enlisted in his service, came forward to volunteer themselves to Clark. As for the white residents of Vincennes, who were mostly French, none came forward to help Hamilton, leaving him with no choice but to surrender both Vincennes and Fort Sackville. Clark initially refused to talk terms with Hamilton, claiming that "the Cries of the Widows and Fatherless on the Frontiers . . . Required [the blood of Hamilton and his men] from my Hands," but, in the end, Clark paroled him, the other whites, and most of the Indians—reserving his vengeance for a select few, three Indian warriors whom he consigned to be "Tomahawked by the Soldiers and flung into the River." Much as Clark had sought before the battle to portray Hamilton as the ruthless Hair Buyer, both patron and partaker of Indian savagery, so Hamilton subsequently described Clark, who (he wrote), after overseeing the butchery of the three Indians in succession, approached him to speak, "his hands and face still reeking from the human sacrifice in which he had acted as chief priest." Thus both Clark and Hamilton made a show of understanding and exploiting Indian culture and war practice only to condemn one another for doing precisely this. Moreover, for all their show of solidarity with the Indians, neither man truly respected Indian culture, Indian war practices, Indian motives, or Indian needs, yet both professed astonished frustration when the Indians failed to climb aboard the imperial—whether U.S. or British—bandwagon.

Clark had hoped that taking the western forts would bring an end to the raids in Kentucky. Although neutralizing the British in the region did entice some Indian leaders to talk peace, the raids continued and became so widespread in 1780 that Clark had to abandon the culminating objective of his campaign, the capture of Fort Detroit, so that he could return to fighting Shawnee and Loyalists closer to Kentucky. He chased off the raiders and burned the Shawnee "capital" of Chillicothe (in modern Ohio) along with many other Shawnee towns. Most damaging of all, he destroyed perhaps ten thousand bushels of corn—the ration on which the Indians relied to survive the winter. This, rather than a direct military victory, brought a long pause in the raiding.

Leading a much larger army than Clark, General Sullivan made less headway against the Indians of northwestern New York in the summer of 1779. If anything, his campaign of destruction served only to enflame the diehards, and on May 21, 1780, Sir John Johnson, son of William Johnson, led a massive mixed Indian-Loyalist raid on the Patriot forts of the Mohawk Valley. His four hundred Tories and two hundred Indians burned Johnstown, New York, on May 23 (some sources say May 21). Later, during the summer, Joseph Brant razed Caughnawaga and Canajoharie, then moved along the Ohio into Pennsylvania, intercepting a one-hundred-man Pennsylvania militia force under Archibald Lochry. Five officers and thirty-five enlisted troops were killed; the rest became prisoners.

This victory achieved, Brant and his men returned to New York, linked up with John Johnson's Loyalists and a Seneca chief named Cornplanter, and—now eighteen hundred strong—swooped down upon the Scoharie Valley on October 15, then marched up the Mohawk River, putting to the torch all that they found. In just five days, Johnson and Brant destroyed as much as Sullivan had in a full month of marching. Wounded while raiding with Johnson, Brant did not return to action until early 1781, when he hit the Mohawk and Cherry valleys. Washington had scant forces with which to oppose him. He sent Colonel Marinus Willett with 130 Continental troops and a handful of militiamen to do the best they could, and, thanks to Willett's skill, the raids were suppressed for the rest of summer. When they resumed in October, Willett responded vigorously and was fortunate enough to kill Walter Butler, the most important Loyalist leader in the region. This brought a brief respite in the war on the near frontier even as the American Revolution itself came to an end with the signing, in Paris, of preliminary articles of peace between the United States and Great Britain on November 30, 1782. The articles included the crown's agreement to cede the Ohio Country—the entire Old Northwest—to the new nation.

Yet while the seaboard celebrated victory and independence, the fighting in the West did not end. Too many people, residents of a civilization partaking of Iroquois, Algonquian, English, and French elements and interests, a civilization mixed together by nearly two centuries of trade, felt themselves without a real stake in either a British Empire or an American Republic. Theirs was an empire of fur, and the terms on which it might achieve peace had not even been contemplated in the negotiations conducted at Paris, a world away from the rivers and forests of the Ohio Country, the places where fur was traded for sustenance and where mere merchandise—presents—bought allies and made enemies.

15

Anthony and Astor

THERE WERE THOSE—THEY were few—who wanted the western war with the Indians to end, even before the Treaty of Paris ended the American Revolution. The most notable of these was George Morgan, the son of Welsh immigrants, who had set up as a fur trader and partner in the mercantile firm of Baynton, Wharton, and Morgan. During the American Revolution, he was commissioned a colonel and given the principal job of Indian agent, assigned to Fort Pitt, where, from 1776 to 1779, he represented the Continental Congress in its diplomacy (or attempted diplomacy) with the Indians of the Ohio Country.

As a trader, Morgan wanted to use the trading model to make peace in the West and thereby free up Patriot resources to concentrate on fighting the war in the East. Morgan well knew that fur traders—especially the French—were capable of comfortably coexisting with the Indians precisely because they had no claim on either Native lands or Native spirits. They wanted to acquire neither empire nor religious converts. The Indians were willing to hunt and trap beaver, and the traders were willing to allow them to be the primary producers of this merchandise. Except for those committed to the Hudson's Bay Company and its factory system, traders were willing to work within the framework of the Indian culture and the Indian production model. In exchange for the pelts, they offered trade goods—value for value, with no political, moral, religious, or real estate strings attached.

Morgan saw that Patriot politicians, administrators, and military men failed to understand the importance of the trading model and therefore mightily resisted adopting it. When the Mingo chief White Mingo reminded American Indian commissioners who had come to negotiate in the Ohio Country that "the ancient custom of our Forefathers"—by which he meant the custom of gift giving—ensured that the parties in a negotiation were "always treated well," the commissioners stubbornly refused to take the hint and instead bristled at what they saw as a demand for bribes. They therefore reported that negotiating with the western Indians was an exercise in extortion. Morgan also recognized that Indians who tried to persuade their brethren to ally themselves with the British often pointed out that the Patriots, even when they were willing to trade, demanded higher prices for lesser merchandise than the British asked for better goods. This was proof, the Indians said, that the Americans were no friends. In 1777, dissension developed within the Delaware tribe over whether or not to side with the Patriots. The argument against the alliance (Morgan recorded) was that the paucity and poorness of American presents and American trade goods would bring down ridicule on any foolish enough to attach themselves to a people "who cannot [even] furnish . . . a pair of stockings or a Blanket."

When Morgan appealed to the Continental Congress and to local settlers, militia leaders, and other military officials to reintroduce gift giving and to do so generously, he was greeted with suspicion and accused of being a secret Tory, perhaps even a Loyalist spy. In 1777, when Morgan went further, suggesting that the surest road to peace in the West was to withdraw from Kentucky, the Continental Army general Edward Hand briefly arrested him, convinced that the British had put him up to suggesting the territorial concession. For his part, George Rogers Clark called for increasing pressure on the hostiles by making threats to force the neutrals and other fence sitters to choose sides. Clark's patron, Virginia governor Patrick Henry, put it this way: "Savages must be managed by working on their Fears."

. . .

The Patriots' aggressive policy in the Ohio Country would prove to be a miserable failure. Morgan proposed conciliating the Indians with presents, an "ancient" custom that had worked well in the past, and he also proposed withdrawing from the contested far frontier in order to concentrate all military effort on combat in the eastern theater, the quicker to win the war's principal objective, national independence from the British Empire. These were strategically rational moves, proposed by a former Indian trader who understood that trading value for value was more likely to produce a successful outcome than extorting value through violence. Yet Morgan's rationality could not prevail over the pervasive irrational need to conquer and kill.

On the Ohio frontier, Indian hating was a more powerful motive than national independence. In part, this was because the white settlers of the far frontier had great interest in acquiring their own independence—in the form of land—but very little interest in acquiring national independence. Their overriding concerns were local and had as little in common with the concerns of such colonial capitals as Boston, Philadelphia, and Williamsburg as they did with London fashions. The irrational roots of the policy of limitless aggression seemed to run even deeper than this, though. After all, immediate, local gain may be strategically shortsighted, but it isn't necessarily crazy. The infamous Gnadenhutten Massacre of March 8, 1782, however, was.

On October 19, 1781, Joseph Brant, representing the Mohawks, and Pimoacan and Pipe, chiefs of the Delaware, met with Abraham, chief of the "Moravian Indians"—also known as the Christian Munsee, members of the Delaware tribal group who had been christianized by Moravian missionaries. Brant and the others tried to persuade Chief Abraham to unite with them in attacking white settlements, but Abraham refused, arguing that the Americans would surely leave peaceful Christian Indians alone. Captain Matthew Elliott, in command of the British garrison at Fort Detroit, then ordered the Moravian Indians to leave their homes (in what is today western Pennsylvania and eastern Ohio) "for their own safety" and to resettle closer to territory covered by the British stronghold at Detroit. Accordingly, Abraham and the Moravian Indians set out for the banks of the Sandusky River in Ohio Country. By early 1782, however, a harsh winter famine compelled them to seek permission to move back temporarily to their mission towns on the Tuscarawas River. The permission granted, they arrived just after Brant and his Delaware allies had raided the area. In February, Pennsylvania militia Colonel David Williamson was ordered to "punish" all of the "hostiles" he could find. As it turned out, Williamson's mission coincided with the Moravian Indians' return.

In March, Williamson and a force of one hundred marched into Gnaddenhutten, a town German Moravians and the Indians affiliated with them had founded on the Tuscarawas River. The English equivalent of its German name, "Huts of Grace," expressed the aspiration of both the Indian as well as the white residents. Encountering Chief Abraham and the forty-seven men, women, and boys gathered with him there, Williamson announced that he had been sent to take them back to Fort Pitt, where they would be protected from all harm. At Williamson's request, Abraham sent runners to the neighboring Moravian Indian town of Salem to fetch the Indians there and bring them back to Gnaddenhutten. No sooner was this done than Williamson ordered the wrists of each Indian bound behind him or her, and when the fifty-two people from Salem arrived, he bound them as well. All were thus confined until the following morning, when Williamson announced to them that were to be executed as punishment for the recent raids. To Abraham's plea that they had refused to take part in the raids, Williamson turned a deaf ear and a stone heart. At nightfall, his men killed a total of ninety-eight men, women, and children, delivering to each a mallet blow to the back of the head. Two boys managed to escape, surviving to tell the grisly tale.

The Gnaddenhutten Massacre was universally condemned, including by the Pennsylvania legislature, but neither Williamson nor anyone else was punished for it. That the atrocity would trigger acts of Delaware vengeance was, of course, inevitable. These raids, in turn, prompted an order to Colonel William Crawford, who was assigned, on May 25, to undertake the so-called Second Moravian Campaign for the purpose of destroying the Moravian Indian, Delaware, and Wyandot towns all along the upper Sandusky River, including the principal village of Sandusky. One of the 480 volunteers Crawford commanded was John Rose, whose real name was Baron Gustave Rosenthal, a Russian nobleman self-exiled from his homeland to escape familial vengeance after he had killed a man in a duel. Rose recorded his impressions of Colonel Crawford and left a picture of what a frontier citizen army was really like:

> [Crawford was] kind and exceedingly affectionate . . . Brave, and patient of hardships. . . . As a Commanding Officer, cool in danger, but not systematical. Like others in the same stations, he wanted to be all in all: by trusting everything to the performance of his own abilities only, everything was but half done, and Everybody was disgusted. . . . Jealous of his military Knowledge & Superiority, but a mere quack in the profession of a Soldier. No military Genius; & no man of Letters.

As to the men of Crawford's command:

> Upon these Volunteer Expeditions, every Man allmost appears on Horseback; but he takes care to mount the very worst horse he has upon the farm. This horse he loads with at least as much provisions as he is well able to carry. No man calculates the distance he is going, or how long he can possibly be absent. As he has provisions enough to maintain at least three Men on the Campaign, he does not stint himself to a certain allowance. Lolling all day unemployed upon his horse, his only amusement is chewing [tobacco], particularly as all noise in talking, singing & whistling is prohibited.

The horses, Rose observed, were actually an impediment to a wilderness campaign, overloaded as they were with provisions, which made it particularly difficult for them to negotiate thickets and swamps. "Add to this that every Man hangs upon his horse to the very moment of attack. Then instead of being disencumbered & ready to defend himself, his first care is his horse. Him, he must tye and look after during an engagement, because all his dependence is in his horse & his horses burthen."

Furthermore, Rose complained, order—"regularity and precaution"—was "looked upon as . . . mere Moonshine." Lack of discipline and their commander's want of skill promised disaster.

Simon Girty was a man of Scots-Irish ancestry who, taken captive by Seneca when he was a child, spent between four and seven years (sources vary) with the tribe before he was returned to his family. At the outbreak of the American Revolution, he declared himself a Patriot, but when the Seneca sided with the Loyalists, so did he, and he was thereafter vilified as a turncoat—a double turncoat, really, betrayer of the American cause as well as his race. Girty served as a liaison between the British and their Indian allies, yet he was also clearly averse to gratuitous killing and was known to have ransomed Patriot prisoners at his own expense. Thus when he approached Crawford under a flag of truce with a warning to turn back, some in Crawford's command implored their leader to listen. Girty explained that Crawford and his men were surrounded by Shawnee and Delaware. Turn back now, he said, before it was too late.

Crawford would hear none of it. Spurning both Girty and his advice, he pressed on until on June 4, near Sandusky, the Shawnee began to pick off isolated members of his force. On June 5, they encircled the militiamen and pinned them down, awaiting the arrival of additional warriors. Crawford attempted to organize a retreat, but his command had dissolved in confusion and panic. Clots of men deserted en masse. Others just wandered off into the woods. Some forty to fifty were known to have been killed or captured, and twenty-eight were wounded. Among those taken captive was Colonel Crawford.

Relationships were seldom cut-and-dried on the far frontier, and Crawford, though he led a punitive expedition, actually had a reputation among the Delaware as a fair-minded and honorable man. He asked his captors to send for Wangomend, a Native religious leader revered as a prophet. Wangomend was a voice of peace, who had been Crawford's guest at Fort Pitt and who was known to be sympathetic to the Americans. He answered Crawford's summons but told him, in sorrow, that he could not intercede on his behalf. Although it was understood that Crawford had not massacred the men, women, and children at Gnadenhutten, it was more than enough to be associated with those murderers. He was therefore beyond saving. At the conclusion of this exchange, a tearful Wangomend bid Colonel Crawford farewell as Chief Pipe tied him to a stake and lit the low fire that would slowly, very slowly, burn him to death. Before the flames consumed his life, a Moravian Indian named Joseph was sent forward with a scalping knife. It was he who took the colonel's scalp while the colonel still had the consciousness to feel it.

Crawford's defeat emboldened others to undertake new raids along the upper Ohio, and these, in turn, prompted a Patriot call for yet another expedition against the Sandusky villages. Joseph Brant, who had been planning an attack against Wheeling, decided to turn his force of eleven hundred Indians and Loyalists back to the Ohio to head off that new Sandusky expedition. En route, on August 16, 1782, a detachment from his force, three hundred Wyandots and Tory rangers, including Simon Girty, surrounded Bryant's (or Bryan's) Station, five miles north of Lexington, Kentucky. After a brief siege, Girty withdrew, destroying crops, killing livestock, and stealing horses as he went. While he retreated, reinforcements from Lincoln and Fayette counties (the latter group led by Daniel Boone) arrived at Bryant's Station. From here, 180 mounted riflemen lit out after Girty's party. At Lower Blue Licks, they caught sight of a few Indians—whereupon Boone, suspecting a trap, argued for holding off the attack until the arrival of reinforcements. Hugh McGary, a blustering major of militia, countered that Girty and his men must not be allowed to escape. Brushing aside Boone's objections, he led the small force in an assault.

Boone, of course, was right.

In no time, the Patriots were flanked in ambush, and in the ensuing battle on August 19, seventy Americans were killed and twenty were captured or wounded in what was the Kentucky militia's costliest defeat to date. It boded the abandonment of the Kentucky frontier—the very thing Morgan had argued for as a matter of deliberate strategy—but neither the Continental Congress nor General George Washington wanted to deliver the Loyalists such a victory. General William Irvine, who had replaced Brodhead as commander of the Continental Army's Western Department, assembled 1,200 regulars and militiamen for an assault on the Sandusky

Shawnee, Wyandot, and Delaware towns. In the meantime, George Rogers Clark mustered an additional force of 1,050 Kentuckians on the Ohio shore opposite the mouth of the Licking River. His objectives were the destruction of the just-rebuilt towns of Shawnee strongholds of Chillicothe and Piqua, and on November 9, 1782, he issued his general orders:

> As an action with the Enemy may be hourly Expected the Officers are Requested to pay the Strictest attention To their duty as Suffering no man to Quit his Rank Without leave as Nothing is more dangerous than Disorder. If fortunately any prisoner Should fall in to our hands they are by no means to be put to Death without leave as it will be attended with the Immediate Masseerce [massacre] of all our Citizens that are in the hands of the Enimy and Also deprive us of the advantage of Exchanging for our own people, no person to attempt to take any Plunder until Orders Should Issue for that purpose under penalty of Being punished for Disobedience of orders and to have no share of Such plunder himself. The Officers in perticular are requested to Observe that the Strictest Notice be paid to this Order, as much Depends on it all plunder taken to be Delivered to the Quarter Master, to be Devided among the Different Batallions in proportion to their Numbers any person Concealing Plunder of any kind Shall be Considered as Subject to the penalty of the Above Order.

Clark was on the move well before Irvine, but, as had happened in Sullivan's campaign in western New York (chapter 14), the Indians eluded him. He burned Chillicothe and other abandoned Shawnee towns, and he destroyed by his estimate ten thousand bushels of corn, but he encountered only twenty of the enemy, killing ten and capturing the others before the preliminary articles of peace between the United States and Great Britain were signed on the thirtieth of the month, and the Ohio Country officially became the property of the United States. At least, that is what the papers drawn up in Paris said. In physical fact, as 1782 was drawing to a close, the English, having just made peace, controlled more Indian allies than they had had in the entire French and Indian War and at any other time in the American Revolution. None of *them* had signed a treaty.

To their Indian allies, the withdrawal of the British when they were clearly at the height of their power in the West was incomprehensible. Nevertheless, the Algonquians for the most part complied with British instructions to end offensive operations, although they appealed to their erstwhile partners to look after their interests in making a final treaty with the Americans. In simply ceding the Ohio Country and the entire Old Northwest to the Americans, the British clearly did no such thing. The Iroquois expressed greater outrage than the Algonquians, protesting that the British were giving away what was not theirs. This, of course, was precisely what the British *and* the Iroquois had jointly done in the Treaty of Fort Stanwix with regard to the Algonquian land in Ohio and Kentucky.

Although the crown did enter into the Treaty of Paris without regard for the interests of its Indian allies, a number of the local British officers did feel some sense of obligation. General Frederick Haldimand believed that simply abandoning the Indians to their fate at American hands was not only morally wrong, it posed a danger to British Canada as well as to the British fur trade, which still extended from Canada into the ceded territory below. Noting that the Paris treaty left the timing and terms of the British evacuation of the western outposts vague, Haldimand and others proposed that garrisons be maintained indefinitely to help ensure good treatment of the Indians. His goal was to maintain rather than end the Anglo-Indian alliances and to enable the continuation of British trade with the Indians on both sides of the border.

The British fur trade had actually prospered during the American Revolution. Not only did the Hudson's Bay Company come into its first great maturity during this period, but a new firm, the North West Company, was founded in 1779, during the height of the Revolution, to compete with it. Both companies were headquartered in British Canada, and both operated north as well as south of the border. In 1787, the North West Company merged with Gregory, McLeod and Co., which brought into the firm the Mackenzie cousins, Roderick and Alexander. The remarkable Alexander Mackenzie led exploration of Canada's vast western territories and established Grand Portage, Minnesota, on Lake Superior, as the company's regional headquarters and its main supply depot for the mountain men who were trapping and trading in the far western peltries. Grand Portage had been a fur-trading center since the seventeenth century, but the North West Company greatly augmented its importance and ensured that Detroit and Michilimackinac would, the Treaty of Paris notwithstanding, continue to function as major British fur-trading posts as well.

Whereas the local British, such as Haldimand, were motivated by a sense of moral rectitude reinforced by a desire to maintain the profitability of the far western fur trade to reassert their role as "fathers" to the Indians, George Rogers Clark observed in a letter to Virginia governor Benjamin Harrison on May 22, 1783, that "we shall be Eternally Involved in a war with some [Indian] nation or other of them, until we shall at last in order to save blood and treasure be Reduced to the necessity of convincing them that we are always able to crush them at pleasure, and determined to do it when Even [ever?] they misbehave." Moreover, Clark believed that, with armies in the field and the war against Britain ended, "a greater Opportunity can never offer to Reduce them to Obedience than the present moment."

As it turned out, the Shawnee, Ottawas, and Miami in the Ohio Country had no intention of being so "reduced." *They* hadn't lost the war between the British and the Americans. Quite the contrary, it seemed to them that their position had never been stronger and that there was no greater opportunity to drive the Americans from their land than the "present moment."

The national government of the newly independent United States made offers to purchase (albeit cheaply) Indian territory, but the Shawnee spurned them all, and, in January 1786, a Shawnee chief named Kekewepellethe, known to the Americans as Tame Hawk, declared emphatically that the Kentucky and Ohio land the settlers desired was Shawnee land and would always be Shawnee land. Richard Butler, the U.S. commissioner endeavoring to conclude a treaty with the Ohio Country tribes, replied to Tame Hawk that, on the contrary, the land was the sovereign territory of the United States, claimed by virtue of the American victory over the Indians' British allies, and that the purchase offer was a generous expression of friendship and goodwill rather than an act of necessity. Under threat of war, and with his people suffering the effects of a hard winter and the loss of the presents they had received from the British, Kekewepellethe at length agreed to relinquish the entire Miami Valley. Almost immediately, however, other Shawnee septs, together with the Miami, repudiated the agreement. Led principally by the war chiefs Blue Jacket (Shawnee) and Little Turtle (Miami), the Shawnee and Miami intensified a campaign of hit-and-run raids that had begun during the American Revolution.

During the fall of 1786, George Rogers Clark raised a two-thousand-man militia force in Kentucky and marched it toward the Wabash Valley, where Shawnee, Miami, and Ottawa warriors had banded together and were meeting with British military officers and fur traders, who, taking advantage of the vague language of the Treaty of Paris, loitered in the Ohio Country.

Clark was no longer the man he had been during the Revolution. Given to strong drink, he was prematurely aged and infirm. Not only did he fail to encounter the enemy, he did not try very hard to do so, and his militia disbanded and returned home as soon as their short-term enlistments had expired. Another force of eight hundred militiamen, under Colonel Benjamin Logan, did attack Shawnee villages on the Miami River shortly after the dissolution of Clark's force, but did so with little lasting effect. In the summer of 1787, Logan conducted a more intensive raid, destroying large stocks of Shawnee provisions. According to Clark's theory of intimidation, this should have reduced them to obedience. Instead, it drove the Shawnee into a closer union with the Miami and drew other tribes into the alliance, including Ottawas, Ojibwa, Kickapoo, and Potawatomis. Together, these tribes, which were periodically joined by the Chickamauga and Cherokee, raided settlements all along the Cumberland River from 1788 on.

What would be known as Little Turtle's War was now in full swing, and by 1790, weary of chronic Indian trouble, settlers appealed for a federal campaign against the Indians throughout the entire Ohio Valley. This prompted mobilization of the "First American Regiment," which had been formed in 1784. In 1790, it was placed under the command of

Josiah Harmar, a not particularly distinguished Continental Army officer during the Revolution but now—by default—the senior commander in the diminutive United States Army. Harmar led 353 regimental regulars and 1,133 militiamen in a westward march during the fall of 1790.

Both Little Turtle and Blue Jacket were exceedingly well informed of Harmar's plan of attack. President George Washington's secretary of war, Henry Knox, fearful that the British in the area would interpret the movements of the First American Regiment as an attack on them, ordered territorial governor Arthur St. Clair to tell Major Patrick Murray, the British commandant at Detroit, that an assault was being launched against the Indians, not His Majesty's subjects. Murray thanked St. Clair for the information—then, like a good father, informed the Indians.

On October 19, Harmar dispatched 150 mounted militiamen under John Hardin in the hope of locating a few hostiles to fight. Little Turtle and his Miami warriors got the jump on Hardin's company, however, springing an ambush that sent it withdrawing in panic and disorder. The mounted troops collided with infantrymen who had been sent as reinforcements and, infecting them with their own fear, sent them into retreat as well. A mere thirty army regulars and nine militiamen stood their ground against the attack. Harmar had no choice but to order a general withdrawal. On October 21, he sent a small body of regulars and four hundred militiamen to act as a rear guard for the retreating First American Regiment. This rear guard, however, was also ambushed, this time by Blue Jacket and his Shawnee. As before, the militia broke and ran, though not before 108 of them had been killed, along with 75 regulars. This encounter was not as one-sided as the first—Blue Jacket also lost at least a hundred warriors—but he held the tactical upper hand and was inclined to return to the fray. He would have done so, too, had it not been for a total lunar eclipse that took place the night following the battle, which Blue Jacket's Ottawa allies took as an evil omen. Against Blue Jacket's anguished protests, they refused to renew the fight, and his Shawnee followed suit. Thus the First American Regiment was saved from likely annihilation.

After Harmar's defeat, the Shawnee and allied tribes staged a series of winter raids—an innovative and daring tactic, since Indians traditionally avoided fighting in the winter. Early in January 1791, Blue Jacket and two hundred Shawnee warriors laid siege to Dunlap's Station, near Cincinnati. They also hit other outposts and even ambushed flatboat traffic on the Ohio River. At the height of violence in 1791, the British fur traders working with both the Hudson's Bay Company and the North West Company volunteered to intercede. The war was disrupting trade, and they began to fear that the incessant raiding would unleash a massive American response, which would drive out fur-trapping Indians and very likely result in the eviction of the British traders as well.

The Shawnee and other Indians listened to the British proposal with interest but without commitment. The Americans, represented by Washington's secretary of the treasury, Alexander Hamilton, summarily rejected the proposal. Rather than treat with "savages" as sovereign nations, Hamilton proposed that the United States should punish them once and for all. This time, the *Second* American Regiment, a force of 2,300 men—half of them temporary soldiers (enlisted for a period of six months)—convened at Fort Washington under the command of Governor Arthur St. Clair. He was an experienced soldier, having fought in the regular British army during the French and Indian War and as a Patriot major general in the Continental Army during the American Revolution. He had, however, suffered court-martial when, on July 5, 1777, he retreated from Fort Ticonderoga, relinquishing it to a British siege without so much as firing a shot. Acquitted, he was returned to duty, but General Washington recognized that his days as a field commander were over. He adopted the man as his aide-de-camp, maintaining, without particular warrant, a high opinion of him as a general. Apparently, he entertained no second thoughts about entrusting to him the new expedition against Blue Jacket and Little Turtle.

St. Clair and his men advanced to the Great Miami River, where they built Fort Hamilton. On October 4, 1791, the punitive expedition pushed off from here, but progress was painfully slow, and the army was poorly supplied. By October 19, the force was still a hundred miles from the Maumee River, its objective. St. Clair paused to erect Fort Jefferson, but during a spell of miserably wet weather, he was plagued by desertions. Fearing that his army would waste away if he delayed much longer, he left behind

120 men to garrison Fort Jefferson (most of these were ill or simply unreliable), dispatched a 300-man patrol to round up deserters, then set off with 1,400 troops to seek out Little Turtle, Blue Jacket, and their warriors.

A full month passed without an encounter. Then, on November 3, 1791, the army made camp on a plateau above the upper Wabash. Doubtless, St. Clair had chosen it because of the visibility it afforded, but, in truth, it was a terrible place for a camp, since it was exposed and quite vulnerable to attack. Little Turtle and Blue Jacket, leading a thousand warriors, took full advantage of the army's bad position. At dawn on November 4, the Indians rushed the camp from three directions. Once again, the Americans were gripped by panic. Many soldiers dropped their weapons and either ran aimlessly or cowered in prayer. The artillery, positioned too high to be of any use, fired without effect, whereupon Blue Jacket led a party of Shawnee against the gunners. St. Clair's second in command, Richard Butler, attempted to rescue the artillerymen, but his detachment of the Second American Regiment was quickly cut down and Butler himself mortally wounded.

After three hours, those who could—about five hundred men in all—fled back down the road they had laboriously cut through the wilderness. They were fortunate, for the triumphant Indians, celebrating their victory with looting and whiskey, were too engrossed to give chase. They were celebrating having just killed 623 officers and men, along with 24 civilian teamsters. A total of 271 soldiers were wounded, whereas Indian losses were just 21 warriors, with about 40 wounded. In proportion to the number of men fielded that day, it stands as the worst loss in U.S. Army history. When news of it reached President Washington, he vented his wrath before Tobias Lear, his private secretary:

Here on this very spot [the president's study], I took leave of him [St. Clair]; I wished him success and honor; you have your instructions, I said, from the Secretary of War, I had a strict eye to them; and will add but one word— BEWARE OF A SURPRISE. I repeat it, BEWARE OF A SURPRISE—you know how the Indians fight us. He went off with that as my last solemn warning thrown into his ears. And yet!! O God, O God, he's worse than a murderer! how can he answer it to his country;—the blood of the slain is upon him, the curse of widows and orphans—the curse of Heaven!

Following his defeat, Arthur St. Clair resigned as head of the army but retained his post as governor of the Northwest Territory. The catastrophe persuaded President Washington to abandon any thought he may have had concerning a conciliatory Indian policy. Although a still war-weary public was inclined toward peace, in 1792 the House of Representatives authorized a larger army—with the proviso that an earnest attempt first be made to conclude a treaty. Washington used this proviso to buy the time necessary to reorganize his shattered western forces, which had been reduced to a mere 750 men. At the president's direction, Iroquois agents, including Chief Red Jacket, were hired to present an American peace proposal at a meeting with the Shawnee and other tribes on the Auglaize River during the summer of 1792. The U.S. government proposed a boundary line along the Muskingum River, beyond which whites agreed not to settle—though tracts already settled would remain unmolested. To this, the Shawnee responded with contempt, asserting that all of the land north of the Ohio River was theirs, and demanding that all Americans settled on it must move and that restitution must be made for the usurpation and spoliation of Kentucky hunting grounds. In reporting this rebuke to the American commissioners, Red Jacket, perhaps reluctant to admit diplomatic defeat, put the response in its best light and announced that the Shawnee, Miami, and other western tribes were willing to consider peace at a conference next year. In the meantime, however, the Shawnee resumed raiding the Ohio Country, and President Washington found himself a new general.

He settled on one of his revolutionary generals, Anthony Wayne, who bore the nickname "Mad Anthony." Contemporary legend interpreted this sobriquet as homage to the commander's fearless impetuosity—which he unquestionably possessed; however, the nickname was the product of a fairly irrelevant set of circumstances. A neighbor of Wayne's who was serving in the Continental Army had deserted, was arrested, and told the authorities to contact General Wayne, who would surely vouch for him. Wayne not only refused to help but denied even knowing the man. Informed of this, the stunned deserter responded, "He must be mad," and the name stuck.

Wayne accepted the commission in April 1792 and set about recruiting his army, which he mustered at Pittsburgh that summer. After assembling a thousand men, he prudently avoided calling the force the *Third* American Regiment and instead christened it the Legion of the United States. He then moved his headquarters twenty miles downstream from Pittsburgh to a campsite he named Legionville. As he recruited more troops, he instituted a program of thorough training while he, in vivid contrast to previous commanders, endeavored to learn all he could about the lives and military tactics of the western Indians he would be up against. Based on this study, he concluded that it was best to pursue a strategy of sustained conflict, to fight the kind of war of attrition that the Indians were least suited to win.

By the spring of 1793, Wayne moved his growing army to Fort Washington, then set up camp—called Hobson's Choice—just outside of it. While these preparations were under way, a final peace commission offered the Indians a considerable array of concessions, which were presented to the Shawnee and their allies on July 31, 1793. Most significantly, the commissioners recanted the previous position of the United States, that the western Indians were a conquered people by virtue of their alliance with the defeated British. They also announced that the government would relinquish all claim to lands north of the Ohio River, except in the immediate vicinity of Cincinnati and the Scioto and Muskingum rivers; for these lands, the government would pay the Indians. The Shawnee replied on August 15, 1793, through the British trader Alexander McKee:

> You agreed to do us justice, after having long, and injuriously, withheld it. We mean in the acknowledgment you now have made, that the King of England never did, nor ever had a right to give you our Country, by the Treaty of peace, and you want to make this act of Common Justice a great part of your concessions, and seem to expect that, because you have at last acknowledged our independence, we should for such a favor surrender to you

our country. . . . Money to us is of no value . . . and no consideration whatever can induce us to sell the lands on which we get sustenance for our women and children; we hope we may be allowed to point out a mode by which your settlers may be easily removed, and peace thereby obtained. . . . We know these settlers are poor, or they would never have ventured to live in a country which has been in continued trouble ever since they crossed the Ohio; divide, therefore, this large sum of money [$50,000 plus a $10,000 annual annuity], which you have offered to us, among these people . . . and we are persuaded, they would most readily accept of it, in lieu of the lands you sold them. . . . If you add also, the great sums you must expend in raising and paying Armies, with a view to force us to yield you our Country, you will certainly have more than sufficient for the purposes of repaying these settlers for all their labor and improvements.

On September 11, 1793, Big Tree, an Iroquois the Americans had hired as a secret agent and courier, informed Wayne of the breakdown of peace talks. Although the general himself had warned against doing battle during the fall, when the Indians were at their greatest post-hunt strength, he believed that delay would communicate weakness and decided therefore to break his own rule and attack immediately. The corruption and incompetence that had plagued the supply of St. Clair's army came back to haunt Wayne. Worse, the army's second in command, Brigadier General James Wilkinson, deliberately sabotaged supply lines, inadequate as they were, in a scheme to overthrow Wayne and take his place. (Wilkinson would prove an inveterate schemer: As a secret agent in the employ of the Spanish and perhaps even the British, he later conspired unsuccessfully with Aaron Burr to force the secession of the western territories from the United States.) During the delay, Wayne built a fort at Greenville, Ohio, and then, farther west, erected Fort Recovery, on the site of St. Clair's defeat. While the American commander thus consolidated his position, many of the allies of the Shawnee and Miami, disgruntled in their idleness, began to desert the cause. Thus, when Wayne, still impeded by lack of supply, failed to get his campaign under way by May 1794, Little Turtle and Blue Jacket decided to strike the first blow.

Their plan was to attack the army's already tenuous supply line, thereby drawing soldiers out of the forts to defend the baggage trains. Once exposed, the Legionnaires could be ambushed, and the chiefs hoped this latest army would follow those of Harmar and St. Clair into ignominious retreat, if not annihilation. With twelve hundred warriors, Blue Jacket and a remarkable young Shawnee warrior named Tecumseh set out from the Maumee River to blockade Fort Recovery. A scout—one of the sixty Chickasaw, traditional enemies of the Shawnee, fighting on the American side—spotted them on June 29. Unfortunately, he knew little English, and the Legion captain to whom he reported, Alexander Gibson, knew no Chickasaw. The June 30 attack on the pack train and its escort of 140 Legionnaires was therefore a total surprise and resulted in a rout. Victorious, Blue Jacket and Tecumseh tried to call off their warriors, but the Ottawas and other allies insisted on advancing to Fort Recovery itself. Wayne directed his artillery (ordnance recovered from the site of St. Clair's defeat) against them, turning them back with the loss of perhaps thirty warriors.

At this point, the grand Indian alliance began to crack after warriors fighting alongside the Shawnee raped and robbed a number of Shawnee women. The alliance with the British traders also faltered when promised aid, including two pieces of artillery, failed to materialize. In the meantime, on July 28, the bulk of the American forces, 2,200 regulars and 1,500 Kentucky militiamen, arrived at Fort Recovery. Wayne ordered the construction of a more advanced post, Fort Defiance, which the augmented army reached on August 8.

Just downstream from this newest fort, Little Turtle was counseling the leaders of his 1,500 warriors that victory over Mad Anthony Wayne was now impossible. It was time, he said, to negotiate peace. Both Blue Jacket and Tecumseh refused to yield, however, and overall command of the forces passed to Blue Jacket; Little Turtle would lead no more than his 250 Miami warriors.

Blue Jacket, the new commander, decided to intercept the Legion at a place opposite the rapids of the Maumee. Pocked with deep ravines and strewn with the trunks of trees that had been blown down by a tornado years earlier, the site was known as Fallen Timbers. Not only would the rugged terrain provide both cover and concealment, the battleground was only five miles from Fort Miamis, a longtime British stronghold the Indians believed would provide sanctuary and succor if the battle went badly.

Wayne, whose scouts had informed him of the Indians' latest position, halted on August 18 a few miles from that position to build Fort Deposit. Here he cached all that was not immediately needed for combat. It was August 20 before he advanced against Blue Jacket. Perhaps this delay was a brilliant tactical stroke gained from his study of Indian customs; perhaps it was just good luck. In either case, the delay made the most of the warriors' custom of fasting before battle in order to put an edge on reflexes and ferocity. The Indians had expected an encounter on the eighteenth, so had advanced to Fallen Timbers without rations on the seventeenth. By the twentieth, the warriors had gone without food for three days. On that day, some absented themselves to look for food; many of the others who remained waiting for the Americans were now weak from hunger.

Blue Jacket's plan was to entrap Wayne in a vast, half-moon-shaped line, but an Ottawa commander acted prematurely, leading his men in a charge against Wayne's advance guard of 150 mounted Kentucky militia. Those men panicked and broke, thereby inciting the front line of Wayne's main body of infantry to do the same. It looked like another rout was in the making, but Mad Anthony was no Arthur St. Clair. In a brilliant display of personal leadership, he rallied his troops—in part by the singularly effective expedient of shooting anyone seen running away—and ordered not a *defense* but an *attack* on the Indians' line, which had been cut up by the hasty action of the Ottawa warriors. Even though Brigadier Wilkinson failed to obey the command to charge (he later claimed he had not heard it), two regiments commanded by Colonel John Hamtramck attacked spiritedly, bloodying their bayonets. It was now Blue Jacket who suffered a rout.

Retreating to their planned fallback position, Fort Miamis, he and his warriors were dealt yet another blow. British commandant Captain

William Campbell, under orders to avoid involvement in the battle, re-fused to admit the Indians into the fort. The father disowned his children.

After taunting both the Indians and the British garrison, Wayne with-drew on August 23, destroying abandoned Indian towns in his path, and at Kekionga, principal village of the Miami, he built Fort Wayne.

In January 1795, his warriors defeated and many of his people now refu-gees, Blue Jacket journeyed to Fort Greenville, in western Ohio near the present Indiana state line, to negotiate a treaty with Anthony Wayne. Formally signed in August 1796, the Treaty of Greenville secured Ameri-can occupancy of lands northwest of the Ohio River, established yet an-other "permanent" boundary of settlement west of the present state of Ohio, and instituted a program of compensation for territory lost ($20,000 as a lump sum and annual $9,500 payments). For their part, the British agreed at last to vacate the Ohio Country. Peace came to this region at last and endured until the outbreak of the War of 1812.

With peace came a resurgence of the fur trade. Even as the leaders of the new American republic celebrated Wayne's victory, a fresh army of fur traders was carrying commerce—as well as smallpox—to the farther Northwest, the land of the Dakotas. Thus was the ground prepared for the greatest of all fur fortunes, that of John Jacob Astor, the signal figure of the trade in the nineteenth century, the man who transformed it from a desperate and daring wilderness enterprise to big business and the ba-sis of a fortune of mythic proportions.

Astor was born in Walldorf, Germany, in 1763, lived for a time in London, where he worked for his brother, a flute maker, and learned En-glish. He immigrated to the United States in 1784, the year after the Treaty of Paris became final, and he started in the fur business at the bottom, trading with Indians, then opened up a small fur goods shop in New York City before the end of the decade. His breakthrough into big business came in 1794–95. In 1794, the Jay Treaty, negotiated by John Jay during the Washington administration, finalized the British withdrawal from the Ohio Country and the Pacific Northwest. This was mandated by the 1783 Treaty of Paris, but it had been left vague as to timing; the Jay Treaty made it specific. U.S. entrepreneurs now had the confidence to enter the American western fur trade without fear of being crushed by the Hudson's Bay Company and the North West Company, and the Jay Treaty also opened new markets for the United States in Canada. In 1796, Mad Anthony Wayne's Treaty of Greenville made the Great Lakes region safe for American fur traders. The combination of the Jay Treaty with the British and the Treaty of Greenville with the Indians presented Astor with an opportunity he seized with a ferocious passion.

Working with both the Hudson's Bay Company and the North West Company, Astor developed the early U.S. trade with China. In this he prospered until President Thomas Jefferson's 1807 embargo threatened to bring his import-export business to a crashing end. Astor turned this catastrophe into yet another unparalleled opportunity by appealing to the president for a charter authorizing a new *American* company, the American Fur Company, which he presented to the powerful New York governor DeWitt Clinton (from whom he sought support) on January 25, 1808, as a way "to embrace in the course of 4 or 5 years the whole of the fur trade & to extend it to the western ocean [the Pacific] . . . and to have a range of Posts or trading houses on the Rout[e] made by Captain Lewis to the sea." Thus Astor portrayed his scheme to monopolize the American fur trade not as the product of personal ambition but as the fulfillment of Jefferson's own vision, the vision that had moved the president to send Lewis and Clark on their western journey and had motivated as well the Louisiana Purchase. Astor made common cause with Jefferson—who had just laced himself and the nation into the economic straitjacket of the embargo—by proposing a venture that would not only perfect the U.S. claim to sovereignty over the continent from sea to shining sea but would make the controversial Louisiana Purchase turn a profit sooner rather than later.

Astor financed fur-trading outposts in the Ohio Country and the Great Lakes region that had been won first from the British and then from the Shawnee and their allies. Next, he pushed out to the virgin fur country of the Pacific Northwest. The enterprise became so large that Astor turned the American Fur Company into one of the first great corporate "trusts" of the nineteenth century, creating the subsidiary South West Company to handle the fur trade in the Midwest and the Pacific Fur Company to run coastal operations. While these competed with both the Hudson's Bay Company and the North West Company, Astor had the great advantage of a continuous and direct line of communication between his far western sources of product and the markets for that product in the East, especially New York City.

In April 1811, Astor's men established Fort Astoria on the Columbia River, which was the first United States settlement on the Pacific coast. The epic overland Astor Expedition of 1810–12, which he financed to establish direct communication with that outpost, opened up the South Pass on the Continental Divide through the Rocky Mountains, thereby pioneering the principal route of the first great national migratory waves into the transmountain West. Although the War of 1812 disrupted American Fur Company operations, Astor was sufficiently diversified to weather the crisis and, resuming his intimacy with the federal government after the war, secured passage in 1817 of protectionist legislation that effectively barred foreign fur traders from U.S. territory.

The American Fur Company became the dominant force in the American fur trade, and the establishment in 1822 of Astor House on Mackinac Island created the new fur-trading capital of the continent. By this time, however, the demand for fur was beginning to level off as fashions changed. In particular, beaver no longer possessed the extraordinary cultural value it had had beginning in Samuel Pepys's seventeenth century. No matter. Astor had already built his fortune, and he used it now to amass vast tracts of Manhattan real estate, which he leased to those who developed it and expanded New York northward, making it an international commercial capital. In the process, John Jacob Astor became the first great personal icon of American capitalism, his wealth and power founded on fur as surely as future fortunes would be founded on gold, on oil, and on steel. When he retired from active management of his fur and real estate empire in the early 1830s, he financed some of the early cultural life of the young republic and left in his will the major endowment for what would become the New York Public Library.

. . .

As Astor helped to create high culture in the East, his industry contributed to the rapid decline of the hybrid Euro-American/Native American civilization that had developed in many of the places defined by the fur trade.

Toward the end of the first quarter of the nineteenth century, in the Far West, the counterparts of the seventeenth- and eighteenth-century coureurs de bois were the "mountain men," figures Washington Irving compared to Robin Hood and the twentieth-century historian Bernard DeVoto to Odysseus and Siegfried. The first mountain men answered the call that trading partners William Henry Ashley and Andrew Henry put out in the February 13, 1822, issue of the St. Louis *Missouri Gazette and Public Advertiser,* for "Enterprising Young Men . . . to ascend the Missouri to its source, there to be employed for one, two, or three years." Jedediah Strong Smith, James Bridger, Thomas Fitzpatrick, Edward Rose, Hugh Glass, James Clyman, and Milton and William Sublette were all hired and became the most celebrated trappers of the Rocky Mountain fur trade: the original mountain men.

Like the coureurs de bois, the mountain men lived in Indian country; unlike them, they did not generally trade with the Indians for beaver but trapped the animals themselves. Thus the fur trade of the Rocky Mountain West did not tend to create the Euro-American/Native American hybrid civilization that developed in parts of the Ohio Country frontier. Instead, the mountain men lived solitary lives of tireless trapping, interrupted only for one month out of every year, when they converged at a designated "rendezvous." This trading pattern had its origin in the winter of 1824–25, when Ashley led an expedition out of Fort Atkinson, Nebraska, bound for the Rockies. The march across prairie and mountain was pounded by wind and snow. Before long, Ashley's men were forced to abandon their wagons. Their horses came near to starving until the men stumbled across a stand of cottonwood, whose bark made lifesaving forage. The Indians they encountered, eager for trade, were mostly friendly, and that contributed to the salvation of expedition as well.

At length, Ashley's men crossed the Rockies south of South Pass at Morrow Creek. After reaching the Green River on April 19, Ashley divided his party of twenty-five into four groups: one to explore the Green; one to trap its tributaries; one to find the source of the river today known as the Colorado; one to trap beavers in the mountains to the west. As he sent his men in all directions, he made plans to meet them fifty miles downriver at a "place of randavoze [rendezvous] for all our parties on or before the 10th July next." It was the first rendezvous in the history of the far western fur trade, and it rapidly developed into a major economic feature of the American Rocky Mountain fur trade and became the defining social institution for the mountain men.

Each year, they would come in from the wilderness to the designated rendezvous in the heart of the mountains. They would meet with Ashley or another company trader to exchange whiskey, guns, knives, and the like for the year's take in beaver. A good mountain man arrived at the rendezvous with three or four hundred pelts—a very fortunate one, with maybe twice that take. Before the trade began its decline, pelts brought between $2 and $4 each and could be resold in St. Louis at a 200 percent markup, but the mountain men seemed satisfied enough with the $2,000 or so they cleared at a time when skilled labor earned perhaps $1.50 a day—though they tended to spend much of what they made during the monthlong rendezvous on liquor, Indian women, gambling, and the goods and supplies they needed for the coming year. Washington Irving, an early and eloquent historian of the western fur trade, wrote that the mountain men had "the manners, habits, dress, gesture, and even walk of the Indian." Their plaited hair was grown long, dangling below the shoulders, where it was tied with otter skins or what Irving called "parti-colored ribands." They wore knee-length hunting shirts made of ruffled calico brightly dyed or of "ornamented leather," their legs wrapped in leggings "ornamented with strings, fringes, and a profusion of hawks' bells," their feet shod in "a costly pair of moccasins of the finest Indian fabric, richly embroidered with beads." Across the shoulder of a mountain man, a blanket was always thrown, typically of bright scarlet, and was "girt around his waist with a red sash, in which he bestows his pistols, knife, and the stem of his Indian pipe."

Emulating the Indian, the mountain men seemed to outdo him in demonstrations of endurance and the love of dangerous adventure. Hugh Glass told all who would listen of how he had been mauled by a grizzly bear and was saved from death by the ministrations of the Sioux. Jim Beckwourth, an African American former blacksmith, claimed to have been made a Crow war chief. On the stories went, many undoubtedly pure fiction. There was, however, nothing but truth in the fact that the work was dangerous. Some five hundred mountain men were killed over the three decades of the trade's heyday—a 25 percent mortality rate. The greatest hazards were natural—illness, injury, exposure to the elements—but hostile Indians also took a toll. The motive in these attacks was not racial vengeance or a desire to halt unwanted incursions onto Native land. There were men, alone, carrying merchandise of great value. The Indians, now and then, killed and robbed them.

While Irving and others of a romantic turn of mind saw the mountain men as marvelous mythic figures, the mountain men saw themselves much as Charles Keemle, a former trapper, explained in the *Missouri Herald and St. Louis Advertiser:*

> The recent expedition of General Ashley to the country west of the Rocky Mountains has been productive of information on subjects of no small interest to the people of the Union. It has proved, that overland expeditions in large bodies may be made to that remote region. . . . The whole route lay through a level and open country, better for carriages than any turnpike road in the United States. Wagons and carriages could go with ease as far as General Ashley went, crossing the Rocky Mountains . . . and descending . . . towards the Pacific Ocean.

That is, they saw themselves as the heralds of American civilization—*white* American civilization—in the Far West. Mountain men even trekked to Washington, where they lobbied Congress and the president to settle, by force if necessary, persistent British claims to the Far Northwest. Ironically, perhaps, it was not the British who ran the mountain men out of business but Astor's American Fur Company. Astor simply bought the Upper Missouri, destroying rivals either through negotiation, absorbing them into the American Fur Company, or by underselling them, in the knowledge that short-term losses would be more than made up by long-term victory.

By 1827, the American Fur Company had a virtual monopoly on the Upper Missouri, and within another decade, the beaver in the region were on their way to extinction—or at least to population levels too low to be of commercial value, especially with the decline in demand for fur. As for the mountain men, they were gone well before midcentury, but they had left behind the routes they had opened to the Far West.

It would not be fur that would bring Euro-American settlement to this region. Other "extractive" lures—gold, silver, eventually oil—and the land itself, sometimes for farming, sometimes (as in the case of the Mormons) for religious expression, would draw hundreds of thousands to the West Coast, the Rocky Mountain West, and the vast space between the Rockies and the Appalachians. The quest to establish an empire of fur was sometimes violent, even to the point of genocide, yet it also presented an opportunity to build a new civilization on the seventeenth- and eighteenth-century American frontier, one that peacefully and productively blended Euro-American and Native American perceptions, values, and interests. Assailed by a thousand cuts for a century and a half, that opportunity finally died in the fight for American independence. The fur trade outlived the American Revolution—at least for a time—but the natural and human ecology of the Middle West, the Far West, and the coastal West conspired with the economic realities of the young republic and with the business model of one of the republic's first significant capitalists to make the revival of that lost opportunity a virtual impossibility. Instead, the story of western settlement in the United States would be marked by the injustice and violence of swindle and conquest, and the western landscape would be marked not by the progress of new civilizations but by one "Indian War" after another and the ineffable squalor of reservations, despised and decried by white and Indian alike.

Bibliography

Abbot, W. W., ed. *The Papers of George Washington: Colonial Series.* 10 vols. Charlottesville: University Press of Virginia, 1983–95.

Adams, Paul K. "Colonel Henry Bouquet's Ohio Expedition in 1764." *Pennsylvania History* 40 (April 1973): 139–47.

Adney, E. T., and Howard I. Chapelle. *The Bark Canoes and Skin Boats of North America.* Washington, D.C.: Smithsonian Institution Press, 1964.

Anderson, Fred. *A People's Army: Massachusetts Soldiers and Society in the Seven Years' War.* Chapel Hill: University of North Carolina Press, 1984.

Anderson, Niles. "The General Chooses a Road: The Forbes Campaign of 1758 to Capture Fort Duquesne." *Western Pennsylvania Historical Magazine* 42 (June, September, December 1959): 109–38, 241–58, 383–401.

Andrews, Charles M. *The Colonial Period of American History.* 1934–38; reprint ed., New Haven: Yale University Press, 1964.

Aquila, Richard. *The Iroquois Restoration: Iroquois Diplomacy on the Colonial Frontier, 1701–1754.* Detroit: Wayne State University Press, 1983.

Auth, Stephen F. *The Ten Years' War: Indian-White Relations in Pennsylvania, 1755–1765.* New York: Garland, 1989.

Axelrod, Alan. *Blooding at Great Meadows: Young George Washington and the Battle That Shaped the Man.* Philadelphia: Running Press, 2007.

————. *Chronicle of the Indian Wars: From Colonial Times to Wounded Knee.* New York: Macmillan General Reference, 1993.

Axtell, James. *The Invasion Within: The Contest of Cultures in Colonial North America.* New York: Oxford University Press, 1985.

Baker-Crothers, Hayes. *Virginia and the French and Indian War.* Chicago: University of Chicago Press, 1928.

Boatner, Mark M. *Encyclopedia of the American Revolution.* New York: D. McKay, 1966; Bicentennial ed., 1974.

Bouquet, Henry. *The Papers of Colonel Henry Bouquet.* Ed. Sylvester K. Stevens et al. 19 vols. Harrisburg: Pennsylvania Historical Commission and Works Progress Administration, 1940–44.

Bourne, Russell. *The Red King's Rebellion: Racial Politics in New England, 1675–1678.* New York: Athenaeum, 1990.

Bradstreet, John. *An Impartial Account of Lieut. Col. Bradstreet's Expedition to Fort Frontenac.* Toronto: Rous & Mann, 1940.

Branch, E. Douglas. "Henry Bouquet: Professional Soldier." *Pennsylvania Magazine of History and Biography* 62 (January 1938): 41–51.

Brand, Irene B. "Dunmore's War." *West Virginia History* 40 (Fall 1978): 28–46.

Brock, R. A., ed. *The Official Records of Robert Dinwiddie, Lieutenant-Governor of the Colony of Virginia, 1751–1758.* 2 vols. Richmond: Virginia Historical Society, 1883–84.

Brooks, Edward Howard. "The First Battle for the Ohio Valley." *Historian* 10 (Autumn 1947): 14–26.

Calloway, Colin G. *The Western Abenakis of Vermont, 1600–1800: War, Migration, and the Survival of an Indian People.* Norman: University of Oklahoma Press, 1990.

Chittenden, Hiram Martin. *American Fur Trade of the Far West,* 2 vols. Stanford, Calif.: Academic Reprints, 1954.

Chronister, Allen, and Clay Landry. "Clothing of the Rocky Mountain Trapper, 1820–1840." In William H. Scurlock, ed., *The Book of Buckskinning* 7:2–41. Texarkana, Tex.: Scurlock Publishing , 1995.

Church, Thomas. *The History of the Great Indian War of 1675 and 1676, Commonly Called Philip's War. Also, The Old French and Indian Wars, from 1689 to 1704.* Ed. Samuel G. Drake. Hartford: Silas Andrus & Son, 1854.

Commager, Henry Steele, and Richard B. Morris, eds. *The Spirit of 'Seventy-Six: The Story of the American Revolution as Told by Participants.* New York: Harper & Row, 1958.

Cook, Sherburne F. "Interracial Warfare and Population Decline Among the New England Indians." *Ethnohistory* 20 (Winter 1973): 1–24.

Corkran, David H. *The Cherokee Frontier: Conflict and Survival, 1740–62.* Norman: University of Oklahoma Press, 1962.

———. *The Creek Frontier, 1540–1783.* Norman: University of Oklahoma Press, 1967.

Cox, Ross. *The Columbia River.* Norman: University of Oklahoma Press, 1957.

Craven, Wesley Frank. "Indian Policy in Early Virginia." *William and Mary Quarterly*, 3d Ser., 1 (January 1944): 65–82.

Cressy, David. *Coming Over: Migration and Communication Between England and New England in the Seventeenth Century.* New York: Cambridge University Press, 1987.

Debo, Angie. *A History of the Indians of the United States.* Norman: University of Oklahoma Press, 1977.

Dederer, John Morgan. *War in America to 1775: Before Yankee Doodle.* New York: New York University Press, 1990.

DeVoto, Bernard. *Across the Wide Missouri.* Boston: Mariner Books, 1998.

Ferling, John E. *A Wilderness of Miseries: War and Warriors in Early America.* Westport, Conn: Greenwood Press, 1980.

Forbes, John. *Writings of General John Forbes Relating to His Service in North America.* Ed. Alfred Procter James. Menasha, Wisc.: Collegiate Press, 1938.

Freeman, Douglas Southall. *George Washington: A Biography.* 7 vols. New York: Scribner's, 1948–57.

Gallay, Allan, ed. *Colonial Wars of North America, 1512–1763.* New York: Garland, 1996.

Gates, Charles M. *Five Fur Traders of the Northwest: Being the Narrative of Peter Pond and the Diaries of John Macdonell, Archibald N. McLeod, Hugh Faries, and Thomas Connor.* St. Paul: Minnesota Historical Society, 1965.

Gilman, Carolyn. *Where Two Worlds Meet: The Great Lakes Fur Trade.* St. Paul: Minnesota Historical Society, 1982.

Hamilton, Edward P. *The French and Indian Wars: The Story of Battles and Forts in the Wilderness*. Garden City, N.Y.: Doubleday, 1962.

Hazard, Samuel, ed. *Minutes of the Provincial Council of Pennsylvania, from the Organization to the Termination of the Proprietary Government*. 16 vols. Harrisburg, Pa.: Theophilus Fenn, 1838–53.

Horowitz, David. *The First Frontier: The Indian Wars and America's Origins, 1607–1776*. New York: Simon and Schuster, 1978.

Hubbard, William. *History of the Indian Wars in New England*. New York: Kraus Reprint, 1969.

Hunt, George T. *Arms for Empire: A Military History of the British Colonies in North America, 1607–1763*. New York: Macmillan, 1973.

———. *The Wars of the Iroquois: A Study in Intertribal Trade Relations*. Madison: University of Wisconsin Press, 1940.

Illinois State Historical Library. *Collections of the Illinois State Historical Library*. Springfield: Trustees of the Illinois State Historical Library, 1915–40.

Innis, Harold A. *The Fur Trade in Canada: An Introduction to Canadian Economic History*. Rev. ed. Toronto: University of Toronto Press, 1970.

Irving, Washington. *Astoria; or, Anecdotes of an Enterprise Beyond the Rocky Mountains*. Ed. Edgeley W. Todd. Norman: University of Oklahoma Press, 1964.

Jaray, Cornell, ed. *Historic Chronicles of New Amsterdam, Colonial New York, and Early Long Island,* First Series. Port Washington, N.Y.: Ira J. Friedman, n.d. [1968].

Jennings, Francis. *The Ambiguous Iroquois Empire: The Covenant Chain Confederation of Indian Tribes with English Colonies*. New York: W. W. Norton, 1984.

———. *Empire of Fortune: Crowns, Colonies, and Tribes in the Seven Years War in America*. New York: W. W. Norton, 1988.

———. *The Invasion of America: Indians, Colonialism, and the Cant of Conquest*. Chapel Hill: University of North Carolina Press, 1975.

Jensen, Merrill. *The New Nation: A History of the United States During the Confederation, 1781–1789*. 1950; reprint ed., Boston: Northeastern University Press, 1981.

Bibliography

Leach, Douglas Edward. *The Northern Colonial Frontier, 1607–1763.* New York: Holt, Rinehart and Winston, 1966.

———. *Roots of Conflict: British Armed Forces and Colonial Americans, 1677–1763.* Chapel Hill: University of North Carolina Press, 1986.

Lee, E. Lawrence. *Indian Wars in North Carolina, 1663–1763.* Raleigh, N.C.: Carolina Charter Tercentenary Commission, 1963.

Lengel, Edward G. *General George Washington: A Military Life.* New York: Random House, 2005.

Mann, Charles C. *1491: New Revelations of the Americas Before Columbus.* New York: Vintage, 2006.

McCardell, Lee. *Ill-Starred General: Braddock of the Coldstream Guards.* Pittsburgh: University of Pittsburgh Press, 1958.

Merwick, Donna. *Possessing Albany, 1630–1710: The Dutch and English Experiences.* Cambridge: Cambridge University Press, 1990.

O'Callaghan, E. B., ed. *Documentary History of the State of New-York.* 4 vols. Albany: Weed, Parsons, 1850–51.

———. *Documents Relative to the Colonial History of the State of New-York.* 15 vols. Albany: Weed, Parsons, 1853–87.

Peckham, Howard H. *The Colonial Wars, 1689–1762.* Chicago: University of Chicago Press, 1964.

Pepys, Samuel. *Diary.* Complete text at www.pepysdiary.com; accessed March 9, 2010.

Phillips, Charles, and Alan Axelrod, eds. *Encyclopedia of the American West.* 4 vols. New York: Macmillan General Reference, 1996.

Prucha, Francis Paul, ed. *Documents of United States Indian Policy,* 2nd ed., expanded. Lincoln: University of Nebraska Press, 1990.

Quinn, David B., ed. *North American Discovery, Circa 1000–1612.* New York: Harper and Row, 1971.

Ray, Arthur J. *Indians in the Fur Trade: Their Role as Trappers, Hunters, and Middlemen in the Lands Southwest of Hudson Bay, 1660–1870.* Toronto: University of Toronto, 1974.

Ronda, James P. *Astoria and Empire.* Lincoln: University of Nebraska Press, 1990.

Russell, Carl P. *Firearms, Traps, and Tools of the Mountain Men.* Albuquerque: University of New Mexico Press, 1977.

Sargent, Winthrop. *The History of an Expedition Against Fort Du Quesne, in 1755.* Philadelphia: Lippincott, Grambo, 1855.

Shea, William L. *The Virginia Militia in the Seventeenth Century.* Baton Rouge: Louisiana State University Press, 1983.

Silver, Peter. *Our Savage Neighbors: How Indian War Transformed Early America.* New York: W. W. Norton, 2008.

Smith, Page. *A New Age Now Begins: A People's History of the American Revolution.* 2 vols. New York: Viking Penguin, 1976.

Smoyer, Stanley C. "Indians as Allies in the Intercolonial Wars." *New York History* 17 (October 1936): 411–22.

Starobinski, Jean, et al. *Revolution in Fashion: European Clothing, 1715–1815.* New York: Abbeville Press, 1989.

Sturtevant, William C., ed. *Handbook of the North American Indians.* 20 vols. Washington, D.C.: Smithsonian Institution, 1978–2008.

Sullivan, James, ed. *The Papers of Sir William Johnson.* Albany: University of the State of New York, 1921–65.

Thwaites, Reuben Gold, ed. *The Jesuit Relations and Allied Documents*, Vol. 22. Cleveland: The Burrows Brothers Company, 1898.

Tilberg, Frederick. *Fort Necessity National Battlefield Site.* National Park Service Historical Handbook Series no. 19. Washington, D.C.: National Park Service, 1954.

Twohig, Dorothy, ed. *George Washington's Diaries: An Abridgment.* Charlottesville: University Press of Virginia, 1999.

Vaughan, Alden T. *New England Frontier: Puritans and Indians, 1620–1675.* Boston: Little, Brown, 1965.

Wainwright, Nicholas B. "George Croghan and the Indian Uprising of 1747." *Pennsylvania History* 21 (January 1954): 21–31.

Wall, Robert Emmet, Jr. "Louisbourg 1745." *New England Quarterly* 37 (March 1964): 64–83.

Washington, George. *Writings.* New York: Library of America, 1997.

Weigley, Russell F. *The American Way of War: A History of United States Military Strategy and Policy.* Bloomington: Indiana University Press, 1977.

White, Richard. *The Middle Ground: Indians, Empires, and Republics in the Great Lakes Region, 1650–1815*. New York: Cambridge University Press, 1991.

Williams, Glyndwr. "The Hudson's Bay Company and the Fur Trade: 1670–1820," *Beaver*, Autumn 1983, 4–86.

Williams, John. *The Redeemed Captive Returning to Zion*. Cambridge, Mass.: Applewood Books, 1987.

Wishart, David J. *The Fur Trade of the American West, 1807–1840*. Lincoln: University of Nebraska Press, 1979.

Index

Index